Readings: A New Biblical Commentary

General Editor
John Jarick

Z E C H A R I A H

ZECHARIAH

Edgar W. Conrad

Sheffield Academic Press

In memory of Matthew

בן אחי

Copyright © 1999 Sheffield Academic Press

Published by Sheffield Academic Press Ltd
Mansion House
19 Kingfield Road
Sheffield S11 9AS
England

Typeset by Sheffield Academic Press
and
Printed on acid-free paper in Great Britain
by Bookcraft Ltd
Midsomer Norton, Bath

British Library Cataloguing in Publication Data

A catalogue record for this book is available
from the British Library

ISBN 1-85075-899-9
ISBN 1-85075-900-6 pbk

Contents

Preface

Zechariah has never been an easy read. The cryptic imagery has even led some such as Mark Love in his excellent and provocative study, *The Evasive Text: Zechariah 1-8* (forthcoming in the *JSOT* Supplement series), to conclude that it is unreadable. I offer my reading in this commentary, therefore, as *one* reading and make no pretences about its being definitive. Indeed, any reading of any text will result in a plurality of meanings. The following reading diverges from the majority of commentaries. Its strategies for interpreting the book emphasize literary rather than historical context. I am interested in reading Zechariah in the larger literary context of the twelve minor prophets and in the larger world of the textuality of the Hebrew Bible. I am not concerned with reading Zechariah as providing information about a world external to it, for example, the sixth-century BCE world of Judah under Persian rule. Nor am I interested in the historical development of either Zechariah or the Twelve as texts, that is, in tracing the stages of their formation. While I am not following the more conventional historical-critical approach in this reading, I have learned an enormous amount from those who have, as is evident in the bibliography at the end of the book.

I have written the commentary based on my reading of the Hebrew text. However, I have not assumed a knowledge of Hebrew on the part of my readers. While I do refer to the Hebrew text frequently, I have attempted to keep the technicalities to a minimum. In order to share a common text with my readers, I have focused my discussion on the New Revised Standard Version (NRSV). When my translation of the Hebrew text varies from that of the NRSV, I have indicated this. My frequent alternative renderings of the NRSV are not meant, therefore, as a running criticism of that translation, but as a point of reference for those who do not read Hebrew.

All citations to chapter and verse are those of the NRSV. The Hebrew Bible diverges from the NRSV in one place (Hebrew Bible 2.1-17 = NRSV 1.18-2.13). There are also, of course, variations in other biblical books to which I refer, and in those instances references are also to the NRSV, which indicates variations to versification in the Hebrew Bible in footnotes.

There are many to whom I offer thanks in supporting this project: the Australian Research Council which made possible an ARC Large Grant for the second half of 1997; the Department of Biblical Studies at the University of Sheffield which graciously offered me a visiting professorship during my sabbatical leave in the first half of 1997; Graham White, my research assistant, who carried out a variety of research and editorial tasks; Michael Carden who read and commented on the manuscript; my other postgraduate students who listened to my thoughts on Zechariah at our monthly gatherings in my home; my wife Linda who has always been a partner in my research; and my colleagues in the Department of Studies in Religion who have made my intellectual pursuits challenging and fun: Philip Almond, Michael Lattke, Ian Gillmann, Richard Hutch, Rod Bucknell, Lynne Hume, Rick Strelan, Peter Harrison and Chris Nichols.

Finally, I offer this book in memory of my nephew Matthew. His 17 years filled all who knew him, including his aunt and uncle in Australia, with a zest for life, with humour and with joy.

Brisbane
3 December 1997

Abbreviations

AB	Anchor Bible
BDB	Francis Brown, S.R. Driver and Charles A. Briggs, *A Hebrew and English Lexicon of the Old Testament* (Oxford: Clarendon Press, 1907)
Bib	*Biblica*
BN	*Biblische Notizen*
BSac	*Bibliotheca Sacra*
BT	*The Bible Translator*
BZAW	Beihefte zur *ZAW*
CBQ	*Catholic Biblical Quarterly*
HeyJ	*Heythrop Journal*
HSM	Harvard Semitic Monographs
JBL	*Journal of Biblical Literature*
JETS	*Journal of the Evangelical Theological Society*
JJS	*Journal of Jewish Studies*
JNES	*Journal of Near Eastern Studies*
JSOT	*Journal for the Study of the Old Testament*
JSOTSup	*Journal for the Study of the Old Testament*, Supplement Series
KJV	King James Version
NCBC	New Century Bible Commentary
NEB	*New English Bible*
NIV	New International Version
NRSV	New Revised Standard Version
OTL	Old Testament Library
OTG	Old Testament Guides
RB	*Revue biblique*
SJOT	*Scandanavian Journal of the Old Testament*
TANAKH	The New Jewish Publication Society Translation according to the Traditional Hebrew Text
VT	*Vetus Testamentum*
VTSup	*Vetus Testamentum*, Supplements
WBC	Word Biblical Commentary
ZAW	*Zeitschrift für die alttestamentliche Wissenschaft*

Introduction

1. Locating the Reading

Perspective

The reading of Zechariah in this commentary is literary. The figure of Zechariah is understood as a character in the text, and the text of Zechariah is interpreted as part of a larger literary whole—the scroll of the twelve 'minor' prophets. To read and to comment on Zechariah in this way has not been common practice in commentary literature. Most frequently the Twelve has been broken up into twelve separate books, and each of these has been commented on in isolation from the others. Indeed, Zechariah has often been further divided into two separate sections, Proto-Zechariah (chs. 1-8) and Deutero-Zechariah (chs. 9-14), each treated separately.

The practice of pulling books apart into independent layers or sources was a consequence of the interpretative aim of historical-critical scholarship to uncover the authentic words of a prophet and to understand those words in their original historical context. Scholars assumed that a prophet's original words were buried in secondary literary accretions. To read and understand prophetic books as literary wholes was generally not considered appropriate since books were understood as collections of disparate materials containing within them data to be used in historical reconstruction.

In the past 20 years or so there has been an emerging interest in the final form of prophetic books, reflecting the broad interest in the final form of books in the Hebrew Bible in general. This has meant a different evaluation of the role of the redactor. Redactors are increasingly being perceived as less like collectors and more like authors who creatively assembled prophetic books to form unified wholes. This changed view of the redactor is summed up by James Nogalski in his *Literary Precursors to the Book of the Twelve*:

> [O]lder redactional work peeled back the layers of the text in an attempt to find the ever elusive original form of a prophetic saying. Recent redactional studies attempt to do the opposite. They attempt to peel back the literary layers of a given text in order to put it back together, assuming this

process provides insights into the thoughts and the situations of those responsible for the present state of the writings.[1]

While I share with the newer redaction critics an interest in understanding prophetic books as literary wholes, my approach is different. The text of Zechariah is read as literature and is used neither as data for reconstructing Zechariah as a historical prophet in the sixth century BCE nor for reconstructing the historical development of the Twelve as a whole. In order to place my commentary of Zechariah in perspective, it will be useful to: (1) contrast my reading of Zechariah with the historical approach used in most commentaries on prophets and prophetic books; (2) outline the literary approach adopted in my reading; (3) give a brief overview of my interpretation of the Twelve as a prophetic book; and (4) summarize my reading of Zechariah in the context of the Twelve.

Studies of Zechariah as Prophet and as Book

Biblical scholarship during this century has associated prophecy with creativity and spontaneity. The spoken word rather than the written word has been the focus of interpretation. Prophetic books have been viewed as blocking access to the essential orality of prophetic speech. Julius Wellhausen, often seen as the father of historical criticism, understood the prophets to be 'awakened individuals' who 'do not preach on set texts; they speak out of the spirit'.[2] For Wellhausen, written texts deaden the vitality of the oral words of the prophets as they existed in their pre-book form. He associates the introduction of the law with the reduction of the original spoken words of the prophets to writing. He says:

> The introduction of the law, first Deuteronomy, and then the whole Penta-
> teuch, was in fact the decisive step, by which the written took the place
> of the spoken word, and the people of the word became a 'people of the
> book'. To *the book* were added in course of time *the books* . . . The notion
> of canon proceeds entirely from that of the written Torah; the prophets
> and the hagiographa [*sic*] are also called Torah by the Jews, though not
> Torah of Moses.[3]

For Wellhausen, then, the writing down of the law had as its consequence the writing down of the words of the prophets. This writing

---

1.   J. Nogalski, *Literary Precursors to the Book of the Twelve* (BZAW, 217; Berlin: W. de Gruyter, 1993), p. 16.

2.   J. Wellhausen, *Prolegomena to the History of Ancient Israel (with a Reprint of the Article 'Israel' from the Encyclopedia Britannica)* (Meridian Books Reprint; New York: World Publishing Company, 1957), p. 398.

3.   Wellhausen, *Prolegomena*, p. 409.

down, this becoming Torah, spelled 'the death of prophecy' (*Prole-gomena*, p. 401). For much of this century historical critics have been preoccupied with the notion that the prophet, buried in the written tomb of the text, needed to be resurrected, to live again. It has been the task of the biblical scholar to open up prophetic books by dissecting their constituent parts through source analysis and form criticism so that the spoken word could be heard once more.

The study of Zechariah for most of this century reflects biblical schol-arship's interest in the historical prophet. The 'prophet Zechariah', not the 'book of Zechariah', has been the focus of attention. Furthermore, the search for the historical Zechariah has been confined to so-called Proto-Zechariah, chs. 1–8. It is only here that the prophet is mentioned by name. The latter part of the book, chs. 9–14, often referred to as Deutero-Zechariah, has normally been associated with another anony-mous prophet (or prophets) coming from a different place and time although the identification of the place and time has been much dis-puted.[4]

Zechariah (along with Haggai) was considered important in historical studies of prophecy in ancient Israel because he was seen to represent a change in the institution of prophecy in the Persian period. Zechariah's 'visions' and the role of the 'angel' as interpreter represented for many scholars the movement away from the immediacy of the spoken word of the prophet suggested by Wellhausen. Older scholars such as Gunkel, who saw prophecy as having its high point in the period from Amos to Deutero-Isaiah, viewed Zechariah as continuing a decline of prophecy beginning with Ezekiel.[5] More recent portrayals of Zechariah, such as those by Paul Hanson in his *The Dawn of Apocalyptic*, perpetuate the

---

4.   R.J. Coggins states succinctly the reasons frequently given for the division of the book into Proto- and Deutero-Zechariah. He says that in chs. 9–14 'the series of visions comes to an end, and references to the restoration of the Jerusalem commu-nity and its temple in the reign of Darius are no longer to be found. The Jewish lead-ers, Joshua and Zechariah, are not mentioned. In chs. 1–8 the prophet Zechariah is mentioned by name four times and the "I" of the visions is clearly identified with him. By contrast the oracles in 9–14 are anonymous, and set out in a markedly different style from the visions of the first section... Finally, there are considerable differences in vocabulary, both with regard to the occurrence of particular characteristic expres-sions in one part but not the other, and in detailed word usage.' See his *Haggai, Zechariah, Malachi* (OTG; Sheffield: JSOT Press, 1987), pp. 61-62.

5.   On this point see M.H. Floyd, 'Prophecy and Writing in Habakkuk 2,1-5', *ZAW* 105 (1993), pp. 462-56.

devaluing of Zechariah (and Haggai).[6] Hanson understands that in the postexilic period there were competing parties representing different social and political contexts. Genuine prophecy was seen to be associated with prophets like Deutero-Isaiah who lacked political power but who produced visions of an idealized future. In contrast Haggai and Zechariah were understood as serving the interests of those in power and as lacking 'the revolutionary element which was always an essential ingredient in genuine prophecy' (*The Dawn of Apocalyptic*, pp. 240-62). Others see in Zechariah the transition from prophecy to apocalyptic.[7]

The prophet, seen as a truly creative individual, whose spoken words represent the origins of a prophetic book, became the primary focus of investigation. Because it was assumed that secondary words were added to an original prophet's spoken words in the process of collection, prophetic books were understood to be composite and were deemed to be unreadable in their present form. Prophetic books themselves were virtually dismissed as objects of study and were understood as composites of data for historical reconstruction.

More recently some scholars have begun to turn their attention to the final form of prophetic books. Terence Collins, who represents the newer appreciation of the redactor as 'author' compiling materials according to his or her own agenda, says, 'Redaction criticism seeks to establish the way in which a body of literary material has been arranged, adapted and shaped into a book'.[8] Furthermore,

> Redaction criticism looks at the process of selection of the material and its organisation but also at the network of relationships that resulted. It observes the relationships that *bind together into a new unity* all the parts of the work. Consequently it includes both a historical and literary aspect in its analysis, but shifts the focus of the historical inquiry from the life and times of the prophets themselves to the life and times of the people who produced the books about the prophets.[9]

It is important to see that while redaction criticism has begun to focus less on prophets as historical figures and more on prophetic books as unified wholes, the significance of the study still rests on creative

---

6.   P.D. Hanson, *The Dawn of Apocalyptic* (Philadelphia: Fortress Press, 1975).

7.   R. North, 'Prophecy to Apocalyptic via Zechariah', in G.W. Anderson *et al.* (eds.), *Congress Volume: Uppsala 1971* (VTSup, 22; Leiden: E.J. Brill, 1971), pp. 47-71.

8.   T. Collins, *The Mantle of Elijah: The Redaction Criticism of the Prophetical Books* (The Biblical Seminar, 20; Sheffield: JSOT Press, 1993), p. 15.

9.   Collins, *Mantle*, p. 16; emphasis mine.

individuals behind the text. The focus has shifted, however, from the prophet as the creative source of a literary tradition to the redactor as the creative fashioner of a unified book. Collins represents this view when he says,

> Books are written by writers, professional scribes, and we would dearly love to know more about the writers who composed the prophetical books—who they were, how they operated and why they did what they did. Redaction criticism tries to answer such questions. We may not succeed in answering the question 'who?' very satisfactorily, except in general terms, but the questions 'how?' and 'why?' are in fact more important, and we can hope to make some progress in that direction by analysing what they actually did ...An examination of the compositional techniques used by the exilic and post-exilic writers in producing their texts can give us some indication, though admittedly incomplete, of their motivation.[10]

This means that redaction critics reading Zechariah do not understand Proto-Zechariah in isolation from Deutero-Zechariah, nor do they perceive Zechariah in isolation from the larger scroll of the Twelve. A prophetic book such as the Twelve is seen as having been gradually shaped through time.

Such a brief overview of studies concerning the historical Zechariah cannot do justice to the complex and pluriform character of the inquiry. I have outlined the sorts of issues raised about the historical Zechariah to make it clear that these are not my concerns. I am not interested in a historical prophet Zechariah during the reign of the Persian king Darius. Nor am I interested in prophecy in Persian times and how it related to prophecy in pre-exilic times. The relationship of the institution of prophecy to apocalyptic writings is not my concern. Rather I am interested in exploring Zechariah as a literary character in the Twelve when read as a literary whole.

The decision to read Zechariah as part of a larger literary work, the scroll of the Twelve, is not arbitrary. While I have gained a great deal from historical-critical studies of Zechariah, I identify in this study with an increasing number of scholars who find it difficult to read biblical narratives and prophetic texts as data for reconstructing the past. This shift away from asking primarily historical questions of biblical texts results in part from the impact of literary criticism on biblical studies. As Philip R. Davies acknowledges in *In Search of 'Ancient Israel'*,[11]

---

10. Collins, *Mantle*, pp. 15-16.

11. P.R. Davies, *In Search of 'Ancient Israel'* (JSOTSup, 148; Sheffield, JSOT Press, 1992), pp. 12-13.

'Awareness of the [biblical] text first and foremost as a literary artifact has replaced the instinct to know its author, time, place and purpose'. He goes on to say that even 'history is a narrative, in which happenings and people are turned into events and characters'.[12] Whoever Zechariah was, or whether an actual individual named Zechariah lived in Jerusalem in the sixth century BCE, is not something that we can determine from the literature in which he appears as a character. Furthermore, information outside the text enabling one to make such a decision is lacking. I read Zechariah, then, as a literary character portrayed in the text, because the literary creation of the Twelve in which he appears as a character, not Zechariah as a historical person, is accessible for study.

The historical analysis of the redactional growth of a prophetic book such as the Twelve raises problems similar to those in connection with the historical Zechariah. Diachronic studies of the Twelve are often mapped out against the story of Israel depicted in the Hebrew Bible. This charting is problematic at a time when it is becoming increasingly clear that the Israel depicted in the biblical text is the construction by a later community of its past.[13] Just as many have become critical of the conception of an Israel encoded in the sources of the historical narratives, conscious of itself, and writing its history as it evolved through time, so we need to become critical of the conception of the Twelve as encoding its own redactional history.

My Strategies for Reading a Prophetic Book

To focus on a prophetic book in its final form apart from reconstructions of its development is not to ignore its discordant character. Indeed, it is possible to conceive of a prophetic book as a composite created from diverse materials at a particular point in time rather than as a document evolving through time. It is possible to imagine the book of the Twelve produced by a later community creating a prophetic past by piecing together existing materials available to its scribes.[14] I would agree with redaction critics such as Terence Collins that the composition of prophetic books 'had much in common with the modern art form of collage, in which the juxtaposition of varied, even dissimilar

12. For a fuller discussion of these issues see pp. 12-20. In addition to literary criticism he also mentions sociology and anthropology as having a major impact on historical research into biblical literature.

13. On this point see, for example, Davies, *Search*, pp. 1-22.

14. See John Barton, 'Reading the Bible as Literature: Two Questions for Biblical Critics', *Literary and Theology* 1 (1987), pp. 135-53. Barton suggests that biblical texts were scribal constructions for community performance.

items, is cultivated as a matter of style'.[15] However, I will adopt a strategy for interpreting this literary collage that differs from that of redaction criticism, which has focused on diachronic history.[16] My aim will be to understand the Twelve in much the same way that one approaches a collage as a work of art in its own right apart from tracing its sources or its development. Just as a contemporary collage requires the observer to configure the parts, so a literary collage, such as the Twelve, necessitates the participation of the viewer/reader in its reception. In interpretation of a collage, equal time and consideration need not be given to every square inch of the composition; rather, certain sections may be highlighted in an effort to configure the whole.

When I speak of configuring the whole, I want to make it clear that I am participating in the construction of the structure I see and that I am not claiming the structure as 'an essential literary context'. I concur with David Carr when he says that 'excessive confidence in the existence of...complete unity in biblical texts—and our need to find it—can blind us to the unresolved, rich plurality built into texts'.[17] I do not claim, then, that *my* way of reading Zechariah and the Twelve in this commentary is *the* way of reading. The reader who reads Zechariah and the Twelve, like the reader of any text, is actively involved in configuring, not discovering, a pattern of coherence.

My reading of the Twelve will also be an exercise in intertextuality since it will be done in conjunction with other texts of the Hebrew Bible, particularly the book of Isaiah. 'The theory of intertextuality insists that a text...cannot exist as a hermetic or self-sufficient whole, and so does not function as a closed system'.[18] Both the inception and reception of texts are influenced by and are, in some sense, a mimesis of other texts, which authors and readers bring to their writing and

15. Collins, *Mantle*, p. 29.

16. For example, Collins understands the origin of prophetic books to be a 'three tiered process'. He says, 'The word "redactors" will be used to refer to those who were responsible for the earlier stages of collection and organization in the "pre-book phrase"; the term "writers" will refer to those who used this redacted material to compose the prophetical books; the term "editors" will refer to those responsible for the subsequent revisions of those books', *Mantle*, p. 32.

17. D. Carr, 'Reaching for Unity in Isaiah', *JSOT* 57 (1993), pp. 61-80 (80). Carr here is speaking specifically of Isaiah but what he says about Isaiah is also applicable to the Twelve.

18. J. Still and M. Worton (eds.), *Intertextuality: Theories and Practices* (Manchester: Manchester University Press, 1990), p. 1. On intertextuality and the Hebrew Bible see D.N. Fewell (ed.), *Reading between Texts: Intertextuality and the Hebrew Bible* (Louisville, KY: Westminster/John Knox Press, 1992).

reading.[19] My reading of the Twelve from an intertextual perspective means that I do not require one text to be prior to the other[20] but understand the relationship between the texts synchronically as a way of aiding the interpretative process. My reading of the Twelve in conjunction with other texts of the Hebrew Bible rather than as an isolated text has influenced the way I have configured it as a prophetic book.

To emphasize the role of the reader in the configuration of the Twelve as a whole distinguishes my reading of the Twelve from that of redaction critics, who ascribe the unity to the intentional design of the redactor who shaped the text. It also distinguishes my reading from the formalist or New Critical reading of the Twelve, which understands the unity of the Twelve as arising out of a close reading of the text, which refuses consideration of the input of either the 'author' or the 'reader'.[21]

Zechariah in the Twelve: An Overview

The Twelve of which Zechariah is a part presents a series of occasions in which the LORD spoke through twelve individuals. These twelve

---

19. Still and Worton (eds.), *Intertextuality*, pp. 1-2.

20. On this point see the comments of my colleague at the University of Queensland, John Frow, 'Intertextuality and Ontology', in Still and Worton (eds.) *Intextuality*, pp. 45-55. He says, 'Intertextual analysis is distinguished from source criticism both by this stress on interpretation rather than on the establishment of particular facts, and by its rejection of a unilinear causality (the concept of "influence") in favour of an account of the work performed upon intertextual material and its functional integration in the later text', p. 46. For another example of the intertextual approach to biblical texts see G. Savran, 'Beastly Speech: Intertextuality, Balaam's Ass and the Garden of Eden', *JSOT* 64 (1994), pp. 33-55. In his article Savran discusses the intertextual relationship between Gen. 3 and Num. 22, the only two stories in the biblical text in which animals speak.

21. An example of a formalist reader is P.R. House, *The Unity of the Twelve* (JSOTSup, 117; Bible & Literature Series, 27; Sheffield: Almond Press, 1990). House says, 'Psychological criticism and reader-response analysis are likewise rejected ... Both types emphasize something besides the text itself. The former tries to understand the psyche of the author, while the latter focuses on how literature affects its readers' (p. 31). In his book House does not satisfactorily address the poststructuralist argument that unity and structure do not emerge out of texts but arise out of reading. House's understanding of the unity of the Twelve has often been criticized because his tri-partite unitary structure of the Twelve—sin (Hosea through Micah), punishment (Nahum through Zephaniah) and restoration (Haggai through Malachi)—is so broad that 'one gets the impression that they could be imposed upon any combination of prophetic writings' (Nogalski, *Precursors*, p. 11).

individuals are placed in a historical setting portrayed as extending from the Judaean King Uzziah and ending with the Persian King Darius. A transition occurs in the Persian setting. The first nine individuals are confined to a more vaguely remembered past and are understood as 'former prophets' to whom God spoke in earlier times. With Haggai, prophets appear in new guise as messengers of the LORD in what is portrayed as a world better known, since it is more precisely dated. The appearance of messengers in the Twelve coincides with the time of return from exile when the LORD himself has returned to the temple under construction. The message of these new messengers is succinctly put by Haggai: ' "I am with you," says the LORD' (Hag. 1.13).

The Persian section of the Twelve closely entwines the three individuals portrayed in this period. The dating of Haggai and Zechariah overlaps so that the activities of these two individuals are interconnected. The foundations of the temple are laid in Haggai, and its construction is completed in Zechariah. Furthermore, Haggai, identified as 'the messenger of the LORD' in Haggai (Hag. 1.13), appears in the opening scenes of Zechariah (see especially Zech. 1.12 and 3.1, 6). The end of Zechariah is linked with Malachi by the repetition of the phrase, 'An Oracle, the word of the LORD' (Zech. 9.1; 12.1; and Mal. 1.1). There are other ways in which Haggai, Zechariah and Malachi are connected. For example, in Haggai the LORD asks most of the questions; in the beginning of Zechariah (Zech. 1-6), Zechariah asks the messenger questions; at the end of Zechariah (Zech. 7-14) and in Malachi, the community is asking questions. Also, as one moves to the end of the Twelve, prophetic messengers lose their named identity.

In the configuration of the Twelve as a whole, then, Zechariah plays a significant role in the emergence of messengers. He is ambiguously linked with the former prophets through a genealogy extending to his grandfather Iddo, the prophet (1.1, 7). He speaks, nevertheless, for the former prophets (see 1.6; 7.7, 12; cf. 8.9). Their words from the past, presented as if the former prophets had been in agreement, are evoked to justify the LORD's actions in the present. Embedded in the middle of this reference to former prophets are scenes depicting what Zechariah sees or is shown, and attached to these sights are sayings of the LORD. While the tradition has been to read these as 'visions', I would rather use a more neutral mode of description—especially since the text itself does not refer to these sights and sayings as 'visions'. I read them as 'seeing-sayings', analogous to Jer. 1.11-16 or Amos 7.7-9; 8.1-3. Almond branches, boiling pots, plumb lines and baskets of summer fruit are items one can see in the surrounding world, and they function as visual metaphors of the LORD's words. Likewise, what Zechariah sees are items in the world in which he is placed, in which Jerusalem is being restored and the temple rebuilt. He is looking at the temple under construction, and temple images become a metaphorical expression of the meaning of the LORD's message, 'I am with you'. This imagery and the associated sayings of the LORD occur in scenes in which Zechariah himself begins to act like a messenger.

From the perspective of the Twelve as a whole, a messenger presence represents a return to the way it was in the days of Jacob when a messenger used to appear to Jacob at Bethel (Hos. 12.4). It is significant, therefore, that when the scenes come to an end, Bethel sends representatives with a question to the priests and prophets in the house of the LORD (7.1-3). Bethel, where the LORD used to speak to a messenger, now sends representatives to the house of the LORD in Jerusalem where the LORD is present with his messenger Zechariah. This event marks a transition to the end of Zechariah and the end of the Twelve. It indicates that the temple has been completed and that Zechariah speaks with a new status (see 6.15; 4.9; cf. 3.8, 9, 11). In the course of Zechariah's answer to Bethel's question, the full implications of the LORD's presence in the temple as 'the master of all the earth' (4.14; 6.5; cf. 5.3, 6) become clear. The whole earth will come to hear the message, ' "I am *with you*," says the LORD' so that in the future 'ten men from nations of every language shall take hold of a Jew, grasping his garment and saying, "Let us go with you, for we have heard that God is *with you*" ' (8.23). This verse at the end of the section of Zechariah in which Zechariah emerges as a messenger emphasizes the LORD's presence 'with you'. Presence 'with' is the central theme of the 'message' Haggai proclaimed when he was first identified as a messenger (Hag. 1.13). In the Twelve messenger presence is tantamount to divine presence, 'God is with you'.

In response to the question from Bethel (7.1-3), Zechariah, as a messenger, provides an answer (Zech. 7.4-8.23) to which the oracles are attached (Zech. 9-14 and Malachi), and this answer is analogous in structure to the earlier scenes in which sayings were attached to questions Zechariah asked about what he was seeing. There is, however, a major difference. While the seeing-sayings were primarily concerned with the LORD's actions seen in temple imagery, Zechariah's answer, which includes the oracles, is concerned primarily with the actions of the northern community. The text is dissonant in that there is a conflict between the world-view presented to the reader through the eyes of Zechariah in Zechariah 1-6 and the world-view reflected in the oracles, which betray the inconsistency between expected and existing realities (see the commentary on 8.6 below).

The oracles highlight a conflict played out on a stage much more localized than that of 'the whole earth'. As the oracles progress, the focus increasingly narrows. The first oracle (Zech. 9-11) is concerned with 'the whole land' surrounding Jerusalem (Judah and Israel in a restored union as well as a union of Aram, Tyre and Sidon and the Philistine cities) rather than 'the whole earth'. However, the oracle closes with a shattering of even this more local expression of the LORD's power. Although the LORD continues to be presented in a dominant role, the LORD's power is challenged by the cryptic reference to the shepherds, the leaders of the various communities. They permit their peoples, the sheep, to wander. It appears that the LORD is not in control of these shepherds as the text would have us believe (Zech. 11.17) and that the LORD is not even master of 'the whole land'—this more limited portion of 'the whole earth'.

'The whole earth' of Zechariah 1-8, which became 'the whole land' in the first oracle (Zech. 9-11), becomes Jerusalem in the second oracle (Zech. 12-14). Even here there is conflict over the LORD's power. The situation has changed from that of the earlier scenes in Zechariah. While earlier in Zechariah the nations were seen as being plundered by the LORD, the LORD is now viewed as gathering the nations against Jerusalem to purge the enemy within. While this oracle still speaks of that day when the nations of the whole earth will come to celebrate the feast of booths in Jerusalem, this view of the centrality of the LORD's power in Jerusalem reads more like a wish than a certainty. As this oracle comes to limit its focus on Jerusalem, the leaders in that community—the prophets of the old order (Zech. 13.2-6)—emerge as being in conflict with the world-view portrayed through messenger eyes in Haggai and Zechariah. The third oracle (Malachi) suggests that priests, too, challenge the messenger construction of the world. In summary, then, the world-view of the messengers who speak in Haggai and Zechariah is in conflict with the world-view of the prophets and the priests in the restored community.

The main theme of Zechariah is 'return' understood in spatial—and local—terms. The LORD will return to Jerusalem to dwell in the midst of those who have returned from being scattered throughout the whole earth. Such a localization of the deity makes it difficult to fit this text into the theological agenda for many communities whose reading relates it to a deity understood in more universal terms. The claims made for the LORD in Zechariah, that he is 'the master of the whole earth' (4.14; 6.5), suggest a universalistic reading. But the claim later in Zechariah is more about a radical localization than a radical universality—'the master of all the earth is with you' in Jerusalem.

My reading of Zechariah, then, contrasts with prevailing readings in the following ways: While Zechariah contains what some see as bizarre imagery in the opening scenes, my reading has understood this imagery in relation to the temple under construction and the restoration of Jerusalem. This imagery itself, associated with the seeing-sayings, constructs a world-view of Jerusalem, inhabited by the LORD, as the centre of the whole earth. Zechariah presents the LORD as master of the whole earth and then localizes this universal power in Jerusalem, where the LORD speaks through messengers. Through this construction of the world the messenger and the message gain authority. When I read Zechariah, I see not angelic beings but prophets in a new guise. What others have seen as visions, I read as seeing-sayings. That is, where others see fantastic forays into another world, I see images of the temple and the city of Jerusalem. Where some have seen most clearly Zechariah's assertion of the universal power of God, I see a claim for human power. While some have seen Zechariah as a stage, even if an initial one, of the history of thought termed apocalyptic, I see it as literature that tells a story portraying prophecy in a new guise in which messengers speak for the LORD who is present with them in the temple in Jerusalem.

2. The Book of the Twelve

The Literary Context for Reading Zechariah

One of the primary features of my reading of Zechariah is that I see Zechariah as an integral part of the book of the Twelve. Looking at certain literary characteristics of the Twelve will clarify the role of Zechariah both in its macro-context of the Twelve as a whole and in its micro-context of Haggai, which precedes it, and Malachi, which follows it.

Configuring the Twelve: Zechariah in its Macro-Context

Reading, Writing and Speaking in the Twelve. I understand that, in the Twelve, spoken words appear in written form. However, unlike historical-critics who understand prophets as speakers whose words have been reduced to writing, I read the text as portraying the LORD as speaker and prophets as writers and readers of the LORD's once spoken words.

The note of the LORD as speaker is sounded at the very beginning of the Twelve, providing the reader with the key for understanding that what is encountered in writing are the words the LORD has spoken. The enigmatic phrase in Hos. 1.2a casts a shadow over the entire text. This odd phrase, which because of its peculiarity captures the attention of the reader, can be translated literally as: 'Beginning of the LORD spoke [was] with [or, 'by means of'] Hosea.' The significance of this phrase is sometimes obscured in translations such as the NRSV, where it is read as a dependent clause in a continuing sentence, 'When the LORD first spoke through Hosea, the LORD said to Hosea...' However, I read it by itself, separated from what immediately follows; and this reading receives support from ancient readers such as the Masoretes[22] as well as more recent commentators.[23]

'Beginning of the LORD spoke [was] with Hosea' can be understood as a kind of introductory sentence for the Twelve as a whole. The Hebrew word translated 'beginning of' is often used to mean the first in a series of occurrences. For example, at the beginning of the book of Judges, it is used to refer to Judah, who 'will go up first' to fight against the Canaanites (Judg. 1.1, cf. Judg. 20.18). It is also used to refer to the first in a series of visions (Dan. 8.1, cf. Dan. 9.21), the first in a series of pitching tents (Gen. 13.3), the first in the series of times that Jacob's sons went to Egypt to buy bread (Gen. 43.20, cf. 43.18), the first in a series of harvests (2 Sam. 21.9, cf. Ruth 1.22), and the first in a series of attacks in a battle (2 Sam. 17.9), among other examples. At the beginning of the Twelve, then, the reader is informed that the LORD's initial speaking with Hosea is the first in a series in which God spoke also with the eleven individuals subsequently encountered.

While the LORD is portrayed in the Twelve as speaking to the prophets, the LORD's words are encountered in writing. The 'durability' of the written word, not the spontaneity of prophetic speech, characterizes the language associated with the prophets. Prophetic proclamation is portrayed as an activity associated with writing down and reading aloud the once spoken words of the LORD rather than with prophetic speaking. The Twelve does not portray in great detail how the spoken words came to the prophet and what the prophet did with them. However, when the Twelve does depict the reception of what the LORD spoke, reception is connected with the production of written words for reading. That the Twelve presents the spoken words of the LORD for reading is clear in some sketches of prophetic activity. It is implicit at the

---

22. The Masoretes, Jewish scholars of the fifth to the tenth century responsible for preserving the Hebrew text, inserted a *pisqā'* between Hos. 1.2a and 1.2b, i.e. a punctuation mark requiring a major pause. Their reading, then, would not support the continuation of the sentence as in the NRSV. On this point see F. Andersen and D.N. Freedman, *Hosea: A New Translation and Commentary* (AB, 24; Garden City, NY: Doubleday, 1980), p. 154.

23. See, for example, F. Landy, *Hosea* (Readings: A New Bible Commentary; Sheffield: Sheffield Academic Press, 1995), p. 21; and H.W. Wolff, *Hosea: A Commentary on the Book of the Prophet Hosea* (trans. G. Stansell; Hermeneia; Philadelphia: Fortress Press, 1974), pp. 8, 12-13.

beginning of Nahum in which the oracle of Nahum is presented as a 'book' for reading: 'An oracle of Nahum. The book of the vision of Nahum of Elkosh' (Nah. 1.1). Prophetic activity as the production of the LORD's words in writing and reading is made explicit in Hab. 2.1-2.[24]

> I will stand at my watchpost,
>   and station myself on the rampart;
> I will keep watch to see what he will *speak* by means of[25] me
>   and what I will bring back[26] concerning my reproof.[27]
> Then the LORD answered me and said:
> '*Write* the vision;
>   make it plain on tablets,
>   so that a *reader* may run[28] with it.'

This passage suggests several important points about the portrayal of prophecy in the Twelve: (1) The LORD speaks by means of a prophet. (2) The prophet communicates those words by writing them down so that they can be read. (3) Prophetic oracles (Hab. 1.1) are tangible things (words written on tablets) that can be brought back by the prophet and carried by readers. (4) The LORD speaks to *prophets* by means of visions.

As I configure the Twelve, then, the prophetic words a reader of the Twelve encounters in writing are not derived from original prophetic speech. On the contrary, reading and writing are fundamental aspects of prophetic proclamation of what the LORD spoke. Hence reading and writing are of central importance in configuring the Twelve as a whole and especially for understanding the placement of Zechariah in that configuration. An intertextual reading of the book of Isaiah and the Twelve helps illuminate this configuration.

Isaiah and the Twelve. The book of Isaiah and the book of the Twelve can be configured in a similar way even though they are clearly not

24. For a more detailed discussion of this passage see Floyd, 'Prophecy and Writing', pp. 462-81. In his article, Floyd is primarily interested in the history of prophecy in Israelite society and sees in this passage evidence of mantic writing.

25. I have changed the NRSV's 'say to' to 'speak by means of' to indicate that the Hebrew of Hab. 2.1 contains the same verb and preposition as Hos. 1.2, 'The beginning of the LORD spoke was by means of Hosea...'

26. NRSV emends the text and translates 'he will answer'.

27. NRSV translates 'complaint'.

28. The NRSV's 'a runner may read' does not reflect the Hebrew in which the verb is best translated 'may run' rather than as a substantive 'runner' and the participle is best translated 'reader' as the subject of the verb. On this point see Floyd, 'Prophecy and Writing', p. 471.

mirror images of each other. Both books construct the past by presenting a time when there were kings in Judah (Isa. 6-39 and Hosea through Zephaniah) followed by a time associated with Persian kings (Isa. 40-66 and Haggai through Malachi). Each book presents prophetic words, set in a period of Judaean royalty and unheeded by the contemporary audience, as written words to be read out to a more accepting community at a time of Persian kingship.

When I read the two books of Isaiah and the Twelve as each having a section dated according to the reigns of the kings of Judah and another section associated with the later time of a Persian king, I am referring to explicit indications of time.29 In the superscription (1.1) to the book of Isaiah, the prophet is associated with kings, who according to biblical narrative, ruled in Judah during the time of Assyrian ascendancy (Uzziah, Jotham, Ahaz and Hezekiah). In narrative, Isaiah is connected with Ahaz in ch. 7, with Hezekiah in chs. 36-39, with the Assyrian king Sargon in ch. 20 and with the Assyrian king Sennacherib in chs. 36-37. As is well known, the book of Isaiah leaps forward after ch. 39 to the end of the Babylonian period when the only king mentioned is the Persian king, Cyrus (44.28; 45.1). The book of the Twelve has a similar configuration. Explicit references to Judaean kings from Hosea to Zephaniah place this section of the Twelve in a period of time from Uzziah to Josiah, coinciding with the rise and fall of Assyria.

Hosea 1.1	Uzziah, Jotham, Ahaz, Hezekiah
Amos 1.1	Uzziah[30]
Micah 1.1	Jotham, Ahaz, Hezekiah
Zephaniah 1.1	Josiah[31]

The book of the Twelve, unlike the book of Isaiah, extends the dating

---

29. It is important to emphasize here that I am not reading as a source critic nor as a redaction critic. I am aware that it is conventional for many critical studies to be more precise in dating than I have been and also to mistrust explicit references to dating. On the one hand, as I have pointed out above, we have to be more cautious in using biblical literature as data for reconstructing history than traditional historical-critical studies have been. On the other hand, my references to Judaean and Persian kings are at a literary level. How these literary time-settings relate to historical periods is not something that is easily addressed. These texts do not simply reflect the past; they also are involved in its creation.

30. Hos. 1.1 and Amos 1.1 also mention the Israelite king, Jeroboam.

31. Five of the individuals in the Book are given no specific dating (Joel, Obadiah, Jonah, Nahum and Habakkuk) so that their literary location in time is determined by the explicit references to kings associated with the dating of other prophets surrounding them in the literary collage.

beyond Hezekiah to Josiah. Narrative in this part of the Twelve (Amos 7.10-17 and Jonah)[32] also provides the Assyrian era as the historical period for this literary collage. When the reader moves from Zephaniah to Haggai, he or she is catapulted in time, as is the case with the book of Isaiah, over the period of Babylonian rule to the Persian period. In this section of the Twelve only the Persian king Darius is mentioned. Unlike the book of Isaiah, and as if to bring the reader from a vaguely remembered past into a better known period of time, the book of the Twelve indicates dating more frequently and more precisely (see Hag. 1.1, 4b-15; 2.1, 10, 20; Zech. 1.1, 7; 7.1). In summary, then, while there are differences in details, both the book of Isaiah and the book of the Twelve have a similar configuration in which explicit references to Judaean and foreign kings create a division between an Assyrian and a post-Babylonian or Persian era.

Reading the Writing of a Prophetic Past. In an earlier book, *Reading Isaiah*, I argued that the vision of Isaiah is a book (Isa. 6–39) within the book of Isaiah.[33] Isaiah is portrayed as a prophet from an Assyrian past, a time when his community is blind and deaf to his message (see Isa. 6.9-10). Therefore Isaiah, like Habakkuk, is ordered by the LORD to write down his vision,

> Go now, write it before them on a tablet,
> and inscribe it in a book
> so that it may be for the time to come
> as a witness for ever (Isa. 30.8).

This instruction to Isaiah is mirrored in an earlier imperative of Isaiah himself: 'Bind up the testimony, seal the teaching among my disciples' (Isa. 8.16). Isaiah's vision is understood to be for another time, unlike his own time, when the blind will see and the deaf will hear (see Isa. 42.18-20 and 43.8, cf. 29.18). As I maintained in *Reading Isaiah*, the book of Isaiah portrays the period of Babylonian decline and Persian ascendancy as the occasion when the command is given for the vision to be read (Isa. 40.6).[34] The legal ambience of Isaiah's written vision, that it is to be a 'witness', a 'testimony' and a 'teaching', and that, like a legal

---

32. Excluding, of course, the narrative about Hosea's personal history, Hos. 1 and 3.

33. E.W. Conrad, *Reading Isaiah* (Overtures to Biblical Theology; Minneapolis: Fortress Press, 1991); see pp. 130-43.

34. See pp. 137-38. The Hebrew verb in this verse is often rendered as 'cry' or 'call', but I translate as 'read', another possible meaning for the word.

document, it is to be 'sealed',[35] suggests that its significance is for a future community whose members will be witnesses for the LORD (see, e.g., Isa. 43.10, 12) in the trial that he will conduct against the nations (see, e.g., 43.8-13). In the book of Isaiah the LORD's words spoken in the past vision of the prophet Isaiah, originating in a period of Assyrian ascendancy, become audible in a future time when they are read to a community at a time of Persian ascendancy.

When the book of the Twelve is read in relation to the book of Isaiah, a similar configuration can be seen. Hosea, Joel, Amos, Obadiah, Jonah, Micah, Nahum, Habakkuk and Zephaniah are books within the larger book of the Twelve. The spoken words of the LORD encountered in writing in these 'books' are understood as significant for another time, when read out in a period of Persian sovereignty. While I alluded to the significance of writing and reading in relation to Nahum and Habakkuk, it is in the Persian section of the book, especially in Haggai and Zechariah, that the former prophets are portrayed as having generated written words from earlier times to be read out in the later period of Persian sovereignty.

Haggai represents a significant point of transition in the Twelve. It marks the end of a section spanning a succession of Judaean kings from Uzziah to Josiah. It also commences a new part, in which the activities of both Haggai and Zechariah are dated much more precisely to the time of the Persian King Darius. Yet strikingly at the end of Haggai and at the very beginning of Zechariah (Zech. 1.2-6) attention is focused again on the former prophets. If the Twelve is seen as a literary collage, it is appealing to interpret references to the former prophets as pointing to the prophets who appear earlier in the book, that is, Hosea through Zephaniah. When Zechariah summarizes the message of the former prophets, the present Persian audience appears to be aware of what the 'former prophets' proclaimed and heeds the call to repentance.

> The LORD was very angry with your ancestors. Therefore say to them, Thus says the LORD of hosts: Return to me, says the LORD of hosts, and I will return to you, says the LORD of hosts. Do not be like your ancestors, to whom the former prophets proclaimed, 'Thus says the LORD of hosts: Return from your evil ways and from your evil deeds'. But they did not hear or heed me, says the LORD. Your ancestors, where are they? And the prophets, do they live forever? But my words and my statutes, which I commanded my servants the prophets, did they not overtake your ancestors? So they repented and said, 'The LORD of hosts has dealt with us according to our ways and deeds, just as he planned to do' (Zech.1.2-6).

35. See also Jer. 32.9-15.

That the former prophets were individuals who lived in the past before Jerusalem was destroyed is even more explicit in the second place in Zechariah where the former prophets are mentioned (Zech. 7.7). Here a rhetorical question implies an affirmative answer.

> Were not these the words that the LORD proclaimed by the former prophets, when Jerusalem was inhabited and in prosperity, along with the towns around it, and when the Negeb and the Shephelah were inhabited?

A précis of what the former prophets said is given in Zech. 7.5-6 and 7.8-10.

For a reader configuring this literary collage, the connection with the earlier section of the book is not hard to see. But how are we to understand how Zechariah's audience in the Persian section of the book came to know what the prophets proclaimed in the earlier section of the book? How does the Twelve portray the reception of earlier prophetic words in later times? The answers to these questions are suggested in Zech. 8.9-13, another passage in which Zechariah is concerned with 'the prophets' (8.9) and 'the former days' (8.11).

> Thus says the LORD of hosts, 'Let your hands be strong—the ones who have heard in these days[36] these words from the mouth of the prophets[37] which[38] were present when the foundation was laid for the rebuilding of the temple, the house of the LORD of hosts' (Zech. 8.9).

The phrase in this passage, 'from the mouth of the prophets', is concerned with writing, not with spoken words such as public preaching. The phrase is an idiomatic expression for dictation,[39] and it is used in

36. My translation is a more literal rendering of the Hebrew than the NRSV's 'you that have recently been hearing'.

37. Since the Hebrew word is singular, I have translated it in the singular. NRSV renders it in the plural as 'mouths'. To translate the word in the plural is to miss its idiomatic usage. See the discussion below.

38. I have translated the relative pronoun as 'which' rather than following the NRSV's 'who'. In my interpretation of this passage, I understand that the relative pronoun refers to 'these words' and not to 'prophets'. The translation of this relative pronoun, which can be rendered either as 'who' or 'which' is important. To translate it as 'who' suggests that it is 'prophets' who were present; to translate it as 'which' suggests that it was the 'words' which were present. I have opted for 'which' because 'from the mouth of the prophets' is an idiomatic expression referring to dictation of words. See the Tanakh for a similar translation.

39. Carol and Eric Meyers (*Haggai, Zechariah 1-8* [AB, 256; Garden City, NY: Doubleday, 1987], pp. 419-20) understand this phrase in Zech. 8.9 to be an idiom meaning 'dictate'. They say, '…the use of "from the mouth of" along with "prophet" or the prophet's name is an idiom (which usually also includes the verb "to write")

Jer. 36.4, 6, 17, 18, 27, 32 in relation to the production of the scroll Jeremiah dictated to Baruch (see also Jer. 45.1). In Zech. 8.9, then, 'from the mouth of' suggests words written from dictation and read out much later, that is, on the day the foundation of the temple was laid. The former prophets are portrayed as being present in the Persian period in the Twelve in a way similar to the way they are present for the reader of the book; they are present as written words. Such a presence, however, does not suggest a silent reader; these words are for the ear, for 'the ones hearing...these words' (Zech. 8.9).[40] Prophetic words from the past are made audible by reading them aloud to later communities.[41]

In a literary sense the time when the words of the former prophets were read aloud, that is, the time 'when the foundation was laid for rebuilding the temple, the house of the LORD of hosts' (Zech. 8.9), can be linked with the depiction of the period of Haggai. There are several reasons to associate that time in the Twelve with Haggai. Language in the larger pericope Zech. 8.9-13 is reminiscent of Haggai: (1) The occasion when these words were heard is described as a time when there as a call 'to rebuild' the temple (Zech. 8.9). Such a command to rebuild the temple is given in Haggai 1.2. (2) The thrice-repeated 'take courage' to Zerubbabel, Joshua and the people (Hag. 2.4) is echoed in the phrase 'let your hands be strong' in which the same Hebrew verb root is used. (3) The LORD's 'I will bless you' in Hag. 2.19 is paralleled by 'you will be a blessing' in Zech. 8.13. (4) The comforting 'fear not' addressed to all assembled in Hag. 2.5 is paralleled by 'fear not' in Zech. 8.13. (5) Finally, the envisioned restitution of produce in Zech. 8.12 is similar to that in Hag. 2.18-19, cf. 1.11.

In the Twelve, then, the occasion of the assembly of the High Priest Joshua, the governor Zerubbabel, and all the remnant of the people, depicted in the Haggai section of the book, is the occasion for reading the writings 'from the mouth of' the former prophets. The dictated

meaning "dictate". Actually, it is only for Jeremiah that such a process is recorded. In 36.4, 6, 17, 18, 27, 32 and 45.1, Jeremiah orders his prophecies recorded on a scroll or book. Jer. 36.4, for example, informs us that Jeremiah summoned Baruch; and Baruch "wrote from the mouth of Jeremiah [i.e. at the dictation of Jeremiah], on a scroll, all *the words of Yahweh which he had spoken to him*".'

40. On the oral dimension of writing in the Old Testament see my 'Heard But Not Seen': The Representation of "Books" in the Hebrew Bible', *JSOT* 54 (1992), pp. 45-59.

41. In *Reading Isaiah* (pp. 84-87) I also argued that the Vision of Isaiah was a prophetic writing that was intended for the ear, i.e. to be read aloud to later communities.

words of the former prophets are present in the Persian period and can be read aloud to the assembled community.

To summarize, then, both the book of Isaiah and the book of the Twelve can be configured as portraying prophetic words as written in former times, when kings ruled in Judah, to be read out at a later time, a time of Persian royal sovereignty. While the two books are similar in that they present prophetic writing as relevant for a later time, there is one major difference. In the book of Isaiah, the legal ambience associated with the preservation of Isaiah's vision is important to undergird its value as testimony in the trial in which the LORD opposes all the nations of the world. The preservation of prophetic writing is portrayed as serving divine needs. In the book of the Twelve the words of the 'former prophets' serve to call the community concerned with the restoration of the temple to return. The preservation of prophetic writings is portrayed as serving human needs.[42]

The End of Prophecy. There is another link between Isaiah and the Twelve emerging out of an intertextual reading of the two books. By the end of each book, prophets disappear from the scene, or to put it more appropriately, prophets appear in a new guise as 'messengers'[43] of the LORD. In the book of Isaiah, the prophet Isaiah drops from the scene after ch. 39. One encounters messengers in Isa. 42.19; 44.26 and 63.9. However, these messengers appear more in the background and are less clearly developed as characters in the book of Isaiah than they are in the Twelve.[44]

I want, therefore, to turn my attention now to the emergence of prophets as 'messengers' in the Twelve because this book, more clearly than Isaiah, develops the significance of this change.[45] The end of a

42. I will develop this point below in my discussion of Zechariah.

43. There is one Hebrew word that has been translated either as 'messenger' as it is in Hag. 1.13 or 'angel' as it is commonly rendered in Zechariah, e.g. Zech. 1.9. As I will argue below, this rigid division reflected in our contemporary translations between human beings (messengers) and heavenly beings (angels) is blurred in Zechariah and elsewhere in the Old Testament. My understanding of the emergence of messengers in the Twelve has affinities with Naomi G. Cohen's views although she approaches the subject from a more historical perspective. See her 'From *Nabi* to *Mal'ak* to "Ancient Figure" ', *JJS* 36 (1985), pp. 12-24.

44. Prophets such as Second Isaiah and Third Isaiah appear only in the post-texts of historical criticism.

45. Space does not permit me to develop the intertextual implications for reading Isaiah in light of my understanding of 'messengers' in the Twelve, and I will take that up in another place.

prophetic past and the appearance of messengers who supplant prophets, begins to become evident in Haggai. Haggai is identified five times as a prophet (Hag. 1.1, 3, 12; 2.1, 10), but he is also the first person to be identified as a messenger (Hag. 1.13). The distancing of prophets as a past phenomenon becomes more evident in Zechariah when he is surrounded by messengers (see Zech. 1.6–6.8).[46] At the beginning of Zechariah, in the pericope in which Zechariah refers to the "former prophets", the rhetorical questions 'And your ancestors, where are they?' and 'And the prophets, do they live forever?' suggest that prophecy as it occurred in former times is ending. Indeed, it is not even clear whether Zechariah should be understood as a prophet. The phrase 'Zechariah, the son of Berechiah, the son of Iddo the prophet' occurs twice (1.1, 7).[47] Such a phrase is ambiguous.[48] It is possible that the phrase 'the prophet' should be interpreted to refer to Iddo, not Zechariah. If that is the case, then we meet the figure Zechariah, surrounded by messengers, who is two generations removed from his grandfather who was a prophet. The end of prophecy is most clearly indicated in an oracle toward the end of Zechariah:

> I will remove from the land the prophets and the unclean spirit. And if any prophets appear again, their fathers and mothers who bore them will say to them, 'You shall not live, for you speak lies in the name of the LORD'; and their fathers and their mothers who bore them shall pierce them through when they prophesy. On that day the prophets will be ashamed, every one, of their visions when they prophesy; they will not put on a hairy mantle in order to deceive, but each of them will say, 'I am no prophet, I am a tiller of the soil; for the land has been my possession since my youth'. And if anyone asks them, 'What are these wounds on your chest?' the answer will be 'The wounds I received in the house of my friends' (Zech. 13.2b-6).

At the end of the Twelve a single messenger is introduced, Malachi (whose name means 'my messenger'); and the only prophets mentioned are Moses and Elijah (Mal. 4.4-5). Moses is clearly a figure of the past whose statutes and ordinances are to be remembered, but Elijah who will be sent again takes on the appearance of a messenger sent from heaven.

46. As indicated above, the word is translated as 'angels' in most English translations.

47. In v. 7 the proper name is spelled somewhat differently in the Hebrew text.

48. The phrase is unique in the Hebrew Bible. No other prophet is introduced in such a way as to identify him as a prophet after first introducing him in a lineage extending back to his grandfather.

To gain some perspective on the appearance of prophets as messengers in the Twelve, it is important to understand how prophecy is characterized in the book as a whole. Confusion about prophecy is an underlying theme in the earlier section of the book concerned with the former prophets, Hosea through Zephaniah. Who is a prophet and who is not? Who is to be heeded, and who is to be ignored? These are questions the Twelve presents as issues.

On the one hand, prophets are singled out for judgment as participants in the official corruption affecting leaders in the community (Hos. 4.4-6; Mic. 3.5-7, 9-11; Zeph. 3.1-4).[49] On the other hand, prophets are sometimes valued positively as carrying out the work of the LORD (see Hos. 6.5; 12.11 [Eng. 12.10]; 12.14 [Eng. 12.13]; Amos 2.11-12; 3.7-8). However one reads these passages, the impression seems to be of a community's difficulty in distinguishing between prophets who are corrupt, leading the people astray, and others who are filled with the spirit of the LORD. 'Who is acting as a prophet ought to act, and who is mad and acting like a fool?'[50] is an unwritten question that pervades the section of the Twelve from Hosea to Zephaniah.

This bewilderment is probably most clearly conveyed by the narrative about Amos that occurs in the middle of his reception of visions from the LORD (Amos 7.10-17)—the well-known story about Amos's encounter with Amaziah the priest of Bethel who accused him of conspiring against Jeroboam, the house of Israel. In Amaziah's dialogue with Amos, Amaziah makes it clear that Amos has spoken not the words of the LORD but the words of Amos. He says, 'The land is not able to bear all *his* [Amos's] words' (Amos 7.10b). As if to underscore the point, Amaziah switches the formula, 'Thus says the LORD', which Amos had been using throughout (see, e.g., Amos 1.3, 6, 9, 13; 2.1, 4, 6; 3.12; and 5.4), to 'thus Amos said'. Furthermore, when Amaziah addresses Amos, he does not call him a 'prophet' but a 'seer'.

> And Amaziah said to Amos, 'O seer, go flee away to the land of Judah, earn
> your bread there, and prophesy there; but never again prophesy at Bethel,
> for it is the king's sanctuary, and it is a temple of the kingdom' (Amos
> 7.12-13).

While Amaziah does say that the activity that Amos is engaging in is prophesying, he does not say that Amos is a prophet. As is well known,

---

49. Again the book of Isaiah is similar because in its pre-Persian or Assyrian section (Isa. 1-39) the unscrupulous practices of prophets are rebuked (see Isa. 3.2; 9.14 [Eng. 9.15]; 28.7; and 29.10).

50. See Mic. 3.8 and Hos. 9.7b.

the Hebrew nominal sentence in Amos's response, 'Not a prophet I, and not a son of a prophet I', adds to the confusion. Should the sentence be translated in English in the present tense indicating that Amos, as Amaziah has suggested, is not a prophet? Or should it be translated in the past tense—'I was not a prophet, nor was I the son of a prophet'—implying that although Amos has not been a prophet in the past, he is now? The ambiguity need not be cleared up. Indeed, the ambiguity is the point of the passage. The prophets in former times in the Twelve are depicted as existing in a time of confusion. 'Who is a prophet and who is not?' is a question never given a clear answer in this section of the book. The prophets through whom the LORD spoke can only be known as genuine prophets in retrospect.[51]

To gain perspective on how the Twelve envisions the end of this confusion as well as the end of prophecy, it is useful to look at prophecy in the Twelve by reading the book from beginning to end. The rhetorical ploy is subtle at first. Not until Hab. 1.1, 'the oracle that the prophet saw', is any one of the named individuals identified explicitly as a prophet. The identification is repeated in Hab. 3.1. In reading on to Zephaniah, one could initially dismiss as insignificant the identification of Habakkuk as a prophet because Zephaniah, like the previous seven individuals named in the book, is not identified as a prophet. At the end of Zephaniah, however, as one crosses a chasm from the time of the Judaean King Josiah (Zeph. 1.1) at the end of Assyrian domination of Judah to the time of the Persian King Darius (Hag. 1.1), one also passes into a time where there can be no doubt that the reader is encountering a prophet. Within three short chapters Haggai is referred to as 'the prophet' five times (1.1, 3, 12; 2.1, 10). Yet, as noted above, Haggai, unlike any of the other named individuals, is identified not only as a 'prophet' but also as a messenger of the LORD (Hag. 1.13).

> Then Haggai, the messenger of the LORD, spoke to the people with the LORD's message saying, ' "I am with you," an utterance of the LORD'.

Haggai can be seen as representing a transition from the end of prophets to the appearance of messengers. When one reads on into Zechariah, prophecy becomes clearly seen as something past. This distancing is

---

51. This is another parallel between the book of Isaiah and the book of the Twelve. In the book of the Twelve the 'former prophets' are presented as figures who were not accepted by their own communities in their own times just as Isaiah's vision was rejected in his own time by a community blind and deaf to its meaning. The rejection of the words of the LORD by the prophet's own community is heightened in the book of the Twelve by the story of the ready acceptance of Jonah's message by a foreign city, Nineveh. See Jon. 3.5.

evident in two ways: (1) as noted above, Zechariah is identified as two generations removed from his grandfather Iddo, who is a prophet (1.1, 17); (2) only from the Persian perspective in the Zechariah section of the Twelve are the nine former individuals to whom the LORD spoke (Hosea through Zephaniah) identified as prophets. Zechariah identifies all the earlier individuals mentioned in the book as 'former prophets' (1.4, cf. 7.7, 12). By the time of Zechariah, the issue of who is or who is not a prophet is finally settled. The design of the book suggests that it is from the perspective of the later Persian time that these former individuals can be understood as prophets.

The Twelve embodies in its structural design the satisfaction of a criterion suggested elsewhere in ancient Israelite literature for determining who is a prophet of the LORD and who is not.

> You may say to yourself, 'How will we recognize a word that the LORD has not spoken?' If a prophet speaks in the name of the LORD but the thing does not take place or prove true, it is a word that the LORD has not spoken. The prophet has spoken it presumptuously; do not be frightened by it (Deut. 18.21-22).

The book is structured in such a way as to make clear that what the LORD spoke to the 'former prophets' (Hosea through Zephaniah) in the past has proved true at the later time of Persian rule.

> But my words and statutes, which I commanded my servants the prophets, did they not overtake your ancestors? So they repented and said, 'The LORD of hosts has dealt with us according to our ways and deeds, just as he planned to do' (Zech. 1.6).

The Twelve shares with Deuteronomy the notion that a prophet is understood to be legitimate if what he or she says comes true.[52]

Furthermore, in the Twelve Zechariah gains authority from what the former prophets said. We are told that in the fourth year of Darius 'the

---

52. A number of passages outside Deuteronomy suggest this criterion for judging the legitimacy of prophets. In Jeremiah's response to Hananiah who prophesied peace, Jeremiah responds, 'The prophets who preceded you and me from ancient times prophesied war, famine, and pestilence against many countries and great kingdoms. As for the prophet who prophesies peace, when the word of the prophet comes true, then it will be known that the LORD has truly sent the prophet' (Jer. 28.8-9). In the well-known passage concerning the prophet Micaiah and his encounter with Ahab in 1 Kgs 22, Micaiah said that the king would not succeed at Ramoth-gilead but would die in battle. When Micaiah is imprisoned for his unfavourable prophecy, he offers the following as the test for determining whether the LORD has spoken. 'If you return in peace, the LORD has not spoken by me' (v. 28).

people of Bethel had sent Sharezer and Regem-melech and their men' to the priests and the prophets to inquire about mourning and practising abstinence. Zechariah's answer to the inquiry is,

> [t]hen the word of the LORD of hosts came to me: Say to all the people of the land and the priests: When you fasted and lamented in the fifth month and in the seventh, for these seventy years, was it for me that you fasted? And when you eat and when you drink, do you not eat and drink only for yourselves? (Zech. 7.4-6).

In the continuation of his response to the question put to him by the people of Bethel, Zechariah supports his answer by claiming that his answer is in accord with what the former prophets had proclaimed.

> Were not these the words that the LORD proclaimed by the former prophets, when Jerusalem was inhabited and in prosperity, along with the towns around it, and when the Negeb and Shephelah were inhabited? (Zech. 7.7).

Zechariah is not directly quoting what any of the former prophets said, but he seeks to ground his answer in the words of the prophets from the past to whom the LORD had spoken and whose words were proved true by subsequent events (cf. Zech. 1.6). His answer receives authority from its foundation in and continuity with a prophetic past. The word of the LORD to Zechariah continues with a kind of précis of the past prophetic messages to show how Zechariah's answer about the present behaviour of the people fits with what 'the former prophets' said about the past behaviour of the people. In both cases the people are presented as self-centred.

> The word of the LORD came to Zechariah, saying, 'Thus says the LORD of hosts: "Render true judgments, show kindness and mercy to one another", do not oppress the widow, the orphan, the alien, or the poor; do not devise evil in your hearts against one another". But they refused to listen, and turned a stubborn shoulder, and stopped their ears in order not to hear. They made their hearts adamant in order not to hear the law and the words that the LORD of hosts had sent by his spirit through the former prophets. Therefore great wrath came from the LORD of hosts. "Just as, when I [Heb. 'he'] called, they would not hear, so when they called, I would not hear," says the LORD of hosts, "and I scattered them with a whirlwind among all the nations they had not known. Thus the land they left was desolate, so that no one went to and fro, and a pleasant land was made desolate"' (Zech. 7.8-14).

From the perspective of Zechariah, prophecy has become a past phenomenon. Although Haggai and Zechariah stand in the tradition of that prophetic past, the prophets are primarily understood to be characters from a former time and prophecy itself is seen to have no future. Prophecy has come to an end in Zechariah as can be seen in Zech. 13.1-6, cited above. The reported speech of the 'potential prophets' in this passage leaves no doubt; they no longer consider themselves to be prophets. Each will speak the first half of Amos's famous nominal sentence, 'Not a prophet I' (Zech. 13.5, cf. Amos 7.14), and the second part of the sentence, 'I am a tiller of the soil' (Zech. 13.5) allows for no ambiguity. Prophecy will come to an end, and communication with the deity will be by means of messengers.

Messengers in the Twelve. How are we to understand the appearance of messengers, which coincides with the disappearance of prophecy, in the Persian section of the Twelve?[53] One way of seeking an answer to this question is to look at the other place where a messenger is mentioned, that is, Hos. 12.4, a passage that occurs near the beginning of the Twelve. This verse, about a messenger who used to appear to the ancestor Jacob/Israel, is part of a larger passage, Hos. 12.2-6), pertaining to the LORD's indictment of the community.[54]

> In the womb he tried to supplant his brother,
>   and in his manhood he strove[55] with God.
> He strove with the messenger and prevailed,
>   he wept and sought his favour;
> he used to find us[56] at Bethel,
>   and there he used to speak[57] with us.[58]

53. See my 'The End of Prophecy and the Emergence of Angels/Messengers in the Book of the Twelve', *JSOT* 73 (1997), pp. 65-79.

54. The incidents in these verses recall occurrences in the life of the patriarch similar to the stories about him in Gen. 25–35.

55. The two verbs, 'supplant' and 'strove' are a play on words in Hebrew suggesting the patriarch's two names, 'Jacob' and 'Israel'.

56. I am reading the object suffix here as a first person plural rather than a third person singular (as does the NRSV) to bring it into agreement with the first person plural suffix on the preposition associated with the following verb, 'with us'.

57. NRSV translates the two imperfects 'he met' and 'he spoke'. Because the context concerns the past, it is appropriate to render the imperfects as iterative imperfects i.e. to indicate what happened repeatedly in the past.

58. 'Us' reflects the Hebrew of the MT and the footnoted reading in NRSV, which in its main translation follows the Greek and Syriac and translates 'with him'. The need to emend the text to read 'with him' seems less necessary when the preceding verb with a suffix, is read 'he used to find us'.

> The LORD the God of hosts,
>> the LORD is his name![59]
> But as for you, return to your God,
>> hold fast to love and justice,
>> and wait continually for your God.

There are a number of links between this passage about a messenger and the later Persian section of the book in which Zechariah is sur-rounded by messengers. The first concerns Zechariah's name in Hebrew in relation to the doxology that concludes the allusion to the time of the patriarch Jacob, 'The LORD the God of hosts, //*the* LORD is *his name*'. The consonantal spelling of Zechariah's name is *zkryh*. 'The LORD' in Hebrew in the doxology represents the *yh* part of Zechariah's name. The use of the word *zkr* for 'name' in the doxology rather than the more usual *šm*[60] suggests the other component of Zechariah's name. Zechariah's very name, then, encapsulates the doxology associated with remembering a past time when a messenger used to speak to the patriarch Jacob: 'The LORD the God of Hosts, //*the* LORD is *his name!*' The MT pointing of the prophet's name, that is, the vowels used to pronounce it, suggest that it be translated as 'the LORD has remem-bered'. The MT meaning of Zechariah's name, too, links the time of a messenger presence in Zechariah with the way the LORD used to speak by means of a messenger in the days of the ancestor Jacob.

Secondly, these verses in Hosea suggest that striving against the LORD is not only an accusation against the ancestor Jacob but also an indictment against the community Hosea is portrayed as addressing.[61] The community has lost the messenger presence of its patriarchal past. 'He [the messenger] used to find *us* at Bethel, //and there he used to speak with *us*'. This community without a messenger presence is directed to return to 'your' God. The call '*to return*' (Hos. 12.6) is not heeded, according to the Twelve, until the Persian period of Darius

---

59. I have italicized words here that will be important in my discussion below. For a more detailed discussion of these matters see my 'The End of Prophecy', pp. 65-79.

60. Andersen and Freedman comment on this unusual use of the word for name: 'The use of *zikrô* rather than the usual *šĕmô* as in Exod. 15.3, is notable. Hos. 12.6 is the only place where *zikrô* substitutes outright for *šĕmô* in credal hymns of this kind. The words are, however, interchangeable, as comparison with Exod. 3.15 shows', *Hosea*, p. 615.

61. On this point see G.I. Davies (*Hosea* [NCBC; Grand Rapids: Eerdmans, 1992], p. 272) who summarizes the way these verses work in the allegation by suggesting that 'the sins of the present generation [are] already foreshadowed and in some sense fixed by those of the national patriarch'.

when Zechariah reiterates the call of the former prophets for the community to return.

> The LORD was very angry with your ancestors. Therefore say to them, Thus says the LORD of hosts: *Return* to me, says the LORD of hosts, and I will *return* to you, says the LORD of hosts. Do not be like your ancestors, to whom the former prophets proclaimed, 'Thus says the LORD of hosts, *return* from your evil ways and from your evil deeds'. But they did not hear or heed me, says the LORD. Your ancestors, where are they? And the prophets, do they live forever? But my words and my statutes, which I commanded my servants the prophets, did they not overtake your ancestors? So they *returned*[62] and said, 'The LORD of hosts has dealt with us according to our ways and deeds, just as he planned to do' (Zech. 1.2-6).

The decision 'to return' occurs only when there is again a messenger presence in the Persian community. Just as the messenger used to be present to speak '*with* us' at a specific place, Bethel, so the Twelve portrays the time of the Persian king Darius as the time in which the 'LORD has remembered' this past time when a messenger used to be present *with* the community. At this time another messenger, Haggai, is concerned with establishing a particular place by summoning the people to rebuild the temple. Haggai, as the messenger of the LORD, announces the presence of the LORD, 'I am *with* you' (Hag. 1.13, cf. Hos. 12.5). The movement in the Twelve is from a former time of prophets, when there was an absence of messengers, to a Persian period where messengers again appear, and the first of these is Haggai. The argument I am proposing, then, is that in the Twelve Haggai, as both messenger and prophet, represents a transition point in the literature between the end of the LORD speaking with his people by means of his prophets (Hosea through Zephaniah) to a period of time when there will be messengers present in the rebuilt temple (Haggai through Malachi), a time when prophecy will come to an end and when prophetic words are encountered only as written words from the past.

The Twelve as a Literary Collage: A Summary View. In this section, I outlined my configuration of the Twelve as a literary collage, particularly as it related to Zechariah in the Twelve as a whole.[63] It will be helpful to draw together the major points of that discussion. The Twelve opens at

---

62. I have changed the NRSV translation, 'repented', to 'returned' in order to show in English translation the repetition of the root *šûb.*

63. To look at the configuration of the Twelve from some other viewpoint, for example from Jonah or Zephaniah, would require one to highlight other features of its shape.

the beginning of Hosea with a sentence introducing the occasion of the LORD speaking to Hosea as the first in a series of times in which the LORD spoke (Hos. 1.2a). This phrase suggests to the reader at the beginning that the Twelve concerns the LORD's speaking. By the end of the book, it has become clear to the reader that the way the LORD speaks has changed. While in earlier times God spoke by means of 'the former prophets' (Hosea through Zephaniah), in the time of the Persian King Darius, when the temple is rebuilt, God speaks through messengers. This change is not understood as something new but as a 'return' to the way it used to be when God spoke by means of a messenger to the patriarch Jacob at Bethel. Haggai represents the beginning of this return. While he is identified as a prophet, he is the first and only individual in the book to be identified as a messenger (Hag. 1.13). Zechariah represents a distancing from the past time of the former prophets. While he is a descendant of a prophet, his grandfather Iddo, he is portrayed as living in a world in which direct communication with the LORD is through messengers. Furthermore, in Zechariah's world the former prophets are present in the same way they are present to readers of the Twelve; they are encountered in writing. From this later perspective Zechariah's community, unlike the community of the past, is able to heed the proclamation of the prophets to return. The people are able to see what their forebears could not see: the LORD dealt with them 'according to their ways and deeds just as he planned to do' (Zech. 1.6). By the time the reader reaches Malachi, the change in the way in which the LORD speaks is evident. While that which the former prophets proclaimed can only be authenticated through the unfolding in time of divine purpose, the LORD speaking through Malachi is dialogical and immediate. The temple, which Zechariah sees being built in the restoration of Jerusalem, provides the place where the LORD speaks directly with his messengers such as Zechariah.

Configuring the Twelve: Zechariah in its Micro-Context

In this section, I want to look at the way Zechariah fits into its immediate context, especially with Haggai which precedes it, but also with Malachi which follows it. As noted earlier, Haggai and the beginning of Zechariah stand out in the Twelve because of recurring phrases of dating that link them to specific periods of time during the reign of the Persian King Darius (Hag. 1.1, 15; 2.1, 10, 18, 20; Zech. 1.1, 7; 7.1). The particularities of these phrases, which in most cases even include the day, has the effect both of emphasizing the significance of the emergence of messengers in the Twelve and of distancing the former prophets who are dated more generally in what is portrayed as a remotely remembered past. Moreover, since the first date mentioned in Zechariah (the eighth month in the second year of Darius, Zech. 1.1) is prior to the last date mentioned in Haggai (the twenty-fourth day of the ninth month in the second year of Darius, Hag. 2.10, cf. 2.20), Haggai and Zechariah are situated in an overlapping period of time.

This shared time frame has significance for my reading. It suggests that in the Twelve Zechariah should be understood as a continuation of Haggai. Rather than sharing only a broad setting in time as do the former prophets in the Twelve, Haggai and Zechariah share consecutive months so that Haggai provides a very specific setting for the literary world in which Zechariah appears. The significance of this dating for reading Haggai and Zechariah can be seen when one examines closely the nine phrases of dating. The following observations highlight the significant differences.[64] (1) In seven instances the dating concerns the time that 'the word of the LORD' came to either Haggai or Zechariah (Hag. 1.1; 2.1, 10, 20; Zech. 1.1, 7; 7.1). (2) In two instances the dating concerns temple construction although reference to the second year of Darius is missing (Hag. 1.15a; 2.18). (3) In Hag. 1.15a the dating also is concerned with the first time Haggai speaks as a messenger (not as a prophet), and in Zech. 1.7 the date concerns Zechariah's interaction with messengers. (4) The last time the date occurs in both Haggai and Zechariah, it dates a word of the LORD that came to either Haggai or Zechariah but neither Haggai or Zechariah is identified as a prophet.

These variations in the use of the phrases of specific dating emphasize the significance of this dating in the Twelve and provide a basis for my configuration of Zechariah. The first thing to note is that when Haggai and Zechariah initially appear in the Twelve, a phrase of dating links them with a time when the word of the LORD came to them as prophets.[65] However, when they are last mentioned, a phrase of dating also occurs but the designation of them as prophets has disappeared (Hag. 2.20 and Zech. 7.1). Secondly, the significance of this specific dating becomes apparent. These dates pinpoint the beginning of the construction of the temple and the first time that a messenger, not a prophet, appears with the message of the LORD.

One can conclude, therefore, that in the Twelve these phrases of dating are significant because they represent the crucial time in the Twelve when messengers begin to appear—the time when the temple is

---

64. There are also some minor differences. For example, the specific day is not mentioned in Zech. 1.1.

65. As I indicated above, Zechariah is introduced as the grandson of Iddo the prophet.

rebuilt. The significance of temple construction and the appearance of messengers in the Twelve is summed up in the message delivered by the messenger Haggai in 1.13. What has changed in the Twelve is that in the time of the former prophets the LORD was distant so that what he spoke to the prophets entailed a period of waiting (see Hab. 2.3). What the prophets proclaimed could only be understood as words the LORD spoke after the passage of time confirmed their validity. At the time of temple construction the LORD is present with the community as he used to be present with the community in the days of the patriarch Jacob (Hos. 12.4). Temple and messengers represent a time when the LORD's word is immediate because temple and messenger presence is tantamount to divine presence.

The time when the work begins on the temple and the messenger speaks, 'the twenty-fourth day of the month, in the sixth month' (Hag. 1.15a) provides the background for reading Zechariah. What Zechariah sees when he speaks with messengers is the restoration of Jerusalem and the temple under construction. Furthermore, when both Haggai and Zechariah last appear as named characters in the Twelve, they have lost the tag of prophet (Hag. 2.20 and Zech. 7.1) because they are modulating into messengers of the LORD and eventually lose their named identity. This occurs when Haggai appears in Zechariah as 'the messenger of the LORD' (Zech. 1.12; 3.1, 6) and when Zechariah appears at the end of the Twelve as Malachi ('my messenger').

I read Zech. 1.1–6.15 as a time when Zechariah sees sights and symbols associated with the restoration of Jerusalem and the construction of the temple, which in turn become metaphorical expressions of Haggai's original message, ' "I am with you" says the LORD' (Hag. 1.13).[66]

On the other side of these sights concerning restoration, it is significant that individuals come from Bethel to ask questions of the priests and prophets of the house of the LORD in Jerusalem (Zech. 7.1-7). The place where a messenger used to speak to Jacob (Hos. 12.4) now sends representatives to the rebuilt temple in Jerusalem.[67] It is significant that it is Zechariah who speaks. It is the last time he will be named in the Twelve. He is not associated with the prophets because he now speaks 'the word of the LORD' as a messenger and his speaking continues in oracles in 9.1–11.17; 12.1-21 and Mal. 1.1–4.6. Zechariah who received answers to questions he posed to 'the messenger who

---

66. A fuller discussion of my understanding of messengers and of what Zechariah sees (his so-called 'visions') follows in two Excursuses.

67. One is also reminded of Amos who was sent from Bethel to Judah by the priest Amaziah (Amos 7.10-15).

spoke with him', now himself a messenger, answers questions posed by the community.[68]

3. Zechariah: A Summary of my Reading

I offer the following as a précis of the more detailed reading of Zechariah that follows. Zechariah opens with Zechariah reiterating to his community the proclamation of the former prophets, which called the community to return to the LORD (1.1-6). Zechariah's addressees do what their fathers refused to do; they return to the LORD. Zechariah's name, which means 'the LORD has remembered', encapsulates the summons to return. Returning to the LORD implies returning both to Jerusalem where the LORD will be present and returning to the past as it is remembered—returning to the way things used to be.

The specific dating in both Haggai and Zechariah portrays them as interlinked in time. The community Zechariah addresses, therefore, is the community identified in Haggai as Zerubbabel the governor, Joshua the high priest and all the remnant of the people. The significance of return for that community has already been introduced in Haggai: (1) Haggai the prophet, unlike 'the former prophets' (Hosea through Zephaniah), appears in a new guise as 'the messenger of the LORD' (Hag. 1.13). This different role, however, is not so much novel as a return to the way it used to be when the LORD spoke to Jacob at Bethel by means of a messenger (Hos. 12.4). (2) Work has begun on rebuilding the temple in Jerusalem (Hag. 1.14), and the foundations of the temple have been laid (Hag. 2.18). Return, therefore, means returning to the temple. (3) Return also means *seeing* the temple restored to its former glory (Hag. 2.3, cf. 2.9).

The opening scenes in Zechariah (1.7–6.15) portray Zechariah in this context of return initiated in Haggai. He sees the restoration of Jerusalem and the temple under construction. In these scenes Zechariah interacts with messengers of the LORD and he himself emerges as a messenger. Furthermore, toward the end of the scenes he enters the temple and sees in the temple imagery the restoration of the temple to its former glory.

The first scenes portray Zechariah outside the temple. He sees horsemen returning from patrolling the earth (1.1-17), workmen who have cut off the horns for the altar (1.18-21) and a young man measuring the width and length of Jerusalem (2.1-5). In these three scenes Zechariah

---

68. The significance of the questions and the oracles will be discussed below in the commentary proper.

ceases to be an observer; he is drawn into the action and becomes an active participant in what he is seeing. Zechariah himself is drawn into the LORD's presence and communicates directly with him (1.18-21). At the end of these three scenes, Zechariah claims that in what is about to happen, it will be evident that the LORD has sent him. When he makes this claim his words and the words of the LORD merge in form and content indicating the convergence of the LORD's words and the words of Zechariah as messenger (2.6-11). This is consistent with the role of the messenger in these scenes, which suggest that messenger presence is tantamount to divine presence.

At the end of ch. 2, and after Zechariah's repeated claim about his special status, there is a call for silence directed to the reader, for Zechariah is about to enter the temple (2.13). In the temple (3.1-10), Joshua is installed as high priest and is charged with special duties by 'the messenger of the LORD', whom I understand to be Haggai. In this scene Zechariah begins to act like a messenger when he, like the messenger of the LORD, gives instructions about Joshua's apparel.

When the scene involving Joshua closes, Zechariah is in the temple viewing temple imagery and learning about its significance from the messenger who spoke with him (4.1-6.8). The need for such instruction is necessary because few in the remnant community had seen the temple in its former glory (see Hag. 2.3). The recurring motif associated with temple imagery is that the LORD is 'the master of the whole earth'. At the end of the scenes in the temple, the horsemen who appeared in the first scene are portrayed as eager to get out to patrol 'the whole earth'. The messenger who spoke with Zechariah indicates that his spirit is at ease with the north country (6.8). This is an important motif in Zechariah, for the reference to the north country signals a change in focus to the north, to Israel, the northern kingdom as it is portrayed in the Hebrew Bible.

After crowns of silver and gold have been made for Joshua and Zerubbabel indicating who will rule in the restored community (6.9-14), and after Zechariah has claimed that the temple will be completed, again sustaining his claim that the LORD sent him (6.15), the book moves two years ahead in time to when Bethel sends representatives to the house of the LORD to ask a question of the priests and prophets (7.2-3). The reference to the house of the LORD indicates that the temple has been completed. More significantly, however, Bethel, the place in the north where a messenger used to speak to Jacob, sends representatives to Jerusalem to inquire of the LORD. Zechariah's answer, as a messenger of the LORD, speaks about the LORD's mastery over all the earth about to eventuate. He concludes by saying that in the days to come 'ten men from nations of every language shall take hold of a Jew, grasping his garment and saying, "Let us go with you, for we have heard that God is with you"'. The whole earth has heard the message first spoken by the messenger Haggai, ' "I am with you," says the LORD' (Hag. 1.13).

To this answer of Zechariah are appended three oracles (Zech. 9–11, 12–14 and Mal. 1–4). All of these oracles are addressed to Israel, that community portrayed in other portions of the Hebrew Bible as the northern kingdom. In these oracles there is a focus on all the land surrounding Jerusalem, but particularly on Israel ('Ephraim' or 'the house of Joseph') attaching itself to Judah and Jerusalem. In the oracles, however, the grand view of the LORD as master of the whole earth begins to be undermined by the realities of the situation. This discrepancy is raised by the LORD himself in Zechariah's answer offered to the men from Bethel (8.16).

The view of the world in which the LORD dwells in the temple in Jerusalem as the centre of power over the whole earth is undermined by opposing leaders in the north (the shepherds) as well as by opposition from within Jerusalem itself (14.2). While the earlier scenes involved with temple construction view the LORD's power as moving out to the whole earth, the oracles depict a retreat to Jerusalem where, especially in the last chapter (Zech. 14), fantastic and unbelievable claims are made about what is to happen in days to come. As the portrayal of the LORD in the days to come appears increasingly incredible it exposes the unreality of the claims about the power of the LORD over all the earth encountered in temple imagery.

Zechariah 1.1-6
Remembering the Past

Introductory Remarks

These opening six verses in Zechariah occupy a significant position in my configuration of the Twelve as a literary collage. At a micro-level they function as a transition from Haggai to Zechariah indicating continuity and commonality. Zechariah is introduced into the Twelve as a character inhabiting a shared world with Haggai. At the macro-level, the six verses perform a key role in a configuration of the Twelve as a whole. These verses provide a literary setting in Persian times that enables the nine individuals, who appear earlier in the Twelve (Hosea through Zephaniah) to be identified as 'prophets'. From the later perspective of the era of the Persian king Darius, the proclamation of these 'former prophets' regarding what the LORD spoke in earlier times can be seen to have come about. After examining the specific dating and the short family genealogy accompanying Zechariah's introduction into the text, I will turn to a discussion of these verses in both their micro- and macro-settings.

Dating the Word (1.1)

Zechariah 1.1 tells us that a word of the LORD came to Zechariah in the eighth month of the second year of Darius. This date is one month prior to the last date given for a word that came to Haggai (see Hag. 2.10, 20), thus portraying the activities of Haggai and Zechariah as overlapping. I read Zechariah, therefore, as clearly linked to Haggai; both Haggai and Zechariah can be interpreted as characters inhabiting a shared world with a specific setting in place and time.

The specific dating in Haggai and Zechariah, which apart from Zech. 1.1 even includes the day of the month, serves to differentiate these two individuals from the previous nine figures encountered in the Twelve (Hosea, Joel, Amos, Obadiah, Jonah, Micah, Nahum, Habakkuk and Zephaniah). Dates given in the earlier part of the Twelve associate the 'former prophets' generally with the reign of one or more kings (Hos. 1.1; Amos 1.1; Mic. 1.1; Zeph. 1.1) and no mention is made of specific days, months and years. Joel, Obadiah, Jonah, Nahum and Habakkuk are given no dating whatsoever and their place in time can only be inferred from their place in the order of books, which are arranged chronologically. The change in the Twelve from general to specific dating for Haggai and Zechariah suggests to the reader that Haggai and Zechariah are being portrayed as belonging to a better known world. From the perspective of the whole, then, the specific dating in Haggai and Zechariah represents them as being separated from a more vaguely remembered past.

Zechariah's Genealogy (1.1)

Zechariah, to whom the word of the LORD comes, is identified in a brief genealogy linking him to his grandfather, Iddo. This truncated family tree is unusual. It provides more information for Zechariah than for anyone in the Twelve apart from Zephaniah. Amos, Obadiah, Micah, Nahum, Habakkuk and Haggai are given no family history whatsoever and Hosea, Joel and Jonah are linked only with their fathers. Zephaniah (Zeph. 1.1) stands alone as having a longer family history than Zechariah. Zephaniah's family history identifies him as a descendant of the Judaean king Hezekiah with whom some of the earlier prophets were associated (Hos. 1.1; Mic. 1.1). This connection with Hezekiah establishes his continuity with the past.

I read Zechariah's extended genealogy, however, as having the opposite effect. The identification of Zechariah, extending back through two generations, suggests distancing and separation from the past. The implications of this genealogical distancing, however, are not so readily apparent in many English translations. The NRSV translates the genealogy as '*the prophet* Zechariah son of Berechiah son of *Iddo*'. A more literal rendering of the Hebrew is 'Zechariah, son of Berechiah, son of *Iddo the prophet*'. Habakkuk (1.1; 3.1) and Haggai (1.1, 3, 12; 2.1, 10), the only two individuals directly identified as 'the prophet' in the Twelve, are given no family history. Zechariah can be linked with a prophet only through his grandfather *Iddo, the prophet*. (See also Zech. 1.7. Iddo is the name of a number of characters in the Hebrew Bible including a prophet in 2 Chron. 13.22 and a seer in 2 Chron. 9.29; 12.15.)

The dating of 'the word of the LORD' and the identification of Zechariah as a descendant of the prophet Iddo in the very beginning of Zechariah suggest detachment from the past. This separation from the world of the past is corroborated by Zechariah's name. In Hebrew Zechariah is a sentence-name meaning, 'the LORD has remembered'. Those reading the text in Hebrew, then, hear about a word of the LORD that came to '*The-LORD-Has-Remembered*'. '*The-LORD-Has-Remembered*', however, suggests not simply distance, separation and detachment but possible recovery, restoration and return.

The Word of the LORD in its Micro-Context

The word of the LORD that came to Zechariah (1.2-6) begins with a sum-
marizing sentence suggesting the past and alienation: 'The LORD was
very angry with your fathers.' The NRSV reads 'ancestors'. While such a
translation may be an attempt to make the text more presentable for
contemporary communities of faith, it should not be permitted to mask
the underlying patriarchal ideology of the Hebrew text. There are no
mothers mentioned in Zechariah's family tree, nor is the LORD concerned abut the ways and deeds of the mothers. The 'your' in this sentence is masculine plural, referring not simply to Zechariah but to
Zechariah and the audience to whom he is instructed to deliver the
LORD's word. Elsewhere in the passage, Zechariah's audience is identified only in the pronominal plural as 'them', 'they', 'our', and so on. If
one were to read only within the confines of the 'book' of Zechariah,
the identity of the audience would be unclear. The problem of the missing antecedent is overcome, however, if one reads these verses, as I
do, as a continuation of Haggai. Zechariah's audience is the same as
Haggai's: Zerubbabel son of Shealtiel, governor of Judah; Joshua son of
Jehozadak, the high priest; and all the remnant of the people. (See Hag.
1.1, 12, 14; 2.2, 4; 'the remnant of the people' is missing in Hag. 1.1 and
in Hag. 2.4 is identified as 'the people of the land'.) Zechariah, then, is
speaking to a group that has already begun to work on the temple, after
having heard the message of the messenger Haggai, 'I am with you'
(Hag. 1.13) reiterated in words of comfort (Hag. 2.4).

The LORD's anger, which alienated him from the fathers, has already
begun to change in Haggai as the LORD speaks words of comfort
through his messenger. I understand 'the word of the LORD' (Zech. 1.2-
6) addressed to Zechariah's community about the actions of the fathers
to be a justification of the LORD's anger in the past and not primarily a
call to repentance as it is usually interpreted. The fathers were to blame,
causing the LORD to be very angry. The context is one in which the
LORD has made a move toward the 'remnant people' by promising
through the messenger Haggai that he will be present with them. The
remnant community has responded by initiating work on the temple. By
the time the word of the LORD is spoken in Zech. 1.2-6, both parties
(the LORD and the remnant people) are turning toward one another.

The word of the LORD that Zechariah is instructed to proclaim to his
audience resonates with his name, '*The*-LORD-*Has-Remembered*', and
suggests restoration. 'Return to me says the LORD of hosts, and I will
return to you, says the LORD of hosts' (1.3). The LORD remembers a

former time and challenges those addressed by Zechariah to return to that past. This restoration is a return to something lost for a long time, for the former prophets proclaimed a similar message to the fathers:

> Do not be like your fathers, to whom the former prophets proclaimed, 'Thus says the LORD of hosts, "Return from your evil ways and from your evil deeds." ' But they did not hear or heed me, says the LORD (Zech. 1.4).

It is at this point that the word of the LORD moves to argument, which can be understood both as the LORD's defence of his past actions and a statement of the consequences of a failure to return:

> 'But they [your fathers] did not hear or heed me', says the LORD. 'Your fathers where are they? And the prophets, do they live forever? But my words and my statutes, which I commanded my servants the prophets did they not overtake your fathers' (Zech. 1.5-6).

The implied answers to the questions are obvious; there can be no rebuttal. Zechariah's community from the later perspective of the time of Darius, a perspective not shared by their fathers, do what their fathers did not do: 'They returned and said, "The LORD of hosts has dealt with us according to our ways and deeds, just as he planned to do." ' (NRSV translates 'they repented'. I prefer to translate the Hebrew word as 'return', the way it is translated by the NRSV elsewhere in the passage. 'Return' has connotations of the restoration of physical nearness, masked by the more theological word, 'repent'.)

When read in the larger context of Haggai, the decision to return to the LORD can be seen as one that has been made on the basis of more than convincing argument about the negative consequences of failing to heed the LORD's call. The LORD, who promises, 'I will be with you' (Hag. 1.13; 2.4), also promises something more tangible,

> For thus says the LORD of hosts: Once again, in a little while, I will shake the heavens and the earth and the sea and the dry land; and I will shake the nations, so that the treasure of all the nations shall come, and I will fill this house with splendour, says the LORD of hosts. The silver is mine, and the gold is mine, says the LORD of hosts. The splendour of this house shall be greater than the former, says the LORD of hosts; and in this place I will give prosperity, says the LORD of hosts (Hag. 2.6-9).

Read in the context of Haggai, the LORD's call to the community to return is occurring in a world that has already begun to change. The LORD has promised through his messenger to be present, temple construction has begun, and prosperity is imminent.

The word of the LORD that came to Zechariah, then, can be understood in its immediate context as a word addressed to the community portrayed in Haggai. However, as I have already indicated, the LORD's word suggests separation from the past and raises a number of questions: Why is Zechariah portrayed as distanced from the 'former prophets', and why is he identified as a descendant of a prophet? What should be made of the implied threats in the questions about the whereabouts of the fathers and the end of the prophets? What does it mean for the LORD to return? What does it mean for Zechariah's audience and their fathers to return? How exactly did the LORD's words and statutes overtake the fathers? The answers to these questions will become clear when this word of the LORD calling on the community to return is understood against the backdrop of the larger configuration of the Twelve.

The Word of the LORD in its Macro-Context

Further insight into the LORD's word in Zech. 1.2-6 can be gained by looking at the 'former prophets', that is, those mentioned earlier in the Twelve (Hosea through Zephaniah) who, the LORD claimed, had called the fathers to return. While the call to return may be implicit in what 'the former prophets' say as a whole, the explicit imperative plural, 'return', is found in only two places in the 'former prophets', Hos. 14.1-2 and Joel 2.12-13. For one configuring the Twelve as a literary collage, these two passages become highly significant for understanding the summons, 'return', in Zech. 1.1-6.

The call to return in Hos. 14.1-2 occurs at the beginning of a chapter in Hosea. Francis Landy (p. 169) describes it as 'the book's culminating statement of the relationship of God and Israel', that is, '[i]t conforms to the agenda of return following catastrophe' found at various points throughout the book of Hosea. In Hosea the theme is developed that God's judgment—the deprivation of 'the grain, the wine and the oil'—will be followed by the restoration of these three things. For example, in the second chapter of Hosea, in which the sadistic metaphor of the unfaithful wife is used to depict the relationship between Israel and the LORD', divine judgment is understood as taking away 'the grain, the wine and the oil' (Hos. 2.8-9). Following judgment leading to catastrophe, the community, imagined in the figure of the impoverished wife, can look forward to the LORD as husband restoring material prosperity again by replenishing 'the grain, the wine and the oil' (Hos. 2.21-22a). The end of Hosea presents a similar linking of return and replenishment.

> Return, O Israel, to the LORD your God,
>   for you have stumbled because of your iniquity.
> Take words with you
> and return to the LORD,

Israel will then be replenished with 'grain, wine and oil':

> His beauty shall be like the olive tree's
>> His fragrance like that of Lebanon.
> They who sit in his shade shall be revived:
>> They shall bring to life new grain
> They blossom like the vine;
>> His scent shall be like the wine of Lebanon (Hos. 14.9; the translation
>> is from the TANAKH).

In Hosea, then, the community is called to return to the LORD in a situation in which the LORD has deprived them of their prosperity, embodied in the imagery of grain, wine and oil.

Similarly, the community in Haggai, to whom Zechariah's call to return is addressed, has been deprived of its prosperity; the LORD has taken away 'the wine, the grain and the oil (Hag. 1.11). The call to return in Zechariah, then, is delivered to a community, similar to the community that the 'former prophet' Hosea summoned to return; both communities are experiencing a lack of prosperity. In Haggai, the deprivation of grain, wine and oil is linked to the temple lying in ruins,

> Thus says the LORD of hosts: Consider how you have fared. Go up to the hills and bring wood and build the house, so that I may take pleasure in it and be honored, says the LORD. You have looked for much, and, lo, it came to little; and when you brought it home, I blew it away. Why? says the LORD of hosts. Because my house lies in ruins, while all of you hurry off to your own houses. Therefore the heavens above have withheld the dew, and the earth has withheld its produce. And I have called for a drought on the land and hills, on the *grain*, the *new wine*, the *oil*, on what the soil produces, on human beings and animals, and on all their labours (Hag. 1.7-11).

The significance of the temple in the call to return in the former prophets is clear from Joel. Joel continues the call to return found in Hosea associated with the restoration of grain, wine and oil. Before developing the way this theme of return emerges in Joel, however, it will be helpful to look at the transitional link between Hosea and Joel in the Twelve.

At the very end of Hosea there is a verse addressed to readers, both actual readers of the text as well as the community addressed by Zechariah who have heard what Hosea proclaimed.

> Those who are wise understand these things;
>> those who are discerning know them.
> For the ways of the LORD are right,
>> and the upright walk in them,
>> but transgressors stumble in them (Hos. 14.9).

Joel's very name embodies the alternative to walk in the ways of the LORD as the upright do or to stumble as the transgressors do. While Joel's name can mean 'the LORD is salvation' and is consistent with what the LORD had spoken to him, its other meanings become significant. In form Joel can be understood also as a Qal active participle representing two completely different verb roots in Hebrew. On the one hand it can mean 'one who acts foolishly' and on the other 'one who acts with determination or one who undertakes to do something' (BDB, 383. The one root is found only in the Niph'al and the other in the Hiph'il). In short, Joel's name encapsulates the alternatives given to the reader at the end of Hosea. 'The word of the LORD which came to ' "*One-Who-Acts-Foolishly/One-Who-Acts-with-Determination*" '.

This word concerns future generations, as is clear at the opening of Joel 1.2-3:

> Hear this, O elders,
>> give ear, all inhabitants of the land!
> Has such a thing happened in your days,
>> or in the days of your fathers [NRSV 'ancestors']?
> Tell your children of it,
>> and let your children tell their children,
>> and their children another generation.

The three generations of reporting are commensurate with the three generations by which Zechariah is removed from the prophets: 'Zechariah, the son of Berechiah, the son of Iddo the prophet' (Zech. 1.1) is now reporting this to a fourth generation.

Like Hosea, Joel speaks of loss and eventual restoration of grain, wine and oil. However, Joel provides the answer to the LORD's question addressed to Zechariah's community, 'But my words and my statues, which I commanded my servants the prophets, did they not overtake your ancestors' (Zech. 1.6)? The Hebrew word translated 'overtake' here can be used in the sense of being overtaken in war (see Hos. 10.9). It is just such a situation of being overtaken by an invading army that is a major theme in Joel. He reports about an attacking army (Joel 1.6) as if it were a succession of locust plagues leaving the land lying waste (see Andiñach, pp. 433-41).

> Before them the land is like the garden of Eden
>> but after them a desolate wilderness,
>> and nothing escapes them (Joel 2.3b).

The description is typical of military invasion. The total destruction of an invading army on the 'day of the LORD' means no grain, no wine and no oil.

> The fields are devastated,
>> the ground mourns;
> for the grain is destroyed,
>> the wine dries up,
>> the oil fails (Joel 1.10).

In such a situation in which the produce of the land is eliminated, the LORD calls on his people to return.

> Yet even now, says the LORD,
>> return to me with all your heart,
>> with fasting, with weeping, and with mourning;
>> rend your hearts and your clothing.
> Return to the LORD, your God,
>> for he is gracious and merciful,
>> slow to anger, and abounding in steadfast love
>> and relents from punishing (Joel 2.12-13).

To return to the LORD is to have grain, wine and oil restored. In response to a community that has returned to the land the LORD will say,

> I am sending you grain, wine and oil
>> and you will be satisfied;
> and I will no more make you
>> a mockery among the nations (Joel 2.19).

At the time of restoration,

> The threshing floors shall be full of grain
> the vats shall overflow with wine and oil (Joel 2.24).

The question, then, with which Joel opens, 'Has such a thing happened in your days, or in the days of your fathers?' is an alternative form of the question asked by the LORD in the word that came to Zechariah, 'But my words and my statutes, which I commanded the prophets, did they not overtake your fathers' (Zech. 1.6)? For Zechariah's audience, Joel provides the basis for answering the question in the affirmative, 'The LORD of hosts has dealt with us according to our ways and deeds just as he planned to do' (Zech. 1.6).

The link with Joel becomes even clearer when Joel is read in the light of the way the community is portrayed in Haggai. As I indicated above, the community in Haggai is portrayed as experiencing the deprivation of grain, wine and oil about which the LORD spoke to Joel. In Haggai, however, the deprivation is caused by drought and not a plague of locusts. The LORD has caused the drought because his house lies in ruins (Hag. 1.1-6). Here there is also an echo of what was heard in Joel. When grain, wine and oil are withheld, offerings cannot be made in the house of God (Joel 1.9, 15). In such a situation, according to Joel, the community is to assemble at the house of the LORD. When the LORD speaks through Haggai to Zerubbabel, Joshua and the remnant of the people, the LORD's house lies in ruins so that it is of the utmost urgency to rebuild it. (See Hag. 1.7-11.)

While the community in Hosea's day did not heed 'the words' of Hosea (Hos. 14.2) and stumbled, it is reported that the community in the prophet Haggai's time heeds his words.

> Then Zerubbabel son of Shealtiel, and Joshua son of Jehozadak, the high priest, with all the remnant of the people, obeyed the voice of the LORD their God, and the words of the prophet Haggai, as the LORD their God had sent him; and the people feared the LORD. Then Haggai, the messenger of the LORD spoke to the people with the LORD's message, saying, I am with you says the LORD (Hag. 1.12).

The close link that Zechariah has with Haggai, understood in the context of what the former prophets proclaimed (specifically Hosea and Joel), helps to answer the questions raised above. The implied threats in the questions about the fathers are more powerful because we know from Joel that because of the LORD's anger the fathers have been overtaken in warfare, which has led to devastation. Zechariah is distanced from the 'former prophets' because in the Twelve a break with the past takes place when messengers speak and temple construction begins. The community hearing the word of the LORD in Zechariah's time as a call to return is living in a time when the LORD has spoken through his messenger, 'I am with you says the LORD'.

'Returning' is given verbal expression in Zechariah, 'So they returned [NRSV 'repented'] and said, "The LORD of hosts has dealt with us according to your ways and deeds, just as he planned to do"'. But 'return' has a spatial dimension. Returning means to return to a place. This physical dimension of return is clear from Joel and Haggai. According to Joel, when the grain, the wine and the oil are lost, it is the time to gather in a place—in the temple, 'the house of the LORD'.

> Sanctify a fast,
>   call a solemn assembly,
> Gather the elders
>   and all the inhabitants of the land
> *to the house of the* LORD *your God,*
>   and cry out to the LORD (Joel 1.14).

That this gathering in the temple for fasting and mourning is a matter of 'returning' to a place involving physical acts of ritual is evident from Joel 2.12-17.

Yet even now, says the LORD,
    return to me with all your heart,
with fasting, with weeping, and with mourning;
    rend your hearts and your clothing.
Return to the LORD, your God,
    for he is gracious and merciful,
slow to anger, and abounding in steadfast love,
    and relents from punishing,
Who knows whether he will not turn and relent,
    and leave a blessing behind him,
a grain offering, a drink offering
    for the LORD your God.

Blow the trumpet in Zion;
    sanctify a fast;
call a solemn assembly;
    gather the people.
Sanctify the congregation;
    assemble the aged;
gather the children
    even infants at the breast.
Let the bridegroom leave his room.
    and the bride her canopy (Joel 2.12-14).

According to Joel it is in such a gathering that the LORD will become jealous for his people and will send them the grain, the wine and the oil so that they 'will no more be a mockery among the nations' (Joel 2.18-19).

'Returning', therefore, has to do with a physical return. To return to the LORD is to return to the temple 'with fasting, with weeping and with mourning' (Joel 2.12). In the time of Haggai, it is clear that 'returning' to the LORD in a time when the temple is in ruins means that the temple must be rebuilt. To return to the LORD is to return to his house. In such a *spatial* setting the LORD will return to his people. The word of the LORD with the imperative call to return means to return to the LORD in the rebuilt temple where the LORD will return to them. When read in the light of both its micro- and macro-settings, the call for return in Zechariah is not a simple call to repentance but a call to return to the temple where the LORD will be present with his people.

The Word of the LORD and the End of the Twelve

It is important in a discussion of the imperative to return in Zech. 1.1-6 to look at the other place at the end of the Twelve in which an imperative plural to return occurs, Mal. 3.7. This passage suggests that 'the return to the LORD' is not as unanimous as Zech. 1.6 implies. As the

Twelve draws to a close, the LORD has this interchange with the community:

> 'Ever since the days of your fathers you have turned aside from my statutes and have not kept them. Return to me, and I will return to you', says the LORD of hosts. 'But you say, "How shall we return?" ' (Mal. 3.7).

The Twelve, then, highlights division in the community and alerts the reader to reconsider the identity of the community that contains only a 'remnant of the people' (Hag. 1.12, 14; 2.2). There appear to be others in the community less convinced about returning to the LORD than those reported in Zech. 1.6.

In Malachi 'returning' continues to be thought of in spatial terms and is associated with the temple. The LORD's answer to those who ask, 'How shall we return?' (Mal. 3.7), is that they are to bring tithes to the house of the LORD. If the community were to return, then the LORD would rebuke *the devourer* (NRSV, *the locust*) so that it 'will not destroy the produce of your soil; and your vine in the field shall not be barren' (Mal. 3.11). This imagery again recalls Joel. Malachi also recalls Hosea. Toward the end of Malachi, the LORD calls for 'a book of remembrance' to be written of 'those who revered the LORD and thought on his name' (Mal. 3.16). The division between 'the righteous and the wicked' (Mal. 3.17), which this book is to record in writing, recalls the alternatives between the righteous and the wicked in Hos. 14.9.

Summary and Transition

The word of the LORD that comes to Zechariah in 1.1-6, then, situates Zechariah in the larger context of the Twelve with the former prophets, especially with Hosea and Joel at the beginning of the Twelve. It also locates Zechariah in its immediate context by providing a link with Haggai which precedes it and with Malachi which follows it. It, therefore, plays a pivotal role in my configuration of the Twelve as a literary collage.

In concluding my comments on these verses I want to make a few general observations about the way these verses, which share a common setting with Haggai, provide background for the next section in Zechariah, 1.7–6.15 in which Zechariah speaks with messengers: (1) The reader has been introduced to a messenger, Haggai, and to the message he speaks, ' "I am with you," says the LORD' (Hag. 1.13). The reader, then, is prepared for messengers who appear throughout this next section in Zechariah along with the message about the presence of the LORD. (2) The appearance of the messenger in Haggai coincides with the work commencing on the construction of the temple (Hag. 1.14).

The reader is also prepared for the continuing link between a messenger presence and temple construction. (3) Finally, Zech. 1.7–6.15 is concerned repeatedly with what Zechariah sees. It is, therefore, not surprising that the reader is also prepared in Haggai for this emphasis on seeing. Haggai says,

> Who is left among you that *saw* this house in its former glory? Is it not in your *sight* [or *seeing*] as nothing?... Once again in a little while... The splendour of this house shall be greater than the former, says the LORD of hosts; and in this house I will give prosperity, says the LORD of hosts (Hag. 2.3-9).

What Zechariah sees in the presence of messengers is the temple being restored.

Zechariah 1.7-17
Scene 1: The LORD's Horsemen

Introductory Remarks

Zechariah 1.7 introduces another word of the LORD that came to Zechariah. He is identified as the son of Berechiah, the son of Iddo the prophet as was the case in 1.1, and the date of this word event is given as three months later than that of the word found in 1.1-6. The name of the month is specified as *Shebat*, and the day of the month is given, the twenty-fourth day—such particulars were not offered in 1.1. While the word in Zech. 1.1-6 comes one month prior to the last word that came to Haggai (see Hag. 2.10, 20), the word in 1.7–6.15 comes two months later.

There are other variations between the word announced in 1.7 and the word that came to Zechariah in 1.1-6. The report of this second word is extended, more detailed, and variegated; and it closes at the end of ch. 6. Furthermore, the word of the LORD reported to the reader is about what Zechariah sees—not simply words the LORD speaks. Zechariah is one of a cast of characters, including the LORD himself. He speaks and asks questions of a messenger who himself is in dialogue with the deity and with other messengers of the LORD. As we shall see, Zechariah at times also speaks directly with the LORD and in other ways becomes a participant in what he sees.

Many commentators understand what Zechariah sees in the extended word in 1.7–6.15 as visions, and, because 1.8 refers particularly to 'the night', as 'night visions'. Because the LORD appears in what Zechariah is seeing, it is commonly understood that Zechariah has a vision of the heavenly council and that the messengers with whom he speaks are 'angels', beings who are members of the heavenly council. My reading is significantly different. I view these messengers not as angelic beings but as prophets, such as Haggai, who appear in a new guise. What has been interpreted as the heavenly council I see as the temple under construction and the restoration of Jerusalem. Certainly what Zechariah sees is extraordinary. It blurs the distinctions that readers often bring to the text. Heaven and earth, the human and the divine, come together in the scenes unfolding before Zechariah's eyes. This merging of worlds captures the full significance of the message of the messenger, Haggai, ' "I am with you," says the LORD' (Hag. 1.13). The LORD is present in the temple. Before commenting specifically on 1.7-17, therefore, I want to discuss in more detail my alternative views on visions and angels.

Excursus: Visions of the Night

Although the scenes in Zech. 1.7–6.15 have often been referred to as 'night visions', neither the term 'vision' nor the phrase 'night vision' occurs in the narrative portrayal of these scenes. The phrase, 'night vision' occurs only rarely in the Hebrew Bible and, when it does, it is disparaged as the illusion of dreaming (see Isa. 29.8 and Job 20.8; in Job 4.13 and 33.15 the connotations are more positive). Significantly, the Hebrew word for 'vision' (*ḥăzôn*) is associated in the Twelve exclusively with the 'former prophets' (see Hos. 12.10; Obad. 1; Mic. 3.6, Nah. 1.1; Hab. 2.2, 3; cf. Joel 2.28) from whom Zechariah is distanced. The only time the term appears in Zechariah, it refers to the end of prophecy when a prophet will be ashamed of his vision when he prophesies (Zech. 13.4).

What and how Zechariah is *seeing*, then, is not appropriately referenced to the former prophets. Haggai, as I indicated above, provides the context for my reading of Zechariah, including what Zechariah sees. When Haggai the messenger of the LORD first spoke, work began on the temple—on the twenty-fourth day of the sixth month (Hag. 1.14-15). One month later (on the twenty-first day, Hag. 2.1), during the construction, Haggai asks, 'Who is left among you that saw this house in its former glory? How does it look to you now? Is it not in your eyes as nothing' (Hag. 2.3)? The next time we hear about someone 'seeing' something it is four months later; on the twenty-fourth day of the month (Zech. 1.7), Zechariah begins to see things. The 'house of the LORD', which had looked like nothing, was beginning to look like something in Zechariah's eyes. The final occasion when a word of the LORD comes to Zechariah is two years later when people from Bethel come to the house of the LORD, by which time it has apparently been completed (Zech. 7.1-3). When Zechariah lifts up his eyes, he sees the temple under construction. He is looking at imagery and activity associated with building the temple. Whether or in what sense temple imagery becomes animated is not as significant as how 'the word of the LORD' accompanying the construction details and fills out the message of Haggai, ' "I am with you," says the LORD'. Temple construction and divine presence can be seen together. When the temple is present, the LORD is present. When the LORD returns to the temple in Jerusalem, the LORD is indeed present 'with you' when 'you' return to the temple. What I see in Zechariah, then, is a radical localization of the LORD's presence.

Excursus: Messengers in Zechariah

The word *mal'āḵ* in Hebrew is rendered in two different ways in English translations—either as 'messenger' or as 'angel'. When one human being sends another human being as a *mal'āḵ*, the word is translated 'messenger' as it is, for example, in Gen. 32.4; Num. 20.14; Deut. 2.26; Judg. 7.24; 11.12; and 2 Sam. 2.5. The problem of translation occurs when the deity sends a *mal'āḵ*. Sometimes the word is translated 'messenger' as the NRSV translates it in the phrase 'Haggai, *the messenger of the LORD*' (Hag. 1.13; see also 2 Chron. 36.15-16 and Isa. 42.19; 44.26). At other times it is translated 'angel' as the NRSV renders it throughout Zech. 1.7–6.15. For example, in Zech. 1.11, 12 the NRSV translates '*the angel of the LORD*', a phrase in Hebrew that is identical to the phrase translated '*the messenger of the LORD*' in the identification of Haggai (Hag. 1.13). The point I want to make is that the distinction we make as contemporary readers and translators between human *messengers* and divine beings, '*angels*', is not clear in the Hebrew Bible. Just as the temple blurs the distinction between heaven and earth, given God's presence in the temple, messengers also blur the distinction between the heavenly and earthly realms (see Cohen, pp. 18-19). When the messenger is present, the LORD is present. This divine presence need not be confined to 'angelic beings' but may be embodied in human beings who are 'messengers of the LORD'. I have made the point that Haggai and Zechariah are portrayed in the Twelve as sharing a common world. If Haggai, the prophet, can be identified also as a '*messenger* of the LORD', I am less inclined than our standard translations and commentaries to understand the '*messengers*' who speak to Zechariah as angelic beings. I also understand 'the messenger of the LORD' who appears in Zechariah's world (1.11, 12) to be Haggai, 'the messenger of the LORD'.

To understand 'messengers' in the Twelve as blurring the distinction between the human and the divine, with the messenger's presence signifying the LORD's presence, fits into the overall way in which messengers of the LORD are portrayed in the Hebrew Bible. A number of passages indicate that to be in the presence of a messenger of the LORD is to see God. This is suggested by the fear associated with seeing a messenger. The danger posed by seeing God when looking at a messenger appears to be what is suggested by the enigmatic phrase uttered by Hagar in Gen. 16.13-14. It is stated explicitly by Manoah who, terrified when he realizes that he and his wife have been talking to a messenger of the LORD , says, 'We will surely die, for we have seen God' (Judg. 13.22). This fear arising from being in the presence of a messenger of

God is found also in other passages (see Gen. 28.16-17; Exod. 3.6; Num. 22.31; Judg. 6.22-23; 1 Chron. 21.16-17).

At the same time these passages suggest the humanness of the LORD's messengers whose presence is tantamount to divine presence. For example, the messengers who appear to Lot (Gen. 19.1, 15) are perceived as men by the men of Sodom (Gen. 19.5), and even the narrator speaks of them simply as men (Gen. 19.12, 16). In Gideon's interaction with the messenger of the LORD (Judg. 6.11-24), the messenger is perceived as human and Gideon does not recognize him as a messenger of the LORD until he vanishes from his sight (Judg. 6.21-22). Finally, in the story of Manoah and his wife, the messenger appears as a human being. The narrator tells us that a 'messenger of the LORD ' appeared to the wife of Manoah (13.3, 13), but when she speaks to her husband about him she refers to him as a 'a man of God', and, although she says that he was like a messenger of God, she is not sure that he is a messenger of God (Judg. 13.6). Indeed, in the ensuing dialogue between Manoah and his wife they both refer to the messenger simply as a man (Judg. 13.8, 10, 11), and the narrator says, lest we miss the point, 'Manoah did not know that he was the messenger of the LORD' (Judg. 13.15). As in the Gideon story, 'the man' is only perceived as a messenger when he vanishes by ascending in a flame (Judg. 13.20). In all of these passages 'messengers' inhabit the world as human beings. What distinguishes them from other human beings is their status as 'messengers of the LORD'. That status is something eliciting fear because when the messenger is present the LORD is present. To be sure, messengers sometimes do extraordinary things, like disappearing in flames of fire, but such powers are often characteristic of religious leaders whose manifestation of the divine expresses itself in extraordinary powers. To be in the presence of a messenger of the LORD is to face the possibility of death.

A number of texts suggests that the appearance of the LORD's messenger establishes a certain *place* as imbued with divine presence. The appearance of a messenger is the occasion for building an altar so that the place becomes the house of God. When Jacob has a dream of a ladder extending between heaven and earth with messengers of the LORD ascending and descending it, he is afraid of the awesomeness of the place and says, 'This is none other than the house of God, and this is the gate of heaven' (Gen. 28.17). Jacob then took the stone that had been his head rest, set it up for a pillar and poured oil on it. He called the place Bethel ('the house of God') and made a vow that if the LORD looked after him, 'this stone, which I have set up for a pillar, shall be God's house' (Gen. 28.22). Likewise, when Gideon realized he was talk-

ing with the messenger of the LORD, 'he built an altar there to the
LORD, and called it, The LORD is peace' (Judg. 6.24). When David
encounters the messenger of the LORD at the threshing floor of Ornan
the Jebusite, the messenger instructs the prophet Gad to instruct David
to erect an altar on the threshing floor (1 Chron. 21.18). David does this
and says, 'Here shall be the house of the LORD God and here the altar of
burnt offering for Israel' (1 Chron. 22.1). What occasioned David's determination to build the 'house of God' at this altar site was that David
saw that 'the LORD answered him at the threshing floor of Ornan the
Jebusite' (1 Chron. 21.28). Messenger presence is tantamount to divine
presence.

This association of messengers with a place imbued with divine presence has significance for my reading of Zechariah. When the messenger
Haggai first spoke, construction began on the temple. It is appropriate
that, when Zechariah sees the temple under construction, he should be
in conversation with messengers. The temple is the place where messengers of the LORD speak.

It is important when attempting to understand Zechariah's encounter
with the messenger who spoke to him that we do not imagine that he is
transported to some other world of experience. The appearance of messengers of the LORD in the world of human beings is portrayed in a
number of different ways: sometimes they call out from heaven (see
Gen. 21.17; 22.11; 22.15); sometimes they appear in dreams (Gen.
28.12; 31.11). Most frequently they just appear in the world of human
activity as does the messenger who finds Hagar by the spring of water in
the wilderness on the way to Shur (Gen. 16.7); the messengers who
come to Lot at Sodom (Gen. 19.1); the messenger with drawn sword in
hand who confronts Balaam and his donkey (Num. 22.22-31); the messenger who went up from Gilgal to Bochim (Judg. 2.1); the messenger
who sat under the oak tree at Oprah (Judg. 6.11); the messenger who
appears to the wife of Manoah and is at first not recognized as a messenger of the LORD Judg. 13.3-21); the messenger who touched Elijah
(1 Kgs 19.7); the messenger whom God sent to Jerusalem to destroy it
(1 Chron. 21.12); and so on. Sometimes the appearance and disappearance of messengers are portrayed in fantastic ways: a messenger appears
in a flame of fire to Moses (Exod. 3.2); a messenger disappears in a flame
from the presence of Manoah and his wife (Judg. 13.20). The point is
that messengers appear in the world of human beings, are involved in
human activities, and are often indistinguishable from human beings
themselves (cf. Judg. 13). When Zechariah interacts with messengers of
the LORD, we can understand the setting to be Zechariah's world, not
some supra-mundane setting.

Furthermore, when the messenger of the LORD appears to an individual, that individual often sees things or the messenger shows the individual something. What is seen is present in the world. Hagar sees a well of water, and she goes and fetches water and gives her son a drink (Gen. 21.19). Abraham saw a lamb caught in a thicket (Gen. 22.13). Even in his dream Jacob sees the animals in his flock (Gen. 31.10). Elijah sees a cake and a jar of water to give him sustenance (1 Kgs 19.6). Sometimes more fantastic things are seen, but what is seen is in the world, to which the messenger comes. Moses sees a messenger of the LORD appear in the flame of fire in a bush burning but not being consumed (Exod. 3.2), and Manoah and his wife see the messenger of the LORD disappear in a flame (Judg. 13.20). Gideon sees fire leap up from a rock and consume meat and unleavened cake, and at this point the messenger of the LORD also vanishes (Judg. 7.21). The point I am making is that, when Zechariah reports what he sees, the reader is seeing things in Zechariah's world.

My reading of what Zechariah sees and of his encounter with messengers is consistent with a world more concrete than the other world inhabited by angels that is more usually associated with Zechariah. Divine presence is associated with both temple building and the reappearance of messengers. The LORD is present because the LORD has returned to the temple to which the community is summoned to return. ' "I am with you," says the LORD' is a promise associated with the temple, an extraordinary sight in Zechariah's world of Jerusalem in the days of Darius—not a view of the LORD in some other world. Indeed, for Zechariah to be making forays into other worlds would in fact contradict the claim that the LORD had returned; it would imply separation from Zechariah's world.

The Twenty-Fourth Day of *Shebat* (1.7-8)

Many commentators understand 1.7-8 to be introducing a series of night visions, which continue until they conclude in ch. 6. There is nothing really visionary, however, about the opening of v. 8. The phrase can be translated, 'I saw the night [or, tonight]' referring to a specific night in which Zechariah saw something. (The NRSV translates this phrase, 'in the night...' However, the preposition 'in' does not appear in the Hebrew text.) To understand the text this way fits the context of the preceding verse, 1.7, which, unlike 1.1, gives the specific day of the month as well as the month's name. The specificity in dating to the night of the twenty-fourth day of *Shebat* suggests an attempt to pinpoint in time what Zechariah saw and not the nature of his seeing. (The dating is similar to that in Hag. 1.15 which specifies the exact date that work began on the construction of the temple, five months earlier, also on the twenty-fourth day of the month.) The precise date, in this passage, culminating in the announcement that the 'house of the LORD will be rebuilt' (Zech. 1.16), is five months to the day after the original date of the commencement of temple construction. Such exactitude raises the question, 'What significance does this date have in the task of building?'

Before answering that question, I want to look at Zechariah's first person report of what he sees in vv. 8-13. I am particularly interested in the characters, the questioning that is a feature of the dialogue that takes place, what is said in the dialogue, and the significance of this report in the literary context of Zechariah in particular and the Twelve in general.

The Cast of Characters (1.8-13)

Any reading of this passage concerning what Zechariah saw (1.8-13) must take account of a certain amount of ambiguity associated with the characters whom Zechariah first observes and with whom he himself becomes a participant. In v. 8 Zechariah tells us that he saw 'a man riding on a red horse'. The second part of the verse appears to give us an added detail about this rider, 'He was standing among the myrtle trees'. In v. 9 Zechariah refers to a second character whom he addresses politely as 'my lord' and identifies him as 'the messenger who talked with me'. Verse 10 then speaks about 'the man who was standing among the myrtle trees'. With the introduction of this character ambiguity begins to emerge in the passage. Is this man in v. 10 the rider mentioned in v. 8? That this man is standing and not mounted on a horse suggests that it could be a different individual. Two observations give weight to this interpretation. First, the pronoun 'he' in the second part of v. 8 may refer to the horse on which the rider was mounted and not the rider himself. Since in Hebrew the pronoun 'he' is the same for the man and the horse, the 'he' in v. 8 could refer to the horse in the sense, 'He [the horse] was standing among the myrtle trees ... and behind him [the horse] were red, sorrel and white horses'. Secondly, the 'man who was standing among the myrtle trees' in v. 10 may be interpreted as pointing ahead to v. 11 and not backwards to v. 8.

In v. 11 we are introduced to another individual, 'the messenger of the LORD' and this person, like 'the man' in v. 10, is described as 'standing among the myrtle trees'. The introduction of this second messenger, 'the messenger of the LORD' also complicates matters. Is he the same 'messenger who talked with me' (Zech. 1.9) or is he a different character? That he may well be a different character is suggested by the

way the LORD, the last in the cast of characters to appear, interacts with
the messengers. While 'the messenger of the LORD' speaks to the LORD
in v. 12, in v. 13 the LORD responds to the messenger who spoke with
Zechariah. Whether the messenger is the same in both instances is
unclear. One other group of characters has a voice in this passage; the
ones sent to patrol the earth speak in v. 11, but we do not know their
number, and the relationship of these characters to one another in the
scene is ambiguous.

Although obscurity will necessarily remain, some light can be shed on
the characters. In Hag. 1.13, the narrator in an aside reports that Haggai
was 'the messenger of the LORD'. When 'the messenger of the LORD'
appears again in these verses (Zech. 1.11, 12), it is possible to see the
messenger as Haggai. There are other reasons for identifying the messenger in Zech. 1.11, 12 as Haggai. Haggai, the messenger of the LORD, first
spoke on the twenty-fourth day of the sixth month when work began on
the house of the LORD (Hag. 1.15). In Zech. 1.7-16 Haggai, the messenger of the LORD, appears again on the twenty-fourth day of the eleventh
month, also the date of a significant event associated with temple construction (Zech. 1.16).

However, whether Haggai is to be identified with the messenger who
spoke with Zechariah is not clear. Indeed, messengers in the Twelve, as
is the case with messengers of the LORD in general in the Hebrew Bible,
do not have a named identity. The passage involving Manoah's interaction with a messenger of the LORD is interesting in this regard. When
Manoah learns that the man with whom he has been speaking is the
messenger of the LORD, he asks him, 'What is your name, so that we can
honour you when your words come true?' The messenger somewhat
evasively says, 'Why do you ask my name?' and then provides his name.
He says, 'It is Wonderful'. (NRSV translates 'It is too wonderful'.) Significantly, the messenger of the LORD who spoke to Manoah has an adjec-
tival name 'Wonderful'; Haggai is an adjective meaning 'Festive'. One
can see Haggai lose his identify in the Twelve. The last time he appears
as a character in the book of Haggai, he loses his title as prophet (2.20)
and in Zech. 1.11, 12 (see also 3.1, 5, 6) he loses his name—if, as I con-
tend, Haggai the prophet, begins to appear in Zechariah simply as 'the
messenger of the LORD'.

The Questioning (1.8-13)

The characters in this scene are in dialogue although the discourse is
primarily a series of questions and answers. The first question is raised
by Zechariah and is addressed to the messenger who talked with

Zechariah, 'Then I said, "What are these [the horses, presumably with riders], my lord?" ' The messenger who talked with Zechariah responds by saying that he will show him what these things are. But it is 'the man standing among the myrtle trees' who gives the verbal response to Zechariah, 'They are those whom the LORD has sent to patrol, the earth'. These riders then speak to 'the messenger of the LORD', 'We have patrolled the earth, and lo, the whole earth remains in peace'. This comment is the basis for a second question now asked by the messenger of the LORD, 'O LORD of hosts, how long will you withhold mercy from Jerusalem and the cities of Judah, with which you have been angry these seventy years?' Although the LORD replies, he speaks to the messenger who talked with Zechariah, not with the messenger of the LORD. Furthermore, although we are told that the LORD spoke 'gracious and comforting words' (v. 13), the words themselves are not cited.

Before commenting on what is said in this conversation between the messenger and the LORD, I want to consider the form of the dialogue, which consists primarily of question and answer, in the larger context of the Twelve, first with reference to the immediate context (in Haggai and Zechariah prior to Zechariah's encounter with messengers), and then in the larger context of the 'former prophets'. In the immediate context, the LORD asks all the questions. In Hag. 1.4 he queries, 'Is it a time for you yourselves to live in your panelled houses, while this house lies in ruins?' The LORD poses a whole series of questions to Zerubbabel, Joshua and the remnant of the people in Hag. 2.3: 'Who is left among you that saw this house in its former glory? How does it look to you now? Is it not in your sight as nothing?' In Hag. 2.12 the LORD instructs Haggai to ask the priests a question, 'If one carries consecrated meat in the fold of one's garment, and with the fold touches bread, or stew, or wine, or oil, or any kind of food, does it become holy?' Haggai then asks the priests another question in 2.13 although it is not clear if this was also prompted by the LORD: 'If one who is unclean by contact with a dead body touches any of these, does it become unclean?' The LORD's queries continue in Hag. 2.15-16, 'Before a stone was placed upon a stone in the LORD's temple, how did you fare?' and finally in Hag. 2.19, 'Is there any seed left in the barn? Do the vine, the fig tree, the pomegranate, and the olive tree still yield nothing?' In Zech. 1.5-6, before Zechariah begins to converse with messengers, it is still the LORD who is hurling questions, 'Your fathers, where are they? And the prophets, do they live forever? But my words and my statutes, which I commanded my servants the prophets, did they not overtake your fathers?'

The point of all this is that in the immediate past, as it is portrayed in the literary world of the Twelve, in the days of Haggai and Zechariah, only the LORD asked questions. Only in 1.8-13 do questions begin to be posed to the LORD, and this occurs in a context in which Zechariah is conversing with messengers. What I am suggesting is that, when messengers begin to appear in Zechariah, two-way communication begins to take place with the LORD in the form of question and answer. It is not just the LORD who poses questions; questions are posed to the LORD, and he begins to answer. The presence of messengers makes this possible.

The situation is significantly different when one examines dialogue in the form of question and answer in the world of the former prophets portrayed in the Twelve. The overwhelming impression is of distance between the deity and the prophet. Speaking involving the deity is primarily one-way. The LORD speaks a word to the prophet who proclaims the LORD's word to the people. Prophetic speech lacks the immediacy of conversation featured in the question and answer dialogue in Zechariah's encounter with messengers. Even in those places in the Twelve in which a conversation is characterized by question and answer (Amos 7.1-8.3; Jon. 4; Hab. 1-2), there are no messengers present to offer explanations to the prophet. The impression one receives is of remoteness so that the activities of the LORD remain a mystery to the prophet.

Amos sees things in his world—locusts devastating crops (7.1), a shower of fire (7.4), a plumb line (7.7-8) and a basket of summer fruit (8.1). The first two things Amos sees (locusts and fire) require no explanation. The last two (the plumb line and the basket of summer fruit) do require explanation, which the LORD provides voluntarily, without probing questions from Amos. In the entire encounter, Amos asks only one question and this occurs on two occasions (7.2, 5), 'How can Jacob stand?' This question, unlike Zechariah's question, is concerned with intercession rather than with an explanation of what he is seeing. Furthermore, Amos only speaks to God on these two occasions and addresses no question to the deity in relation to the last two things he sees (the plumb line and the basket of summer fruit). While Amos is an intercessor, not unlike 'the messenger of the LORD' who asks the LORD a question in Zech. 1.17, he does not receive an explanation from the LORD about the meaning of the LORD's actions encapsulated in the things he sees. For Amos, the situation is different from that in which a messenger questions the LORD in Zechariah. The LORD is remote. Sanctuaries will be laid waste rather than built (Amos 7.9), and the LORD's absence will give rise to wailings in the temple (Amos 8.3).

From the perspective of the configuration of the Twelve as a literary whole, it is important to note that the series of four things that the LORD is showing Amos is interrupted by an account of Amos's encounter with the priest Amaziah at *Bethel* (Amos 7.10-17). In Amos's day (and in Hosea's) there were no messengers at Bethel as there were in the days of Jacob (Hos. 12.4). In the world of the former prophets, the LORD's activities are not explained through question and answer. In such a world the status of prophetic authority is itself open to question as is evident in the encounter between Amos and Amaziah (7.12-14). In the Twelve, prophetic proclamation, as I have argued above, is clarified only with hindsight when subsequent generations can confirm the meaning of the LORD's activities through experience of what the LORD *has done* by turning away from his people. In Zechariah's world what the LORD *is doing* is confirmed through messengers who offer explanations of the LORD's activities, the LORD who has returned and is present 'with you' in Jerusalem. Later on in Zechariah after Zechariah's encounter with messengers, it is significant that Bethel sends representatives to the house of the LORD in Jerusalem to ask questions (see Zech. 7.1-3).

This difference between the world in which the LORD spoke to the former prophets and Zechariah's world, in which the LORD speaks through messengers, is also accentuated in the question and answer interaction that takes place between Jonah and the LORD in Jonah 4. The difference between Amos and Jonah is that, while Amaziah could not accept Amos as a prophet, Jonah could not accept himself in this role. The interaction between Jonah and the LORD results in neither explanation nor understanding. Both Jonah and the LORD pose questions without answers. Jonah's initial question is offered as an explanation of why he fled from the LORD. He was angry that the LORD had changed his mind about the calamity that he said he would bring upon the Assyrians and he questions the LORD, 'Is not this what I said while I was still in my own country' (Jon. 4.2)? The LORD's retort is to pose questions that Jonah is not able to answer rather than to provide Jonah with clear answers to his questions. The LORD asks Jonah, 'Is it right for you to be angry' (4.4)? Then after providing a bush to give him shade, he says again, when it withers the next day, 'Is it right for you to be angry about the bush?' When Jonah says that he is angry enough to die, the LORD then poses another question,

> You are concerned about the bush, for which you did not labour and which you did not grow; it came into being in a night and perished in a night. And should I not be concerned about Nineveh, that great city, in which there are more than a hundred and twenty thousand persons who do not know their right hand from their left, and also many animals? (Jon. 4.10-11).

Jonah does not respond to this question. Jonah is in a world of questions without answers. What the LORD is attempting to accomplish in the great scheme of things is uncertain.

Habakkuk is the other place in the former prophets in which a prophet raises questions. Here again the interchange suggests distance and a lack of immediacy. The first questions that Habakkuk raises concerns the LORD's inaction in a time of violence and wrongdoing.

> O LORD, how long shall I cry for help,
>   and you will not listen?
> Or cry to you 'Violence!'
>   and you will not save?
> Why do you make me see wrong-doing
>   and look at trouble? (Hab. 1.2-3).

The LORD's answer (Hab. 1.5-6) is that he is doing something about these things. He is raising up the Chaldeans who will correct the problems. But the LORD's response suggests that these things will not be immediately apparent to Habakkuk. Habakkuk would not believe what the LORD is doing even if it were recounted to him (Hab. 1.5):

> Look at the nations, and see!
>   Be astonished! Be astounded!
> For a work is being done in your days
>   that you would not believe if you were told.

Indeed, Habakkuk's questioning response to the LORD's answer is astonished disbelief. Habakkuk asks, 'Are you not from of old, /O LORD my God, my Holy One?' (Hab. 1.12). Put simply, Habakkuk questions how the violent, such as the Chaldeans, can put an end to violence.

> Why do you look on the treacherous
>   and are silent when the wicked swallow
>   those more righteous than they?
> Is he then to keep on emptying his net,
>   and destroying nations without mercy? (Hab. 1.13, 17).

The answer to Habakkuk comes in the form of a vision, which he is instructed to write down (Hab. 2.1-3). The vision does not produce an immediate answer for the present, and Habakkuk is instructed to wait for it (Hab. 2.3). This delay suggests that Habakkuk, unlike Zechariah, is in a situation of confusion. The interchange between the LORD and Habakkuk undergirds the point I have already made about vision in the Twelve. Vision characterizes the time of the former prophets, not the time of Zechariah. Vision suggests a time of waiting in which the meaning of the LORD's actions can only be determined in time to come. The situation in Zechariah is different; the LORD's presence suggests immediate understanding. What the LORD is doing concerns what is happening now, that is, on the twenty-fourth day of the month of *Shebat*.

When read in the larger literary context of the former prophets, Zechariah's world with its messenger presence is significantly different from the world of earlier times. Divine presence is both more immediate and more intimate. Zechariah is participating in a conversation involving both messengers and the LORD himself. We are reminded again that in Zechariah's time, 'the LORD has remembered' (Hos. 12.5) and that this time resembles the time when the LORD used to speak to Jacob by means of a messenger. This world in which messengers ensure more immediate communication with the LORD is not presented as a *new* world. Rather it is a world of '*return*' to the beginnings—the way it was in the days of Jacob when the LORD used to speak by means of a messenger at Bethel. In a world returning to 'the beginning', the divine is more immediately accessible, at least to some like Zechariah, who, like the LORD himself, speaks with messengers.

The Conversation (1.7-17)

Having considered the characters participating in the dialogue and the nature of the dialogue as characterized by question and answer, it will now be helpful to look in more detail at what was seen and what was said. What Zechariah sees is a rider mounted on a red horse standing in front of other horses of assorted colours: red, sorrel and white. At this point in the scene the messenger who spoke to Zechariah appears. He comes on the scene unannounced. His appearance is perhaps less abrupt when read in the context of, and as a continuation of, Haggai, because Haggai has already been introduced as a messenger of the LORD.

Zechariah asks this messenger who talked with him, 'What are these', that is, the mounted rider standing in front of other variously coloured horses. The messenger says that he 'will show Zechariah what they are'. This showing (literally, 'causing to see'), however, has more to do with hearing than with seeing. When the messenger shows Zechariah what 'these' are, a clearer description of the rider and horses does not occur. Instead, Zechariah begins to hear the characters speak. 'Showing' gives the impression that Zechariah is being escorted closer to the scene so that it is possible to overhear what is said in the myrtle trees. Zechariah hears 'a man standing among the myrtle trees' speak: 'They are those whom the LORD sent to patrol the earth.' And then, Zechariah hears: 'We have patrolled the whole earth, and lo, the whole earth is at peace.'

This report seems to be addressed to another character who appears unannounced on the scene, 'the messenger of the LORD'. Zechariah is gradually being pulled into the scene, and what he overhears progressively discloses the significance of what he originally saw. The messenger of the LORD intercedes with the LORD—a conversation we can assume Zechariah overhears because he is reporting it. The messenger of the LORD asks, 'O LORD of hosts, how long will you withhold mercy from Jerusalem and the cities of Judah, with which you have been angry these seventy years?' Significantly, when the LORD responds, Zechariah does not report what the LORD says but only describes the LORD's response as 'gracious and comforting words'. The LORD's words are transmitted through messengers. The messenger who spoke with Zechariah transmits the words to Zechariah, and the words become the basis of the proclamation the messenger instructs Zechariah to declare. At this initial point in the unfolding scenes in Zechariah, the LORD's words to Zechariah are mediated by a messenger, and Zechariah does not have direct access to the LORD himself.

Before looking at what Zechariah is to proclaim, I want to point out a feature of the conversation that links 'the messenger of the LORD' in Zechariah with Haggai. When 'the messenger of the LORD' hears that the whole earth remains at peace and asks the LORD how long he will withhold mercy from Jerusalem and Judah (Zech. 1.11-12), words of the LORD proclaimed earlier by Haggai come to mind. On two different occasions (Hag. 2.6-9 and 2.20-23) Haggai said that as a consequence of rebuilding the temple, the LORD would shake up the nations, that is, disturb world peace, pour prosperity into Jerusalem, and install Zerubbabel, the governor, as his chosen one. Haggai said that these things would happen 'in a little while' (Hag. 2.6) or that the LORD was 'about to' (Hag. 2.20) do these things. This 'little while' in which the LORD is 'about to' act against the nations is relevant to the horses and riders Zechariah is seeing and hearing. Horses and riders out on patrol connote preparation for war, and this scene resonates with the words of Haggai concerning the overthrow of nations and their horses and riders (Hag. 2.22).

The Proclamation (1.14-17)

After Zechariah has seen this cast of characters and after he has overheard what they were saying to each other, the messenger who talked to Zechariah tells him to proclaim (Zech. 1.14) what the LORD said. Apparently, Zechariah is to proclaim the gracious and comforting words that the LORD spoke in response to the question, '[H]ow long will you withhold mercy from Jerusalem and the cities of Judah, with which you have been angry these seventy years?' (1.12).

Zechariah is instructed to make an additional proclamation (see 1.17), and the words Zechariah is to proclaim echo themes in the preceding literary context both at the beginning of Zechariah and in Haggai. At the beginning of Zechariah, the LORD said, 'Return to me ...and I will return to you' (1.3). In 1.6 it is reported, 'So they returned'. In the proclamation that comes as a consequence of what Zechariah has heard and seen, the LORD is quoted as saying, 'I have returned to Jerusalem' (1.16). The call for Zechariah's audience to return as a precondition for the LORD to return has been accomplished. In the first 17 verses of Zechariah, then, it is reported that Zechariah's community has done what their fathers had not done; they have returned to the LORD. As a consequence the LORD has returned to them.

I have made the point that this 'returning' is associated with place. In the days of Jacob, the LORD used to speak to Jacob at a specific place, at Bethel. In the time of Zechariah the LORD's return is to Jerusalem. More specifically the LORD will return to his house, which '*will be built*' in it (1.16). That a measuring line '*will be stretched out*' undergirds the notion of construction. I have italicized the verbs '*will be built*' and '*will be stretched out*' to draw attention to the description of this construction in the passive mood. The absence of active builders is accompanied by the concealment of the audience in Zechariah who are to be the recipients of Zechariah's proclamations. Although the community was identified in Haggai as Joshua, Zerubbabel and the remnant of the people, that is, a minority within the community associated with an elite, the governor and the high priest, they are not identified or given a voice in Zechariah. The silence of this community in Zechariah suggests that 'returning' involving temple construction is not wholeheartedly accepted in the world depicted. Certainly, what Zechariah saw and is to proclaim in 1.7-17 has links with the temple building agreed to by this community in Haggai. The concern of the 'messenger of the LORD' that the whole earth should be at peace (Zech. 1.12), coupled with the LORD's anger against the nations, goes hand in hand with Haggai's notion that the LORD will overthrow the nations of the world so as to restore wealth to the temple in Jerusalem. Indeed, it is the point of the second proclamation that Zechariah is to make that the LORD will restore prosperity to Jerusalem (1.17).

The major theme of these two proclamations, then, is that 'returning' for both parties has to do with returning to the temple. But the entire passage (1.7-17) is also about 'returning' to the past, before the time of the former prophets, when there was communication with messengers making divine presence more immediate and more intimate.

Summary and Transition

This passage (Zech. 1.7-17) begins a series of scenes in which Zechariah sees a variety of things. The date is five months to the day after work began on the construction of the temple (Hag. 1.15). I understand that what Zechariah is seeing in the scenes unfolding before his eyes is the temple beginning to take shape in a way which will outstrip its former glory. The temple that initially looked like nothing (Hag. 2.3) is beginning to look like something. The riders who announce that the 'whole earth remains at peace' mark the beginning of the end of the short period of time Haggai mentioned would pass, before the LORD shook the heavens and earth, bringing the treasures of the nations to the house of the LORD so that the prosperity of this house would be greater than that of the former house of the LORD (Hag. 2.6-9; Zech. 1.16).

Zechariah sees the horses and riders at a place where the LORD's messengers are present, which means that the LORD also is present. The horses and riders in Zechariah's world who are patrolling the whole earth are not, as I understand them, mounted celestial beings. I understand that Zechariah sees them in his own world in much the same way that Hagar sees a well of water, Abraham a lamb, and Elijah a cake and a jar of water when messengers are present in their world. The temple is gaining shape before Zechariah's eyes. What he sees becomes a metaphorical expression of the LORD's message, 'I am with you' because the LORD is returning to Jerusalem to dwell in the temple which will be filled with the prosperity of the nations.

As a reader imagining the scene against the larger background of the Twelve, I also see something else happening. When Zechariah is shown what he sees, he enters in and becomes part of the scene so that he himself stands in the LORD's presence and overhears the question the messenger of the LORD asks. The interaction between Zechariah and the messengers, which brings him into the LORD's presence, raises a significant question when seen in the larger context of the Hebrew Bible in which messengers of the LORD are present. Why does Zechariah exhibit no fear? Why is Zechariah not afraid like Hagar, Manoah and his wife or Gideon, that he will die? A way of gaining an answer to these questions is to understand Zechariah in relation to Elijah, who also exhibited no fear in the presence of the LORD's messenger. While Elijah was terrified of Jezebel's messengers (1 Kgs 19.2-3), he, like Zechariah, was not afraid in the presence of the messenger of the LORD (1 Kgs 19.4-9; see also

2 Kgs 1.3, 15). The impression one gains from this is that Zechariah and Elijah (unlike Hagar, Manoah and his wife and Gideon) themselves gained the status of messengers, blurring the distinction between the human and the divine. At the end of the Twelve we are told that the LORD will again send Elijah (Mal. 4.5-6). While prophets do not live forever (Zech. 1.5), prophets like Elijah attain an extraordinary status as messengers. As the scenes unfold in Zechariah, Zechariah is drawn ever more into the scenes until he himself performs and speaks as a messenger of the LORD.

The LORD as Character

It is revealing to look at the way the LORD is portrayed in both the initial word that came to Zechariah (1.1-6) and in the proclamations that Zechariah is to make (1.14-17). He stands in marked contrast to the portrayal of other characters. He does almost all the talking and in doing so reveals more about himself as a character than we learn about the other characters who appear.

Up to this point we know very little about Zechariah as a character apart from his identification as a descendent of Iddo. He is presented primarily as a mouthpiece asking questions and speaking words of the LORD. Also, neither the messenger who spoke to Zechariah nor the messenger of the LORD appear as individuals for whom their narrative portrayal provides insight into their characters. Furthermore, the portrayal of the community is repressed and nameless in Zechariah, appearing only as a pronominal 'them' in 1.3. Even in Haggai they are identified only as a Joshua, Zerubbabel and the remnant of the people. They appear only to be obedient to the LORD. They fear the LORD (Hag. 1.12), and they work on the house of the LORD (Hag. 1.14). When they do speak, they only do so to acknowledge that the LORD was justified in his actions, 'The LORD of hosts has dealt with us according to our ways and deeds, just as he planned to do' (Zech. 1.6).

While the portrayal of the other characters is repressed, the LORD is given more detailed description. The description primarily discloses his emotions and the overwhelming passion is anger. Throughout 1.1-17, which depicts a change through 'returning', the LORD remains angry. Significantly, however, the object of that anger changes. In 1.2 the LORD is 'very angry' and that anger was directed at the fathers. In 1.12 the anger is with Jerusalem and the cities of Jerusalem and presumably its present inhabitants. In 1.16 the LORD is still 'extremely angry' but the anger is now directed against the nations.

Why is there the need for the LORD to redirect the source of his anger to others? What more can we learn about other characters who appear—Zechariah, the messenger who spoke with Zechariah, the messenger of the LORD, the community? We will need to keep these questions in mind as the scenes unfold.

Zechariah 1.18–2.13
Scenes 2 and 3: Four Horns and a Measuring Line

Introductory Remarks

This passage contains two scenes. In the first scene (1.18-21) Zechariah says that he 'lifted up his eyes' (NRSV 'I lifted up my eyes, and I saw') and saw four horns, and in the second scene (2.1-5) he reports that he 'lifted up his eyes' and saw a man with a measuring line in his hand. These two scenes are followed by words of the LORD (2.6-12) and conclude with words of Zechariah (2.13).

While these scenes followed by the LORD's words share similarities with the preceding passage (1.7-17), there are differences. Here Zechariah interacts differently with the characters (the LORD and the messenger) than he did in the scene involving the horsemen. Also, the words following these two scenes entangle Zechariah's words with the LORD's words, whereas the words of the LORD in 1.14-17 remain clearly and distinctly the LORD's. In this entanglement of words Zechariah claims his status as a messenger sent by the LORD. Finally, the words of Zechariah concluding this scene suggest a climactic moment in what Zechariah sees.

The Four Horns (1.18-21)

Having been given two proclamations to make about the LORD's intentions to build the temple and to make his cities prosper again (1.14-17), Zechariah lifts up his eyes and sees four horns. Later the LORD shows Zechariah four blacksmiths.

The Interaction of Characters

Before considering the significance of these four horns and the blacksmiths, I want to discuss the interaction of the characters in the scene. When the preceding scene concerning the horsemen unfolded, 'being shown' meant that Zechariah moved closer into the arena of the action, close enough to overhear what was being said. In the present scene concerning what he saw, Zechariah becomes even more involved in what he is seeing. In the earlier scene only messengers interacted with the LORD. The messenger of the LORD asked the LORD a question, and the messenger who spoke with Zechariah instructed Zechariah to proclaim the LORD's words. In this scene in which Zechariah sees four horns, however, his interaction with the LORD becomes more direct. Intermediaries between Zechariah and the LORD prove not to be necessary.

Zechariah's account of what he sees begins in 1.7-12. After he sees something (in this case four horns), he says to the messenger who talked with him, 'What are these' (1.19)? The polite form of address, 'my lord', found in 1.9 is missing, suggesting that Zechariah is becoming more familiar with the messenger who talked with him. Another clear departure from the earlier scene occurs. In response to Zechariah's question about the horns, the messenger simply tells Zechariah what they are: 'These are the horns that have scattered Judah, Israel and Jerusalem' (1.19). The LORD himself, not the messenger as in the earlier scene, *shows* Zechariah something: 'Then the LORD showed me four blacksmiths.' After being shown the blacksmiths, Zechariah asks, 'What are they coming to do?' (Zech. 1.21). There is no polite address. Zechariah simply utters the question abruptly, and the LORD responds with an explanation of the horns and the blacksmiths, 'These are the horns that have scattered Judah, so that no head could be raised; but these have come to terrify them, to strike down the horns against the land of Judah and to scatter its people'. Zechariah is directly interacting and conversing with the LORD. The LORD, not the messenger as in the earlier scene, shows things to Zechariah; and Zechariah, not the messenger as in the earlier scene, asks the LORD a question. Zechariah, who was having a conversation with a messenger in the previous passage and at the beginning of this one, is now having a conversation with the LORD.

In this scene, then, conversation with a messenger modulates into a conversation with the LORD. Such a shift from speaking with messengers to direct dialogue with the deity is a feature of other texts involving messengers of the LORD in the Hebrew Bible. For example, in Judges 6 the conversation between the messenger of the LORD and Gideon (6.11-13) modulates into a conversation between the LORD and Gideon (Judg. 6.16-18). A similar situation occurs in Genesis 18. Although here the messengers of the LORD are referred to simply as men, the conversation with the three men at the beginning of the chapter becomes a conversation with the LORD at the end of the chapter. (Note also the similarity in the language in Gen. 18.1 with the scenes in Zechariah: 'and he [Abraham] lifted up his eyes and he saw there three men . . . ') Speaking with the messenger of the LORD is tantamount to speaking with God because when the messenger is present the LORD is present. Zechariah is portrayed, then, as being in a world like that of the fathers, a world in which the divine is more immediately accessible when the messenger is present.

The Four Horns and the Blacksmiths

I have been arguing that Zechariah is looking out on a world in which the rebuilding of the temple, portrayed as commencing in Haggai, is taking place. The LORD's horsemen, seen patrolling the earth in the first scene (Zech. 1.7-17) suggest an imminent 'shake up' of the nations concurrent with temple construction (Hag. 2.6, 21). When read in the context of temple construction, the 'four horns' suggest that Zechariah is literally looking at the four horns of the altar (Exod. 27.2; see also Exod. 4.7, 18, 25, 30, 34; Ps. 118.27). However, in the Hebrew Bible 'horn' can be used as a symbol both of a nation's capacity to destroy and of the coming destruction of a nation, symbolized in the image of a horn being cut off (see Jer. 48.25). The four horns of the altar, which Zechariah is seeing during temple construction, symbolically suggest the coming destruction of the nations—the horns that scattered Judah, Israel and Jerusalem—now at peace. This symbolism of the four horns recalls the LORD's promised actions in the time of Amos concerning the altars of Bethel.

> On that day I punish Israel for its transgressions,
> I will punish the altars of Bethel,
> And the horns of the altar shall be cut off
> and fall to the ground (Amos 3.14).

Furthermore, these nations who are at *ease* (Zech. 1.15), are like those who were at *ease* in Amos's day and who think that they have taken the horns (the nations) for themselves (Amos 6.1, 13)—they will themselves be terrified and struck down.

To understand the four horns as appearing to Zechariah in a time of temple construction helps explain the appearance of the 'artisans' (NRSV 'blacksmiths') or 'workers' the LORD shows to Zechariah. What is suggested, then, is that the artisans have cut off the horns for the construction of the altar, that is, for the purpose of temple construction. Building the temple goes hand in hand with destruction of the nations whose horns scattered Judah, Israel and Jerusalem. The artisans at a time of construction come to signify the destruction of the horns, that is, the nations that scattered Judah.

When Zechariah sees the four horns (and I understand that what he sees is the altar under construction), I am perceiving this as a 'seeing-saying'. What Zechariah is seeing in his world becomes a visual metaphor of the LORD's message, 'I am with you'. The horns of the altar

provide the symbolic expression of how the building of the temple will
result in the striking down of the nations, who had lifted up 'their horns
against the land of Judah to scatter its people' (1.21).

For Zechariah to see an altar built in a world where messengers
appear echoes other scenes in the Hebrew Bible. Often when messengers appear an altar is erected and the place becomes the space where
the house of the LORD/God is built (see Gen. 28.10-22; 1 Chron. 21.18-
22.1; cf. Judg. 6.11-24). The building of an altar at the commencement
of temple construction, then, is consistent with another text, in which
an altar is erected in the place where a messenger of the LORD
appeared. It becomes the site where the temple will be built.

> David built an altar [at the threshing floor of Ornan where the messenger
> appeared]... He called upon the LORD, and he answered him with fire
> from heaven on the altar of burnt offering... Then David said, 'Here shall
> be the house of the LORD God and here the altar of burnt offering for the
> LORD (1 Chron. 21.26–22.1).

A Measuring Line (2.1-4)

The Interaction of Characters

In this scene Zechariah sees a man with a 'measuring line' measuring the
width and length of Jerusalem. Before considering more specifically
what Zechariah saw, it will be important again to look at the interaction
of characters in the scene and to compare and contrast this scene with
previous ones. In the first scene, in which Zechariah saw a mounted
horseman, Zechariah interacted solely with the messenger. In the second scene, in which Zechariah saw four horns, he directly asked the
LORD a question about the artisans that the LORD had shown him. In
this scene, however, Zechariah is less an observer, asking questions
about what he sees, than a participant in the action. Zechariah asks a
question of the man whom he sees with a measuring line in his hand,
'Where are you going?' The man answers Zechariah, 'To measure Jerusalem, to see what is its width and what is its length'. The ensuing conversation between two messengers (the messenger who spoke with
Zechariah and another messenger who comes out to meet him) suggests
the influence of Zechariah on events. One of these messengers (presumably the one who spoke to Zechariah although the referents for the
pronouns are not clear) gives an order to the other one, 'Run, say to that
young man: Jerusalem shall be inhabited like villages without walls,
because of the multitude of people and animals in it'. That the messenger who spoke to Zechariah is to run to deliver a message suggests that
there is some urgency. The impression one has is that this instruction to

be delivered to the young man eventuates because of what the young man had said in answer to Zechariah's question. In the first scene Zechariah had overheard conversations involving messengers. In this scene messengers overhear a conversation Zechariah is having with a character he sees. Zechariah has become a full participant in what he sees; he is not simply an spectator.

The Scene
For Zechariah to see a man with a measuring line in his hand fits the background of temple building and the restoration of Jerusalem developed in the earlier scenes. The theme of measuring Jerusalem picks up similar imagery in 1.16: that temple construction involves the restoration of Jerusalem. That Jerusalem will be a city like a village without walls (or 'an open country' or 'open region') brings to mind a point made in the earlier passage—that comforting Zion and choosing Jerusalem will result in all the LORD's cities overflowing with prosperity (1.17).

Why is it so urgent that the messenger *run* to the young man to tell him that Jerusalem will be inhabited like a village without walls? The text gives no ready clear answers. However, given the fact that the young man is to be told that Jerusalem will be an unwalled city or an open region, it is possible to understand that the young man is wasting his time. If there will be such a multitude inhabiting Jerusalem that it will be like a village without walls, an open region, then there is no need to measure its width and its length. There will be no length or width to it.

It is possible, of course, to understand that the 'young man' in the passage is Zechariah. If that is the case, then Zechariah is being told the meaning of what he sees, that Jerusalem will be like an open region, a village without walls. I find such a reading more problematic than one which recognizes that the young man is someone other than Zechariah. Nowhere else is Zechariah referred to as a 'young man'. Furthermore, the word 'young man' often carries the connotations of inexperience as it does in Jer. 1.7. To attempt to measure a city without walls would be the action of an inexperienced youth; hence, an interpretation of the 'young man' as the man with the measuring line is plausible. More importantly, however, as the scenes involving messengers have been unfolding, Zechariah is presented as being more and more involved in the activities he sees. To understand the 'young man' as referring to Zechariah would be inconsistent with this portrayal of Zechariah as an increasingly active participant in the dialogue. Nowhere else does anyone refer to Zechariah in the third person.

The Words of the LORD and the Words of Zechariah (2.5-12)

The words of the LORD following the two scenes of the horns and the man with the measuring line differ significantly from the words of the LORD that follow the first scene involving the mounted horseman (1.14-17). After the first scene, the messenger who spoke with Zechariah instructs Zechariah to make two proclamations. Significantly, this is the only time that the messenger of the LORD performs this function. After Zechariah's direct communication with the deity in the scene involving the four horns (1.20-21), and after he questions the young man with the measuring line (2.1-4), words come immediately to Zechariah without messenger mediation (2.5-12). Zechariah's status is changing. The close relationship Zechariah has established with the LORD is evident in the repeated statements in which Zechariah is claiming special status as having been sent by the LORD (2.8, 9, 11). Zechariah does not need the mediation of a messenger because he himself is now claiming the status of a messenger *sent* by the LORD.

It will be helpful to analyse the series of the LORD's words as they occur in 2.5-12. The 'sayings of the LORD' in 2.5 and 2.6 are the LORD's words. Like the words of the LORD following the first scene involving the mounted horseman (1.14-17), these words of the LORD are sayings of the LORD about what Zechariah was seeing. The LORD's words in 2.5 relate to the scene involving the measuring line and the words in 2.6 to the scene concerning the four horns. What is distinctive about these words of the LORD in 2.5 and 2.6 is that they are *not* mediated through a messenger. They simply emerge as words of the LORD directly accessible to Zechariah. The words of the LORD in 2.5 and 2.6 are followed by Zechariah's own words (2.7-9, 10-12) in which he gives directives to others. (Zech. 2.13 may be understood not as words of Zechariah, but words addressed to the reader by the narrator who is suggesting a dramatic change in the scene.) To support his commands, Zechariah bases his own words on words which the LORD had spoken. Whereas the messenger who spoke to Zechariah was giving him instructions in 1.14-17, Zechariah is now giving directives to others. By receiving words of the LORD, apart from the mediation of a messenger, and by giving directions to others, Zechariah himself is beginning to act like a messenger.

A Saying of the LORD (2.5)

In this scene and the previous one, what Zechariah sees is associated with sayings of the LORD. However, the sayings are separated from the scene and follow it. This *saying* of the LORD in 2.5 is associated with what Zechariah was *seeing*: a man with a measuring line in his hand who is ready to measure Jerusalem. The sight of the young man, who is assuming a conventionally walled city, is the occasion for the LORD's identification of the city as being without walls in the usual sense. The LORD's words communicated by the messenger are: 'I will be a wall of fire around it' and 'I will be the glory within it'. The imagery of 'fire' here recalls other places in the Hebrew Bible in which a messenger/the divine presence is associated with fire: the messenger who appeared to Moses 'in the flame of fire out of a bush...that] was blazing' (Exod. 3.2); the messenger who appeared to Gideon and caused fire to spring up from a rock and consume the meat (Judg. 6.21); the messenger who appeared to Manoah and his wife and who ascended in the flame of the altar; and finally the prophet/messenger Elijah who is to come again (Mal. 3.5-6) and whose ascension into heaven is associated with horses and a chariot of fire (2 Kgs 2.11). The symbolism of fire here suggests both the presence of messengers and the presence of the LORD. While the LORD will be present in the unbounded borders of Jerusalem, he will also be present in the middle of the city. 'Glory' is used in many places in the Hebrew Bible to refer to the LORD's presence in the temple. For example, Ezekiel sees the glory of the LORD moving from Jerusalem (Ezek. 11.23) and returning to the temple (Ezek. 43.1-5). The LORD's glory is also associated with his *fiery* presence at Sinai (Exod. 14.4, 17-18; 24.16-18; 34.25-29). What Zechariah saw, then, in the young man pointlessly measuring the breadth and length of Jerusalem is a symbolic expression of the LORD's 'fiery' presence around and at the centre of Jerusalem.

The Saying of the LORD (2.6)

This *saying* of the LORD is related to what Zechariah was *seeing* in the scene in which Zechariah saw four horns and the four artisans. The imperative call, 'flee', directed at those who have been spread abroad by the LORD like the four winds of heaven, directs action that should follow from an understanding of the symbolic significance of the four horns and the artisans. The LORD is cutting off the horns, the nations, to which the people of Judah have been scattered, so that they can escape and return to Zion. Here the interplay of responsibility—was it the four horns of the nations or the four winds of the LORD that scattered the people?—echoes the LORD's words in the first scene in which the nations were seen as being engaged in expressing the LORD's anger (1.15) and acting on his behalf. What Zechariah was seeing (the four horns and the four artisans who can be seen as coming to cut off the horns) and what the LORD is saying ('flee') give expression to the idea of return. Dispersal to the four corners of the earth has been reversed; now there is chance for flight to Jerusalem. 'The land of the north' from which the people shall flee may be understood as the symbolic place of Diaspora rather than a specific location.

Escape to Zion (2.7-9)

Following the first scene with the mounted horseman, the messenger gave Zechariah an order to proclaim what the LORD had to say. Following the two scenes associated with the horns and the measuring line, sayings of the LORD come immediately to Zechariah (2.5 and 2.6). The command to escape to Zion from daughter Babylon (2.7-9) is from Zechariah, who is now giving an imperative command as a messenger of the LORD. He bases that command on words of the LORD. Zechariah's words are beginning to mirror the LORD's words, suggesting the blurring of boundaries between the messenger and the LORD. Zechariah's words, 'Up! Escape to Zion, you that live with daughter Babylon', so clearly resemble the LORD's words, 'Up, up! Flee from the land of the north', that one can easily become confused about who is speaking. Is it Zechariah or is it the LORD? When the messenger speaks, the LORD speaks. Notice, however, that the general tone of what the LORD says about fleeing from *the north* becomes geographically specific in what Zechariah says in his imperative call to those who live with *daughter Babylon* to escape *to Zion*. This shift from the general to the specific is significant for Zechariah who is presenting his own agenda as one who has access to the LORD's words. His directive to those who dwell in Babylon will elicit a response, as becomes clear when people arrive from Babylon (see 6.9-14). Moreover, these returnees are carrying wealth (silver and gold), the prosperity of the nations alluded to by Haggai (Hag. 2.8-9) and by the LORD (Zech. 1.17). One can begin to see that in his new status as messenger Zechariah is claiming the power of the LORD whose words are immediately accessible to him.

Zechariah's specific imperative to 'escape' to Zion from daughter Babylon is supported by a reference to the LORD's more general words regarding the nations who plundered the people of Judah. 'For thus said the LORD of hosts (after his glory sent me) regarding the nations that plundered you: "For [NRSV 'truly'] one who touches you touches the apple of my eye".' Zechariah's specific call to escape from Babylon is based on these more general words of the LORD, regarding the nations who plundered the people of Judah.

Notice in these words that Zechariah is not only evoking the authority of the LORD's words but is also affirming his own status—'after his glory

sent me'. This phrase is enigmatic. The NRSV translation can be rendered more literally as 'after glory, he sent me'. This more literal translation suggests its significance. Given the context in the earlier saying of
the LORD that 'I will be glory within it [Jerusalem]' (2.5), the phrase can
be understood as meaning 'after glory', 'after presence', the LORD was
in the middle of Jerusalem, and he sent Zechariah. Indeed, the words of
Zechariah in the remaining verses in ch. 2 suggest a movement into the
temple, that is, a movement into the glorious presence (the glory) of the
LORD.

The phrase 'one who touches you touches the apple of *my* eye'
is also not entirely clear. Actually, the Hebrew text reads 'one who
touches you touches the apple of *his* eye'. This confusion between 'my'
and 'his' may also suggest the convergence of the LORD's and Zechariah's words. Even when Zechariah quotes the LORD speaking in the
first person, he can make a pronominal slip. While the meaning of the
phrase 'apple of my/his eye' is not entirely clear, the overall sense of the
passage is: whoever strikes you strikes me. Or, the phrase can be understood in still another way: whoever strikes you strikes himself (his own
eye). To put this another way, 'apple of his eye' could be understood to
refer to the person who touches you. In more colloquial terms, 'whoever touches you, hurts himself in the place where it most hurts'.

In further support of his call to escape from Babylon, Zechariah cites
the LORD's words, 'For [NRSV 'see now'] I am about to raise [or wave]
my hand against them, and they shall become plunder for their own
selves'. Given the confusion in the previous phrase, 'his/my eye', it is
not totally clear who the 'I' is in this phrase. Is it the LORD or is it
Zechariah? The ambiguity, however, is significant in a world in which
the messenger's presence is tantamount to divine presence and the
LORD's words converge with the messenger's words. Whoever is going
to raise his hand, it is clear from the things that Zechariah has been
seeing and the things that the LORD has been saying that the LORD is
about to shake the nations up (see Hag. 2.6; Zech. 1.21), making escape
possible.

After Zechariah's summons to escape, based on the words of the
LORD that he is 'about to raise his hand', to turn the tables on the
nations, Zechariah asserts, 'Then you will know that the LORD of hosts
has sent me'. Why should Zechariah make such a claim? I think that it
has to do with the fact that the shake up is 'about to' occur. Indeed, the
entire experience of what Zechariah has been seeing and what the
LORD has been saying supports this answer. The report of the mounted
horsemen that 'the whole earth remains at peace' has angered the
LORD. The horns of the nations are about to be struck down. The man

with the measuring line in his hand means that Jerusalem is about to be inhabited. That things are happening or are 'about to happen' in Zechariah's world is what distinguishes him from the former prophets. For example, Joel foresaw a day when every one who calls on the name of the LORD should *escape* 'for in Mount Zion and in Jerusalem there shall be those who escape, as the LORD has said…' (Joel 2.31-32). The difference between Joel and Zechariah is that for Zechariah escape is about to happen. The LORD not only is about to plunder the nations but has also returned to and is present in Jerusalem. In Joel's world escape will only happen in the distant future (see Joel 3.1-3). What would only unfold in the course of time as words foreseen by a former prophet of the LORD is about to happen in Zechariah's world. He can therefore claim that 'you will know that the LORD has sent me'.

Sing and Rejoice (2.10-12)

This second imperative call of Zechariah is also characterized by specificity. This time his words are addressed to daughter Zion, not to those who live in daughter Babylon. After his summons to 'Sing and Rejoice' a reason is given for his imperative, and again it is based on the words of the LORD. The same construction is used in Hebrew as in v. 9, suggesting that the LORD is 'about to do' something: ' "For, I am about to come and I will dwell in your midst", says the LORD'. These words of the LORD echo his earlier words, 'I will be the glory within it' (2.5). The LORD says further, 'many nations shall join themselves to the LORD on that day, and shall be my people, and I will dwell in their midst'. The words of the LORD indicating that Jerusalem will be filled with people of all nations resonate with what Zechariah had seen—a man mistakenly measuring a city that will be an open region, without walls.

Things are 'about to' happen in Zechariah's world. This 'about to' is what distinguishes Zechariah from the former prophets. Zephaniah also spoke of a time for 'daughter Zion//daughter Jerusalem' to 'sing and rejoice', but the time for singing and rejoicing referred to future events, not things about to happen. Zephaniah says,

> *Sing* aloud, O daughter Zion;
>   shout, O Israel!
> *Rejoice* and exult with all your heart,
>   O daughter Jerusalem (Zeph. 3.14).

But this rejoicing is because of what will happen 'on that day' when 'the LORD your God, is in your midst' (Zeph. 3.16-17). 'That day' in Zephaniah is in the distant future. 'That day' in Zechariah (2.11) is imminent: 'I am about to come and dwell in your midst' (Zech. 2.10). It is this 'about to' that distinguishes Zechariah from Zephaniah and supports his claim, 'And you shall know that the LORD of hosts has sent me to you'.

This last claim of Zechariah about his status is followed by the declaration: 'The LORD will inherit Judah as his portion in the holy land, and will again choose Jerusalem' (2.12). As previous commentators have pointed out, this is the only time in the Hebrew Bible that the LORD 'inherits' land and the only time that the phrase 'the holy land' is used. The distinctiveness of these words give rise to speculation. Why is the land identified as holy? Why is the LORD 'inheriting Judah as his portion?' Who is gaining from the land being holy and who is profiting from the LORD's inheritance? There is not space to answer these questions here but I will take them up in the Afterword.

Be Silent (Zech. 2.13): Summary and Transition

This passage concludes with words that have a similar formal structure to the words Zechariah spoke in 2.6-9 and 2.10-12. That is, they open with an imperative followed by a clause introduced by the word 'for', giving a reason for the imperative call to do something. Yet they are quite different. Zechariah does not quote the LORD's words as a reason for his summons to 'all people' to be silent. Zechariah 2.13 provides a transition to what Zechariah next sees, Joshua standing before the messenger of the LORD, and suggests the place in which subsequent action will occur.

In order to understand the significance of this third imperative call by Zechariah, it will be helpful to review how each of the previous scenes begins. In the first scene, Zechariah says, 'In the night I saw a man riding on a red horse' (1.8); in the second scene he says, 'And I lifted up my eyes and I saw four horns' (1.18); in the third scene, he says, 'I lifted up my eyes and I saw a man with a measuring line in his hand' (2.1); and in the fourth scene, which we have yet to consider, Zechariah does not lift up his eyes and see anything. Rather we are told, 'And he [the identity is not clear] showed me Joshua, the high priest, standing before the messenger of the LORD' (3.1, my translation). This fourth scene suggests that Zechariah is being shown things.

All of this is important for understanding the words, 'Be silent, all people, before the LORD; for he has roused himself from his holy dwelling'. Perhaps, one should understand this as a kind of narrator's aside to the reader rather than words of Zechariah. The words sound like a liturgical call to silence before a solemn act. Something dramatic is happening at this point in the narrative. Zechariah has previously seen the initiation of temple construction in the building of the altar (1.18-21). *Now* Zechariah is about to stand in the LORD's presence in the temple. When the scenes opened, Zechariah was out among the myrtle trees. Now what the LORD was about to do, he has done. He is dwelling in the midst of his people. These words, then, are addressed to the readers who have moved into the temple with Zechariah. Zechariah (and the reader) is standing in the LORD's presence in the temple.

These words also recall words of the former prophets. A similar call to silence is found in Hab. 2.20,

> But the LORD is in his holy temple;
> > let all the earth keep silence before him!

To read this text in the light of Zech. 2.13 suggests a major difference between the time of Zechariah and the time of Habakkuk. The call for all the earth to be silent in Habakkuk is followed by a prayer of Habakkuk about the mighty works of the LORD in the past. According to the prayer, this is a time for Habakkuk to quietly wait (Hab. 3.16). When the call for 'all people' to be silent occurs in Zechariah, the waiting is over. The LORD is present in his temple.

Zechariah as Character

Zechariah begins to emerge as a character in this scene, which begins with his seeing the four horns and the measuring line and ends with the call to silence because of the LORD's presence in the temple. Zechariah is no longer just a humble observer seeking explanation or a mouth-piece speaking the words of the LORD. He becomes increasingly in-volved in the scenes, interacting directly with the LORD who shows him things and even converses with him. The sayings of the LORD are not mediated through a messenger but come to Zechariah directly. Follow-ing the two sayings of the LORD (2.5, 6), Zechariah himself begins to speak in his own words. The words mirror the LORD's words and the imperative instructions he gives ('escape' and 'sing and rejoice') are based on the words of the LORD. Furthermore, when Zechariah speaks, he makes claims about his own special status as one sent by the LORD. Zechariah himself has become a messenger. In his claims about his status we can begin to see the significance of the emergence of messen-gers in the Twelve. Messengers, unlike the former prophets, have immediate access to the LORD who is about to act in such a way as to confirm the status of the messenger. Messengers, unlike the prophets, will not be required to wait to have their status confirmed. Zechariah, then, is becoming a messenger with direct access to the LORD, and this will become publicly manifest in what the LORD is 'about to do'.

A messenger presence represents a return to the way it used to be in the days when a messenger used to speak to Jacob at Bethel. The authoritative voice and messenger status Zechariah is claiming for himself in these verses means a return to the way it used to be—encapsulated in the meaning of Zechariah's name, 'the LORD has remembered'.

Zechariah 3.1-10
Scene 4: Cleaning Up the Priesthood

Introductory Remarks

This scene focuses on Joshua, the high priest, and the return of cultic personnel. In this scene Zechariah sees the dirty linen being removed from Joshua, the high priest, and his guilt taken away. Joshua was encountered earlier in the Twelve when Haggai called on Joshua along with Zerubbabel and the remnant of the people to rebuild the temple (Hag. 1.1, 12, 14; 2.2). According to Haggai, Joshua, along with Zerubbabel and the remnant of the people, 'obeyed the voice of the LORD their God, and the words of the prophet Haggai, as the LORD their God had sent him; and the people feared the LORD' (1.12). Joshua, then, as I pointed out above, appears to be included in the ambiguous 'they' who 'returned and said, "The LORD of hosts has dealt with us according to our ways and deeds, just as he planned to do"' (1.6).

The Cast of Characters (Zech. 3.1-5)

Again, it will be helpful to identify the cast of characters, their involvement in previous scenes, and the interaction between them. Just as significant, however, is the character who does not appear—*the messenger who talked with Zechariah*. This character played a significant role in the first scene. Zechariah posed questions to him, he showed Zechariah things, and he even instructed Zechariah to proclaim the words of the LORD. In the second and third scenes he recedes into the background as Zechariah's involvement increases. In this scene he plays no role whatsoever. He will not return again until the beginning of the next scene in 4.1.

Another character, *the messenger of the LORD*, whom I have identified as Haggai, reappears in this scene; he was present in the first scene but was absent in scenes two and three. In the first scene he was the figure who asked the LORD, 'O LORD of hosts, how long will you withhold mercy from Jerusalem and the cities of Judah, with which you have been angry these seventy years?' He is very active in the present scene. He gives instructions to remove the filthy clothes from Joshua and articulates the LORD's 'contract' with Joshua. In some ways Joshua is central to this scene, but he is a passive character. Things are done to him. He is clothed in new apparel, and the messenger of the LORD addresses him with a lengthy exhortation. He himself does nothing and says nothing.

A new character, *the satan* appears for the first and only time in Zechariah. The word appears with the definite article in Hebrew. Since 'the satan' refers to a role of one of the LORD's messengers and is not a proper name, I have rendered it with the definite article and with a lower case 's'. NRSV translates it 'Satan'. This character should not be understood as the devil, a divine being in opposition to the LORD, as Satan came to be understood in later times. The use of the definite article, 'the' suggests that 'satan' is not a proper name but indicates rather a vocational function, and the phrase is similar to phrases such as 'the prophet', 'the messenger' or 'the priest'. This character performs a particular task as a messenger of the LORD. What the satan does is clear from the first verse (3.1): 'Then he showed me the high priest Joshua standing before the messenger of the LORD and the satan standing at his right hand *to accuse* him.' The word the NRSV translates 'accuse' is in Hebrew the same word root as the noun 'satan'. The satan, then, is standing by the right hand of Joshua 'to satan him'.

What does it mean 'to satan' someone? In Job (1.7, 8, 9, 12; 2.1, 2, 3, 6,7) the satan tests Job in a wager he makes with the LORD. However, Job is absent when this wager takes place and unaware of the wager. In Zechariah the satan is standing beside Joshua 'to satan him'. If we turn to another text in which the satan appears, it becomes clear that the role of the satan is not simply to accuse but sometimes to carry out orders of the LORD to inflict bodily harm including death. For example, the messenger of the LORD plays the role of the satan in the story in which God's anger is kindled against Balaam at Balaam's refusal to obey the LORD's word. At that time 'the messenger of the LORD took his stand in the road to be a satan to him [Balaam]' (Num. 22.22). When the messenger carries out the role of the satan, he stands in the road 'with a drawn sword in his hand' (Num. 22.23). In the story, Balaam is unable to see the messenger and is ultimately saved by the donkey, who unlike Balaam, is able to see the messenger. When Balaam does see the messenger of the LORD, he is greatly alarmed and with good reason. The messenger says,

> Why have you struck your donkey these three times? The donkey saw me, and turned away… If it had not turned away from me, surely just now I would have killed you and let it live (Num. 22.32-33).

Just as a messenger can appear in the world to protect someone, as the messenger did in guiding Israel through the wilderness (see, e.g., Exod. 14.19; 23.20, 23), so he can appear as the expression of the

LORD's anger to inflict bodily harm, 'to satan' someone (see also 2 Sam. 24.16, 17; 1 Chron. 21.15, 27).

Also appearing in this scene involving Joshua and the satan are the LORD and Zechariah. As in the second scene, they both have speaking parts. However, in scene two, they spoke to each other; here they do not. The LORD rebukes the satan, and Zechariah gives an order concerning Joshua. In the preceding scene, Zechariah's words mirrored the LORD's words. In this scene, Zechariah speaks in a way that mirrors the words of 'the messenger of the LORD'.

The Setting (Zech. 3.1-5)

The setting for this scene is indicated at the close of ch. 2. The grandeur of this occasion is accentuated by Zech. 2.13: 'Be silent, all people, before the LORD; for he has roused himself from his holy dwelling.' With this scene Zechariah (and the reader) move from outdoors into the temple itself, toward the presence of the LORD who has returned there. Zechariah, who made a claim about his status as being sent by the LORD in the previous scene (2.8, 9, 11) has entered into the presence of the LORD. The consequence of Haggai's message, ' "I am with you," says the LORD' helps explain the solemn imperative, 'Be silent'.

After Zechariah had entered into conversation with the LORD in scene 2 (1.20-21), and after the LORD had shown him the four smiths (or artisans), his account of what he saw pushed others to the periphery as he progressed toward centre stage in the LORD's presence. The present scene opens, 'Then he showed me the high priest Joshua standing before the messenger of the LORD, and the satan standing at his right hand to satan him'. In the unfolding series of scenes this 'he' can only be the LORD. The only other character to show Zechariah anything was the messenger who talked with Zechariah (1.9), and he does not appear with Zechariah in this scene. He will not come on stage again until 4.1 at which time he will become increasingly active. The LORD who had shown Zechariah the smiths in 1.20 is now showing him Joshua, the satan and the messenger of the LORD.

The question can be posed, 'How is the LORD showing Zechariah this sight of the high priest standing before the messenger of the LORD and the satan?' How the LORD shows Zechariah these things is not easily answered. But the view before Zechariah's eyes becomes more understandable when this scene is read as something he sees in his own world. The situation is similar to the way the LORD shows Amos things in his world (locusts, fire, a plumb line and a basket of summer fruit, Amos 7.1, 4; 8.1). In a similar way the LORD asks Jeremiah about things

he sees in his world (an almond branch and a boiling pot, Jer. 1.11, 13).
What Zechariah sees is a scene in the temple in which the LORD shows
him the messenger, the satan (i.e. another messenger) and Joshua, the
high priest. Zechariah hears what the LORD says, but he is not shown
the LORD. The LORD is speaking because, as we have seen, the LORD
speaks when the messenger speaks (see Gen. 16.13; 28.10-11 and Exod.
3.1-12).

While this passage centres on Joshua, its significance is found in what
it reveals about the other characters. We are given no insights into the
character of Joshua. Like a mannequin he is dressed in new attire, and
with no chance for rebuttal he is given a stern lecture about his
behaviour. Similarly, the satan is given no voice, he appears in the scene
primarily to be rebuked by the LORD.

In his rebuke of the satan, the LORD asks him, 'Is not this man a brand
plucked from the fire?' 'Fire' here recalls the LORD's description of himself as being a 'wall of fire' around Jerusalem (2.5). The question implies
that the satan is responsible for Joshua's former condition from which
he needed to be rescued. Among the former prophets, the LORD himself
takes credit for turning people into brands rescued from the fire. He
describes his own activity that way in Amos 4.11. The LORD says,

> I overthrew some of you,
>> as when God overthrew Sodom and Gomorrah,
>> and you were like a brand snatched from the fire;
> and yet you did not return to me, says the LORD.

In rebuking the satan for behaviour that is like his own, the LORD
reveals insights into his own character as it has been portrayed elsewhere in Zechariah.

The LORD again is portrayed as an angry god. The first time the LORD
is introduced in Zechariah, Zechariah says that he was '*very* angry' with
the fathers (1.2). Later we are told that that anger was maintained as a
70-year rage (1.12). When the LORD decides to return, to patch things
up (1.16), he begins to identify others who are to blame for his anger.
The first object of his redirected anger is the nations. He says that he
was '*extremely* angry' with the nations, but was '*only a little* angry'
with the fathers (1.15). In this scene centring on Joshua the LORD continues to divert blame for his anger to others. That Joshua is in such a
bad state, like 'a brand plucked from the fire' (1.2) is the satan's fault.
Satan is responsible, blamed, and is scolded by the LORD.

This passing of responsibility to 'the satan', however, can be seen as
problematic when understood in the light of other passages in which
the LORD gives orders to messengers 'to satan' someone. The LORD

sends his messengers 'to satan' precisely when he becomes angry as was the case with Balaam discussed above. The messenger performing the role of a satan does not act out of his own accord; he does not have free reign over his activities. For example, when the LORD becomes angry with David when he takes a census of the people (2 Sam. 24; see 1 Chron. 21), the LORD's messenger carries out the LORD's threat of pestilence resulting in 70,000 dead. When the messenger moves toward Jerusalem to destroy it, it is the LORD who stops him from killing (2 Sam. 24.16; see 1 Chron. 21.15). The satan is not a messenger of the LORD with independent power; he carries out the LORD's intentions.

In his rebuke of the satan, the LORD also makes the claim that he has chosen Jerusalem (3.2), repeating the promise from the last scene (2.12). Here the LORD presents himself as a changed character. He has returned home to his house in a rebuilt Jerusalem. Many nations will join themselves to the LORD (2.11).

The scene next moves from the LORD's rebuke of the satan to focus on removing Joshua's dirty clothing and attiring him in new apparel (3.3-5). At this point in the scene both the messenger of the LORD and Zechariah are performing similar roles. They, like the LORD in the preceding verses, have speaking parts while Joshua, like the satan, remains silent. In what they say to and about Joshua, they reveal more about their own characters than they do about Joshua, the object of their speech. The most important consequence of their speaking is that it implies their superior status over the high priest Joshua who has no voice.

According to the scene, Joshua is standing before the messenger of the LORD dressed in filthy clothes. The messenger instructs those standing in his presence to take off the dirty clothes of Joshua. That this act has symbolic significance is clear from the words the messenger speaks, 'See, I have taken your guilt away from you, and I will deck you with festal apparel'. At this point Zechariah, who in the last scene claimed his special status as a messenger, now speaks like a messenger, 'Let them put a clean turban on his head'. Haggai, the messenger of the LORD, launched temple construction when he first spoke as the messenger of the LORD (Hag. 1.13-15). Now in this scene Zechariah is preparing Joshua, the high priest, to carry out his role in the rebuilt temple. Furthermore, Zechariah, whose status at the beginning of the book was ambiguously linked with his grandfather Iddo (1.1, 7), is emerging unambiguously as a messenger of the LORD.

Zechariah is normally not considered a messenger in an earthly setting. He is seen as participating in the 'heavenly council' through vision. However, it has been recognized that the figure of Joshua does not belong in the heavenly council. I interpret this passage not as vision but as temple activity, with Zechariah, like Haggai, acting as a messenger of the LORD in the instalment of the high priest. In this scene the satan is involved in temple ceremony and, as will become clear later, is presented as a human being with a role to perform. Apart from Haggai no other prophet in the Hebrew Bible is specifically named as a messenger of the LORD. Messengers speak to prophets as they do to Elijah (2 Kgs 1.3, 15), but prophets are not messengers. The only other place in the Hebrew Bible linking prophets and messengers is 2 Chron. 36.15-16. With the appearance of messengers in the Twelve, the situation has changed. In the rebuilt temple heaven has come to earth, and messengers of the LORD will go out from there. Prophets appear in a new guise. This is the beginning of the end of prophecy in the Twelve. Immediate access to the LORD through his messengers in the rebuilt temple makes the vision of prophets obsolete (see Zech. 13.1-6). As I indicated above, vision of things to come requires waiting, and waiting characterizes the time of the 'former prophets'. In the time of the rebuilt temple prophetic figures such as Haggai and Zechariah will go out from the temple as messengers of the LORD. The message of the messengers is ' "I am with you," says the LORD' (Hag. 1.13).

Haggai's and Zechariah's status is enhanced in their roles as messengers of the LORD, and in this scene they are placed in a position of authority vis-à-vis the high priest Joshua. As the scene unfolds, the reason for Joshua's silence becomes clear. Joshua is being installed and admonished in his role as high priest. The reclothing of Joshua in 3.3-5 appears as a ritual act of installation. Joshua is made to wear the apparel signifying his new role as high priest. The admonition in 3.6-10 concerns the responsibilities of the newly installed priest for the wider community, primarily for 'the Branch', who will be the subject of the next scene (4.1-14). Significantly, as we will see, 'the Branch', although spoken about, will never appear in any of the scenes as a character, not even as a voiceless character, like Joshua.

The ritual act of replacing Joshua's filthy clothes symbolizes removal of the 'guilt' of the high priest. 'See I have taken *your* guilt away from *you*' (3.4). According to the NRSV, Joshua will be reclothed with 'festal apparel'. The Hebrew word for 'festal apparel' is used only here and in Isa. 3.22. In the latter passage it occurs in a list of luxury goods. That Joshua is clothed in such opulent garb is reminiscent of Haggai's claim of much wealth in the rebuilt temple (Hag. 2.6-9; see also Zech. 1.17). Reclothing him with festal apparel symbolizes his ritual purity. As many commentators have pointed out, the Hebrew word translated 'guilt' can refer to both the transgression and the guilt that comes as a result. The importance of the dirty clothes can be recognized in graphic terms when it is pointed out that the word translated 'filthy' can refer to human excrement (Deut. 23.13).

After this symbolic and ritual cleansing of Joshua, Zechariah himself enters the ritual activity and says, 'Let them put a new turban on his head'. As commentators have often pointed out, the Hebrew word for turban is not the usual word used for the turban a priest wears in the Hebrew Bible. The more usual word for the priest's turban is *mṣnpt* (see, e.g., Exod. 28.4, 37, 39. 29.6; 39.28, 31; Lev. 8.9; 16.4). The word used here is *ṣnyp*. They both have, of course, the same word root. The significance of Zechariah's comment will become clear in the discussion of the admonition in 3.6-10.

The Admonition to Joshua (Zech. 3.6-10)

The admonition the messenger of the LORD makes to Joshua requires some extended commentary. On the one hand, it is important to look at the way this admonition contributes to the unfolding picture of restoration in Zechariah. On the other hand, these words spoken by Haggai, the messenger of the LORD, his last words in Zechariah, resonate with the larger literary context of the Twelve, particularly with Hosea and Micah at the beginning and with Malachi, 'my messenger', at the end.

The words of the messenger of the LORD addressed to Joshua, the high priest, begin by focusing on Joshua's responsibility for administering the temple and its courts. I want to offer my own more literal translation of these verses because they are not only important for understanding the charge given to Joshua, but they are also important for understanding the role of the messengers in the Twelve as 'men'.

> Thus says the LORD of hosts, 'If you *go* [or *walk*] in my ways, and if you keep my requirements, then also you will rule my house and have charge of my courts. And I will give you *goings* [or *walkings*] among these *standing ones*. Now listen Joshua, you and your colleagues, the *sitting ones* before you, because they are *men* of portent, because I am about to bring my servant the branch' (Zech. 3.7-8).

If Joshua follows the conditional 'requirements' (or 'priestly duties', the connotation of the Hebrew word in Num. 3.7, 8, 25, 28, 31, 32, 36, 38) to '*go* (or '*walk*') in the LORD's ways and keep his priestly duties, then he will have '*goings*' [or *walkings*] among the '*standing ones*'. We are not given a list of those who were standing. However, that it included individuals other than the messenger of the LORD is indicated by 3.4. Clearly those standing were not Joshua's 'colleagues' or 'associates' because they were 'sitting ones' (3.8). But we know that the messenger of the LORD was standing (see 3.5; NRSV renders the Hebrew 'standing by'. But the Hebrew can simply be rendered 'standing'. As I understand the word in this context the emphasis is on the fact that the messenger of the LORD was *standing*, not on his being in the vicinity, *standing by*). Joshua and the satan were also standing (3.1). One might imagine that Zechariah, who speaks as a messenger in this scene, was standing also. The text, however, does not make this explicit. That the high priest will have access to those who, like the messenger of the LORD, *the standing ones*, suggests that Joshua will also gain the status of messenger by walking among messengers. He also will go in and out of the LORD's presence as a messenger from the temple.

The identification of the messengers, *'the standing ones'* as *'men* of portent' is the clearest statement in Zechariah that the messengers are portrayed as *'men'*, not as angelic beings. The word translated 'portent' ('omen' in the NRSV) should be understood in the sense of a 'sign' of something that will happen. It is used this way in other places in the Hebrew Bible for human beings as 'a sign and a *portent'* of things to come (see Isa. 8.18 and 20.3). Haggai, the messenger of the LORD Zechariah, a messenger of the LORD, and potentially Joshua, the high priest, are a sign that the LORD is *about to bring* the Branch whom the LORD calls, 'my servant'. The high priest, Joshua, is about to be joined by the civil authority, the Branch (Zerubbabel), who will be the subject of the next scene. Haggai, the messenger of the LORD, has already referred to Zerubbabel as 'my servant' (2.23). Furthermore, there seems to be a play on words in relation to Zerubbabel's name 'seed of Babylon' and 'branch', which can also be translated 'shoot' or 'sprout'. What the LORD is about to bring is the governor, 'the seed of Babylon', who is about to shoot or sprout as the governor of Judah. That Zerubbabel appears nowhere in the scenes as a character in Zechariah suggests that this 'seed' is still in Babylon and not present in Zechariah's world. He is only about to come and to begin growth as governor. Although 'branch' is used for a future Davidic monarch in some texts outside the Twelve (e.g. Jer. 23.5), Haggai always designates Zerubbabel by the Persian term of 'governor' (1.1, 14; 2.2; 21). That Zerubbabel is about to come and that he is not present as a character in Zechariah, makes one wonder in what sense Zerubbabel was present in the community addressed by Haggai (see Hag. 1.1, 12, 14; 2.2, 4, 20). Perhaps his was a political rather than a physical presence among the remnant who returned.

The messenger of the LORD then says that he has set a single stone with seven facets (or eyes) before Joshua on which the LORD will engrave an inscription. The importance of this stone is that it will play a role in the removal of 'the guilt of this land in a single day'. In other words the ritual act of removing Joshua's guilt by replacing his filthy clothes with fine apparel is matched by the ritual act of setting before Joshua a stone symbolizing the removal of the guilt of the entire land. This text resonates intertextually with Exod. 28.36-38 (see Petersen, *Haggai and Zechariah 1-8*, pp. 211-12) which speaks about an ornament placed on the turban of the high priest, Aaron, with an engraving, 'holy to the LORD'. Furthermore, it will have the symbolic function of taking on the guilt of the entire congregation of Israelites. Clearly there are differences between Exodus 28 and Zechariah 3, and I am not maintaining that either passage directly influenced the other. However, when read in the light of the Exodus passage, Zechariah 3 gains clarity. Zechariah's participation in the ritual in which he ordered that a clean turban be placed on the head of Joshua is associated with the important role of the priest in taking on the guilt of others. The link with Exodus suggests that the stone in front of Joshua may be for his turban so that he can perform the function similar to that associated with Aaron. Joshua as high priest will be involved in removing the guilt of all the land. The significance of the seven facets or eyes is not clear in this passage, but it becomes clearer in the following scenes in which the LORD is portrayed as 'the master of all the earth, who sees all that is happening in the earth'.

The charge to Joshua by the messenger of the LORD ends by saying that on the day when the Branch comes and when the guilt of the land is removed, friends and colleagues will invite one another to come under their vines and fig trees. This image of coming together under the vine and fig tree reverberates with a passage in Micah (4.1-4). Micah was looking forward to 'days to come' (4.1) when nations would come up to the house of the LORD (4.2, cf. Zech. 2.11), and he sees this as a time of universal peace (4.3) when the nations

> . . . shall sit under their own vines and under their fig trees,
> and no one shall make them afraid;
> for the mouth of the LORD of hosts has spoken (Mic. 4.4).

These things that the former prophet Micah prophesied are now taking place or about to take place in Zechariah's world.

Before ending my discussion of the exhortation to Joshua by the messenger of the LORD, I want to turn to the two conditions that Joshua the high priest is required to meet: 'if you walk in my ways' and 'if you keep my requirements [or carry out your priestly duties]'. What it means to walk in the ways of the LORD or to keep his requirements is not spelled out in Zechariah 3. The larger context of the Twelve, however— particularly Hosea and Micah at the beginning of the Twelve, and

Malachi, at the end—helps us to understand these priestly duties.

The duties of a priest are given explicitly in Mal. 2.5 when Malachi quotes the LORD's words about his covenant with Levi.

> My covenant with him was a covenant of life and well-being, which I gave him; this called for reverence, and he revered me and stood in awe of my name.

But the priests, according to Malachi, have not followed the covenant the LORD made with Levi (Mal. 2.8-9). This passage in Malachi implies that the two conditions stipulated for the high priest's position—to walk in the ways of the LORD and to carry out his duties of instruction (Torah)—have not been met. In other words, by the end of the Twelve, the new world of return portrayed in Zechariah is put in jeopardy by the priesthood. Comparing Malachi 2 with Zechariah 3 is suggestive. It was implied in Zech. 3.7 that the priest was to be a messenger of the LORD also and it is stated explicitly in Mal. 2.7 that the priestly role is that of a messenger of the LORD. Whereas Joshua was to be responsible for removing the 'guilt/iniquity' of the whole land, according to Zech. 3.9, it is implied in Malachi that the priests are not carrying out such duties (Mal. 2.8-9). When the scene concerning Joshua the high priest opened in Zechariah, the satan was 'rebuked' for what he had done to Joshua. In Mal. 2.3 the offspring of the priests are being rebuked because the priests did not heed the conditions the LORD had set down for them. In Zechariah 3, when Joshua stood before the messenger of the LORD, Joshua's clothes filthy with excrement were to be removed. In Mal. 2.3 the LORD is spreading the dung of the priests' offering on their faces, making them filthy again.

In the beginning of the Twelve, there is a vision of the priests' role in the temple. Micah envisions the day when the nations will go to 'the house of the LORD' so that they may 'walk in his ways' and so that they may gain 'instruction' (Torah) (Mic. 4.2). Indeed, the reader is instructed early in the Twelve—at the end of Hosea (14.9)—that returning to the LORD is a matter of walking in his ways (see Landy, p. 169).

> Those who are wise understand these things;
> > those who are discerning know them.
> For *the ways of the LORD* are right.
> > and the *upright walk* in them,
> > but transgressors *stumble* in them.

On the other hand, at the end of the Twelve, Malachi suggests that the whole agenda of the return is being put into jeopardy by the priests, whose behaviour is the antithesis of this instruction to the reader at the end of Hosea. While Levi had '*walked*' with the LORD in integrity and *uprightness*, the present priests are cursed because the LORD says,

> 'You have turned aside from the *way*; you have caused many to *stumble*
> by your instruction; you have corrupted the covenant of Levi,' says the
> LORD of hosts, 'and so I make you despised and abased before all the
> people, inasmuch as you have not kept *my ways* but have shown partiality
> in your instruction' (Mal. 2.8-9).

Looking ahead in this literary collage, then, the restoration of the LORD
depicted in Zechariah is not one of perfect return. The ambiguous 'they'
addressed by Zechariah may indeed be only the 'remnant of the people'
in Haggai's audience (1.12, 14; 2.2). That remnant may only be loosely
associated with Joshua the high priest since the priests at the end of
Malachi have not adhered to the conditions of priesthood. Since Zechariah does not lay eyes on Zerubbabel, this 'seed of Babylon' may not
even have taken root in Zechariah's restored community.

Summary and Transition

The scene we have been discussing begins with the LORD showing
Zechariah something rather than Zechariah on his own initiative looking
up and seeing something. As I have indicated in my discussion of the
previous scenes, when Zechariah is shown something, he moves into
the arena of the action. Here the action centres on the high priest
Joshua. Zechariah moves into the temple. What he sees in the subsequent scenes involves temple imagery because he is in the presence of
the LORD who has 'roused himself in his *holy dwelling*' (Zech. 2.13).
The action of the LORD *rousing himself* in his holy dwelling matches
the action of the people who, when the messenger first spoke, were
'*stirred up*' (Hag. 1.14) to begin to work on the house of the LORD.
(The same Hebrew word is used in both places.) It is appropriate that
Haggai, the messenger of the LORD, is present in both scenes in which
both the LORD and the people are '*stirred up*' into action so that temple
construction can ensure divine presence.

In this scene, Zechariah speaks like the messenger of the LORD when
he orders that a clean turban be placed on Joshua's head. He belongs to
that group of men, 'men of portent', who are standing before Joshua.
According to the admonition of Haggai, the messenger of the LORD,
these men—these messengers—are a sign that the LORD is about to
bring his Branch, Zerubbabel, the seed of Babylon. This is the last time
Haggai, the messenger of the LORD, speaks in Zechariah. Significantly,
when Haggai last spoke in the 'book' of Haggai, he also spoke a word of
the LORD about Zerubbabel, as one chosen by the LORD. Zerubbabel
does not appear even as a passive character in Zechariah. This absent

Zerubbabel, singled out by Haggai (the LORD's messenger) both in Hag. 2.20-23 and in the present scene, suggests that this governor of Judah is more important in the way the messengers see what is happening in their world. Where is Zerubbabel? Was he present when the community began to work on the temple (Hag. 1.14)? Is it because of his absence that a special word is directed to him by Haggai? This absent Zerubbabel will be associated with what is seen—and the seeing that arises from this seeing—in the next scene in which Zechariah, like Haggai, also receives a word of the LORD to speak to Zerubbabel (4.6-7).

The Messenger of the LORD as Character

In this scene we are introduced in more detail to Haggai, the messenger of the LORD, as a character. What we learn about him concerns his status, as was the case with Zechariah in the last scene.

Unlike the LORD whose portrayal as a character gives us insight into his emotions, primarily described as anger and passion, we learn very little about the emotional make-up of either Haggai, 'the messenger of the LORD', or Zechariah. The status of 'the messenger of the LORD' (Haggai) is reflected in the role he plays in this scene. He has special status among those other messengers who are present in this scene, including Zechariah and the satan. As the scene opens he takes centre stage with Joshua the high priest and the satan standing in front of him. He stands at the centre of the scene when the LORD speaks. Again, we are reminded of this blurring of distinctions between divine and human in a world where messengers appear. When a messenger is present, the LORD is present. When a messenger speaks, the LORD speaks. Haggai's special status is confirmed, when he, as one of the 'men of portent', admonishes Joshua the high priest to follow his priestly duties and to walk in the way of the LORD. When Haggai, the messenger of the LORD first spoke the LORD's message, ' "I am with you," says the LORD' (Hag. 1.13), a claim was being made about his special status as *the* messenger of the LORD. That special status as *the* messenger of the LORD is confirmed by his central role in this scene.

Zechariah 4.1-14:
Scene 5: Stirring Up Zechariah

Introductory Remarks

In the previous scene Zechariah entered into the temple where the LORD had roused himself. Zechariah positioned himself as one of those standing before Joshua and his seated colleagues. Zechariah, along with Haggai, the messenger of the LORD, is one of the 'men of portent'. The present scene as well as the remaining ones (in 5.1–6.15) all take place in the temple, where the messenger who spoke with Zechariah returns. Because of the temple setting, I read the things Zechariah sees in the remaining scenes as furnishings of the temple, such as the golden lamp-stand in the present scene, or other features of temple construction. The imagery associated with what Zechariah is seeing can be understood as metaphorical expressions of what the LORD says.

At the beginning of this scene, the messenger 'wakened' Zechariah as 'one is wakened from sleep'. The Hebrew word translated '*wakened*' is the same word used in Zech. 2.13 when the LORD '*roused himself*' in his holy abode. Zechariah is now *roused* to action in the temple just as the LORD was roused to action in his holy dwelling. The same Hebrew word is used in Hag. 1.14 when the spirit of the LORD '*stirred up*' the community to begin work on the temple, and in all of these places the verb concerns the notion of stirring up or rousing to activity. The question this raises for understanding the present scene is, 'What is the activity Zechariah is being stirred up to do?' I will argue that Zechariah is to speak the LORD's word to Zerubbabel about completing temple construction (see 4.9). Zechariah as messenger is associated with the end of temple construction, completing the task of Haggai, the messenger of the LORD, who was associated with initiating work on the temple (Hag. 1.13-14).

While the previous scene dealt with the installation of Joshua as high priest, this scene focuses on the governor Zerubbabel, whose task will be to finish building the temple. As both this present scene and the previous one envisage the completion of the temple and the restoration of the community through the religious and civil authorities, it is important to note how the symbolism of prosperity, which will follow restoration, is reflected in what is seen. The symbolic significance of what Zechariah sees has clear links with the prosperity envisaged by

Haggai when he exhorted Joshua, Zerubbabel and the remnant of the people to rebuild the temple.

As I pointed out in discussion of Zech. 1.1-6, the imagery of 'return' in the Twelve, from the very beginning in Hosea and Joel, is accompanied by the notion of abundance and prosperity symbolized by the return of the grain, the new wine (sometimes associated with the vine) and the oil (sometimes associated with the olive tree). It is precisely these things that were missing, according to Haggai, because of the drought occasioned by the temple remaining unbuilt (Hag. 1.11). Also, according to Haggai, this agricultural produce associated with the grain, the olive tree and the vine began to reappear when the foundation of the temple was laid, dated exactly as the fourth day of the ninth month.

> Consider from this day on…[s]ince the day that the foundation of the LORD's temple was laid, consider: Is there any seed left in the barn? Do *the vine, the fig tree*, the pomegranate, and the olive tree still yield nothing? From this day on I will bless you (Hag. 2.18-19).

At the end of the previous scene ('Cleaning Up the Priesthood') we discussed the very last words addressed to Joshua, concerning the removal of the guilt of the land. This removal suggests that the land can become fertile once more, and members of the community will invite one another to come under *the vine* and the *fig tree*. In that scene, Joshua is being reminded by the messenger of the LORD of the fertility that will return when restoration is completed. In the present scene focusing on Zerubbabel, the symbolism of fertile abundance is seen in the image of the two olive trees with the two spikes of grain (4.11-12). To translate the spikes of grain on the olive trees as branches (as does the NRSV) conceals the symbolism. The usual translation of the Hebrew as 'spikes of grain' is found in Gen. 41.5, 6, 7, 22, 23, 24, 26, 27, and other places. What Zechariah sees are two olive trees with two spikes of grain. The source of oil (olive trees) and the source of grain (spikes of grain) are symbolically significant. The images of *oil* and *grain* complement the imagery of the vine (the source of the *new wine*) used at the end of the previous scene, completing the triad of images associated with prosperity in a time of 'return'.

The Cast of Characters

In this scene the messenger who spoke with Zechariah (absent in the previous scene) returns (4.1). The interaction is only between Zechariah and this messenger; there are no other participants. It will be recalled that previous scenes presented Zechariah as becoming progressively more active as a participant. After his repeated refrain, 'you shall know that the LORD of hosts has sent me' (2.9, 11, cf. 2.8), and after his participation in the ritual concerning Joshua (3.5), Zechariah himself, whose relationship with the former prophets was an ambiguous one, speaks and acts as a messenger in the restored community. Indeed, the interaction between Zechariah and the messenger who talked with him suggests that the messenger is taking on the role of instructor to Zechariah.

This role of the messenger in instructing Zechariah is evident in two ways in the present scene. First, there is a noticeable change in the pattern of questions that typifies the interaction between Zechariah and the messenger in previous scenes. It will be recalled that scene one began when Zechariah saw a man mounted on a horse standing in front of other horses. Zechariah asked the messenger a question, 'What are these, my lord?' The second scene was similar. After lifting up his eyes and seeing four horns, he asked the messenger, 'What are these?' When the messenger returns in the present scene (having been absent in the third and fourth scenes), the interrogative pattern has changed. The messenger, not Zechariah, begins the questioning. This pattern will occur later in the scene (4.11-13) and also in scene six (5.2). The messenger asks Zechariah to identify what he sees, 'What do you see?' (4.2). Zechariah describes what he sees and then asks the messenger, 'What are these my lord?' a question similar to the one he asked in 1.9 and 19. The messenger's response here differs from his response in scenes two and three. Rather than provide an immediate answer, the messenger asks Zechariah another question, 'Do you not know what these are?' (4.4). Given the increasing involvement of Zechariah, especially in the preceding scene, the messenger's question implies an element of surprise on the part of the messenger. Zechariah, who is becoming more and more accustomed to being in a world in which messengers of the LORD are present, might be expected to know what these things are. There is also another dimension to the surprise of the messenger, and this follows from the notion that what Zechariah sees is the continuation of temple construction begun in Haggai. Haggai had said, 'Who is left among you that saw this house in its former glory? How does it look to you now? Is it not in your sight as nothing?' (Hag. 2.3). This verse implies that many in the Persian community of Haggai and Zechariah had never seen the temple as it looked in the days of its former glory. The question of the messenger in response to Zechariah's question suggests that he had expected that Zechariah would recognize what he sees. His surprise is that Zechariah does not know what the temple's restoration to its former glory looks like or what it means. Later on in this passage the contrast between the trifling beginning of the temple

and its restored grandeur is alluded to (4.10). The change in the pattern
of questioning, then, is one indication of the messenger's tutorial role
that typifies the question and answer between Zechariah and the
messenger.

The second indication of the messenger's mentoring here has to do
with the opening of this scene. The scene begins by reporting that the
messenger who spoke to Zechariah returned and 'wakened' Zechariah
'as one is wakened from sleep' (4.1). The use of the simile here does not
suggest that Zechariah was literally asleep or that he was dreaming, as
some commentators have interpreted this verse. The word translated
'wakened' is also used in the sense of 'to rouse or stir up someone to
engage in an activity' (see Joel 3.9 where it is used in the sense of to *stir
up*' warriors; and Isa. 45.13 where it is used in the sense of *stirring up*'
Cyrus). When the messenger *stirred up* Zechariah, then, he roused him
to action.

Significantly, this same verb, as pointed out above earlier is used in
Hag. 1.14 when

> the LORD *stirred up* the spirit of Zerubbabel son of Shealtiel, governor of
> Judah, and the spirit of Joshua son of Jehozadak, the high priest, and the
> spirit of all the remnant of the people; and they came and worked on the
> house of the LORD of hosts . . .

In Haggai, this 'stirring up to activity' came immediately after 'Haggai,
the messenger of the LORD, spoke to the people with the LORD's message, saying "I am with you," says the LORD' (1.13). Similarly in Zechariah 4, immediately after Haggai, the messenger of the LORD, speaks—
in this case addressing Joshua in a ceremony in which Zechariah partici-
pated (3.6-10)—the messenger who spoke with Zechariah is stirring up
Zechariah to activity. This activity concerns work being done on the
temple and Zechariah's role in that activity. In this passage (4.9), as in
2.6-12, Zechariah claims again to the implied readers, 'then you will
know that the LORD of hosts has sent me to you'. Zechariah's claim
about being sent will be reinforced when Zerubbabel, whose hands
have 'laid the foundation of this house', 'shall also complete it' (4.9).
When Haggai first spoke as a messenger (Hag. 1.13), the spirit of the
LORD roused Zerubbabel to begin work on the temple. In this scene,
Zechariah is stirred up into action to deliver the LORD's word to
Zerubbabel to complete it.

The Scene

After being stirred up by the LORD, Zechariah responds to the messenger's question, 'What do you see?' by saying that he sees a lampstand

made entirely of gold with a bowl on top of it. Seven lamps with seven lips are on it, and an olive tree is seen on both its left side and its right side. To see a golden lampstand in a temple might be expected. It is consistent with my reading of Zechariah as lifting up his eyes and seeing things in the temple. Temple furnishings include lampstands. For example, the plans that David gave to Solomon for building the temple included 'the weight of the golden lampstands and their lamps, [and] the weight of gold for each lampstand and its lamps' (1 Chron. 28.15). See also 2 Chron. 4.7, 20, which reports that Solomon included golden lampstands in his furnishings of the temple and 1 Kgs 7.49, which speaks about 'the lampstands of pure gold, five on the south side and five on the north, in front of the sanctuary'. My point is not that any other particular text of the Hebrew Bible influenced the portrayal of a lampstand in Zechariah, but that a golden lampstand in a temple need not be interpreted as a 'vision' but as a thing seen in the material world.

That such lampstands are adorned with intricate patterns of assorted images is clear from Exod. 25.31-40, describing the lampstand to be made for the tabernacle, the temple in the desert.

> You shall make a lampstand of pure gold. The base and the shaft of the lampstand shall be made of hammered work; its cups, its calyxes, and its petals shall be of one piece with it; and there shall be six branches going out of its sides, three branches of the lampstand out of one side of it and three branches of the lampstand out of the other side of it; three cups shaped like almond blossoms, each with calyx and petals, on one branch, and three cups shaped like almond blossoms, each with calyx and petals, on the other branch—so for the six branches going out of the lampstand. On the lampstand itself there shall be four cups shaped like almond blossoms, each with its calyxes and petals. There shall be a calyx of one piece with it under the first pair of branches, a calyx of one piece with it under the next pair of branches, and a calyx of one piece with it under the last pair of branches for the six branches that go out of the lampstand. Their calyxes and their branches shall be of one piece with it, the whole of it one hammered piece of pure gold. You shall make the seven lamps for it; and the lamps shall be set up so as to give light on the space in front of it. Its snuffers and trays shall be of pure gold. It, and all these utensils, shall be made from a talent of pure gold. And see that you make them according to the pattern for them, which is being shown you on the mountain.

What Zechariah sees, then, is a golden lampstand, a sight one would expect to see in a temple.

After Zechariah's inquiry to the messenger about what these things are, and after the messenger's surprise that Zechariah does not know, the messenger responds by saying that these things are the word of the

LORD to Zerubbabel. Here again what Zechariah sees is understood as a metaphorical expression of a saying of the LORD (4.5-7). This occasions a second word that comes directly to Zechariah concerning Zerubbabel and his own status vis-à-vis Zerubbabel (4.8-10a). Sayings of the LORD associated with what Zechariah sees are now coming directly to the messenger, Zechariah. The scene concludes with the messenger explaining further the meaning of the objects Zechariah sees, including further questions of Zechariah and the surprise of the messenger at Zechariah's lack of understanding.

What Zechariah has been seeing in previous scenes has been associated with sayings of the LORD. Words of the LORD concluded earlier scenes: words of the LORD in 1.14-17 close the first scene, words of the LORD in 2.6-12 close the second and third scenes, and words of the LORD in 3.6-10 close the fourth scene. A word or saying of the LORD (6.9-14) will also conclude the sixth (5.1-4), seventh (5.5-11) and eighth (6.1-8) scenes. To encounter the LORD in what one is seeing is to encounter his words. It is significant that in this scene words of the LORD come in the middle (4.6-10a), not at the end, of the scene. They appear to interrupt the explanation of the imagery of the lampstand. It's almost as if the messenger is getting ahead of himself. He gets to the saying before he completes his explanation of the imagery of the lampstand. Perhaps this is occasioned as part of the tutoring as Zechariah learns his messenger role. 'This is the word of the LORD to Zerubbabel' is an indirect answer—a clue to help Zechariah understand that the lampstand, as only one piece of temple furnishing, may be a 'small thing' but signifies that Zerubbabel will complete the temple.

For whatever reason, the sayings of the LORD are incorporated into the scene in a way that is similar to the way the word of the LORD in the previous scene involving the high priest Joshua is integrated into that scene. Both the last scene and this one concern future leaders, Joshua and Zerubbabel. Just as the previous scene concerned the conditions of priesthood, so this scene concerns the responsibilities of Zerubbabel, the governor, for rebuilding the temple. In the previous scene, the LORD's words were addressed directly to Joshua. Zerubbabel, however, is not present in the scene as Joshua was in the last scene. Zerubbabel's absence suggests the action Zechariah is roused to perform. He is to speak the LORD's words to the absent Zerubbabel whose task will be to complete the temple. When this happens, Zechariah claims, 'you will know that the LORD of hosts has sent me to you' (4.9).

I will return to this point at the end of this chapter and in the Afterword, but I now want to focus on those things in the scene which I have not yet mentioned. In order to understand what Zechariah sees in this scene and the following ones, it is important to understand that Zechariah has moved into the temple. What he sees, he sees in the house of the LORD still needing to be completed.

An important feature of the lampstand, which Zechariah sees, is that it is made entirely of gold, 'all of it' as the Hebrew text makes clear (4.2). As noted above, this scene has to do with the return of prosperity to the temple. That Zechariah is looking at a solid gold lampstand suggests that the treasure of the nations, the gold and the silver, that Haggai said would pour into the temple (Hag. 2.6-9) has already begun to flow. Haggai had suggested that on the twenty-fourth day of the ninth month (Hag. 2.18) the restored community had already begun to experience prosperity associated with the vine, the olive tree and the grain. Zechariah, who is to speak the word of the LORD to Zerubbabel about the completion of the temple, is already beginning to see that the splendour of the rebuilt temple will exceed that of the former (Hag. 2.9). Of course, Zechariah, as suggested above, had never seen anything like this before: a lampstand with a bowl on top of it with seven lamps each with seven lips and with an olive tree on either side of it; and 'all of it' of solid gold. It is not surprising, then, when the messenger asks, 'Do you not know what these are?' that Zechariah should reply, 'No, my lord'.

The LORD's word to Zerubbabel can be understood as a ceremony involving the governor that matches the ceremony involving Joshua the high priest in the previous scene. It contains both words and actions. The words appear first: 'Not by might, nor by power, but by my spirit, says the LORD of hosts. Who [NRSV 'What'] are you O great mountain? Before Zerubbabel you shall become a plain.' These words are followed by the anticipated actions of Zerubbabel, 'he shall bring out the top stone amid shouts of "Grace, grace to it!"' Just as Haggai had been responsible for stirring up Zerubbabel, Joshua and the remnant of the people to begin work on the temple, and just as Haggai, the messenger of the LORD, had been active in the ceremony restoring priesthood, so Zechariah is to play a key role in a ceremony concerning the role of the governor Zerubbabel in completing the building of the temple.

The effortlessness of Zerubbabel in accomplishing his goal is stressed. Before Zerubbabel a great mountain will become a plain. The imagery here can be taken in two ways, but these need not be exclusive of each other: (1) The great mountain can be understood as the heap of rubble remaining from the destruction of the former temple, a heap that will be cleared like a plain before the governor in the massive task of rebuilding. (2) The Mountain here can also symbolize the mountain of problems associated with temple building. Zerubbabel's task in completing the temple is addressed with anthropomorphic symbolism,

'Who are you, O great mountain? Before Zerubbabel you shall become a plain.'

As in the last scene, the words of the messenger are accompanied by ceremonial activity. Zerubbabel is to bring out a stone described as the 'top' (literally 'head') stone. The context (see v. 9) suggests that this stone has to do with temple construction, but how it relates specifically to temple structure is not clear. This ritual activity associated with temple building will be accompanied by repeated shouts of 'Grace, grace be to it'. Again, we are not given the identity of those who are shouting these words, but the participation of the remnant of the people in laying the foundation of the temple (Hag. 1.14) would suggest the participation of this same remnant in the ceremony at the completion of the temple.

The text now moves from the word of the LORD to Zerubbabel to a word that comes to Zechariah, 'The hands of Zerubbabel have laid the foundations of the house; his hands shall also complete it'. This word to Zechariah makes clear that the previous word addressed to Zerubbabel has to do with the completion of the temple construction. Also, the completion of the temple construction will be a confirmation of Zechariah's role. Zechariah addresses the implied reader or audience, 'Then you will know that the LORD of hosts has sent me to you'. Those who had seen the insignificance of the beginnings of the temple construction under Haggai (Hag. 2.3) will now see the splendour of its final construction. Those individuals who 'despised the day of small things shall rejoice, and shall see the plummet in the hand of Zerubbabel' (4.10). Whereas Haggai was involved in initiating temple construction, Zechariah is involved in its completion. Indeed, even what he is now seeing, a lampstand made entirely of gold, is an indication of return to former splendour. In the unfolding scenes Zechariah has moved into the temple and distanced himself from the former prophets. He has become a messenger of the LORD, and this will be demonstrated when 'the hands of Zerubbabel' complete the temple.

The messenger who talked with Zechariah, having announced the word of the LORD associated with what Zechariah saw, turns in 4.10b to offer an explanation of the symbolic meaning of the lampstand Zechariah has seen. The seven lamps refer to the eyes of the LORD, ranging throughout 'the whole earth'. The significance of God's seeing *the whole earth* can only be understood in the larger literary context. Passages in Haggai and Zechariah concerned with '*the whole earth*' and with the generation of wealth in the restored temple have to do with shaking the nations. When it was reported that '*the whole earth* remains at peace' (Zech. 1.11), the LORD became angry with the nations. In Haggai it is reported that the LORD will shake the heavens and the earth

so that kingdoms will be overthrown and their wealth of silver and gold
will pour into the temple (Hag. 2.6-9). Furthermore, in Haggai the overthrow of the nations will result in Zerubbabel's assumption to power
because the LORD has chosen him (2.20-23). The LORD has been aroused
to action (2.13), and the symbolism of his eyes ranging through all the
earth suggests the shaking of all the nations that will pour their wealth
into Jerusalem. A similar phrase concerning the LORD's eyes 'ranging
through the whole earth' occurs in 2 Chron. 16.9 in the sense of protecting 'those whose heart is true' to the LORD. While the passage may
have implications concerning protecting those who are to return, the
primary symbolism of the passage in Zechariah concerns the wealth and
prosperity that will come to Jerusalem.

Zechariah's next question about the two olive trees with the two
spikes of grain that pour out gold sustains the association of wealth with
the temple completion. The NRSV translates the Hebrew word 'gold' as
'oil' in 4.12, apparently following many commentators who understand
that 'gold' refers to the colour of olive oil to be poured into the lamp.
While this clearly is a possible interpretation, the mixed symbolism of
riches associated both with fertility (olive oil, grain and new wine) and
with mineral wealth is consistent with the envisaged future following
temple completion, especially in Haggai. The gold and silver of the
nations pouring into the house of the LORD will be matched by the
increase of fertility in the land (read Hag. 2.6-10 with Hag. 2.18-19). The
linking of the spikes of grain and the olive tree symbolize future
prosperity that will be embodied in the oil and grain associated with
return and temple completion.

The messenger explains that the two olive trees with the spikes of
grain (as branches) are 'the two sons of the oil [NRSV 'anointed ones']
who stand beside the LORD of all the earth'. The translation of the
Hebrew here can sometimes obscure differences in the Hebrew text and
be misleading. The following observations about word usage are given
to clarify the situation for those who are reading Zechariah in an English
translation such as the NRSV on which I base my remarks. (1) The word
translated 'branch' by the NRSV in 3.8 has the sense of 'shoot' or 'bud'
and is sometimes used to refer to the shoot of a future Davidic king as it
is in Jer. 23.5. The word translated 'branches' by the NRSV in 4.12, as I
have already indicated, means 'ears or spikes of grain'. It carries no connotations of royalty. (2) The word translated 'anointed ones' by the
NRSV is not the word for 'anointed one' or 'messiah' in Hebrew. In fact,
the NRSV translation renders two Hebrew words which can be translated more literally as 'sons of oil'. The word for 'oil' here is not the
word used for the oil of anointing. 'Sons of oil', then, also has no royal

connotations. In short while the 'branch' in 3.8 (and also 6.12) may have royal connotations, these connotations are not to be found in the imagery in Zechariah 4, which is concerned more with the symbolism of fertility and prosperity following return and the rebuilding of the temple.

The Hebrew word for 'oil' here, as I have indicated, is not the word used for the oil of anointing but rather the word used throughout the Twelve to symbolize fertility and prosperity following return. The 'two sons of the oil'—associated with a return to fertility and prosperity—can only refer to the two leaders that have been the focus of the last two scenes, Joshua the high priest and Zerubbabel the governor. They stand beside 'the master of *the whole earth*', the LORD, whose eyes, ranging through the whole earth, are symbolized by the seven lamps with seven lips. When Zechariah looks at the golden lampstand, he is looking at a restored temple in which the LORD of *the whole earth* is present, flanked by the high priest Joshua and the governor Zerubbabel.

Concluding Overview and Transition

This scene, in which the messenger arouses Zechariah to activity and in which the messenger is acting as a kind of mentor, is the first of the final four scenes in the temple which are concerned with explaining temple images as Zechariah sees them. In order to gain perspective on the climactic character of this and the following scenes, it will be helpful to review what has transpired since the time a messenger first appeared in the Twelve.

The first messenger to speak in the Twelve is Haggai in Hag. 1.13. This is significant in the Twelve because it signals the transition in the LORD's speaking by means of prophets to his speaking by means of messengers. It is occasioned by the response of Zerubbabel, the governor, Joshua the high priest and the remnant of the people to obey 'the voice of the LORD their God, and the words of the prophet Haggai, as the LORD their God had sent him and the people feared the LORD' (Hag. 2.12). It is precisely at this point in the Twelve, when the community obeys the voice of the prophet, that Haggai appears as 'the messenger of the LORD' with the 'LORD's message, saying, "I am with you," says the LORD' (2.13). The message Haggai speaks is significant because it summarizes the change from the time of the 'former prophets' in which the LORD was more distant to the time of the appearance of messengers, when the divine is present: ' "I am with you," says the LORD'. Haggai the prophet has become Haggai the messenger. It is important to note that this appearance of the messenger of the LORD initiates temple construction.

> And the LORD stirred up the spirit of Zerubbabel son of Shealtiel, governor
> of Judah, and the spirit of Joshua, son of Jehozadak, the high priest, and
> the spirit of all the remnant of the people and they came and worked on
> the house of the LORD of hosts, their God (Hag. 1.14).

This all happened on 'the twenty-fourth day of the month, in the sixth month' in the second year of Darius (Hag. 1.15).

Two months later Zechariah, the descendent of Iddo the prophet, speaks. When Zechariah appears with the LORD's word calling on the people to *return* (Zech. 1.1-6), they have already *returned* to the LORD. The opening of Zechariah, then, is not so much a new beginning as an extension of a time when the messenger of the LORD has already appeared. It occasions Zechariah's encounter with messengers. It is this encounter that clarifies Zechariah's own status, which is ambiguously linked to prophecy through his grandfather Iddo (Zech. 1.1). As I have indicated in the developing scenes, Zechariah moves from observing at the periphery to active involvement until he himself takes up the role of a messenger. The messenger of the LORD asked the LORD a question in the first scene (Zech. 1.12); Zechariah asks the LORD a question in the second scene (Zech. 1.21). It is after this initial engagement that Zechariah begins to maintain to his implied audience that 'you will know that the LORD of hosts has *sent* me' (Zech. 2.9, 11, cf. 2.8). Haggai had been '*sent*' by the LORD (Hag. 1.12) just prior to his appearance as the messenger of the LORD. Zechariah in making this claim, is asserting his own standing as a messenger '*sent*' by the LORD .

By the end of the third scene it is reported that 'the LORD has stirred himself [NRSV 'aroused himself'] from his holy dwelling' (Zech. 2.13). In the following scene the LORD participates in installing Joshua as high priest, and the messenger of the LORD (Haggai) appears, taking an active role in preparing Joshua for his role as high priest in the restored community. In this scene Zechariah speaks just as the messenger of the LORD speaks (3.5).

In the next scene, Zechariah is 'stirred up' like one 'stirred up' from sleep. He now has a clear role to perform as a messenger; Zechariah will speak the word of the LORD to Zerubbabel about completing the temple of the LORD. The temple at the beginning of construction was insignificant in appearance (Hag. 2.3), but will exceed its former splendour when it is finished by Zerubbabel (Zech. 4.10).

What Zechariah has been seeing, then, is temple construction. As the scenes develop Zechariah moves into the temple and into a new role as a messenger. The LORD will actually be present when his messenger Zechariah is present. When the temple is completed 'you [the reader] will know that the LORD of hosts has sent me to you'.

We have also seen the roles of the high priest Joshua and the governor Zerubbabel in temple construction. Joshua, not Zerubbabel, will have access to those who are messengers of the LORD. He has responsibility to rule the LORD's house and to have charge of his courts. Zerubbabel has the task of completing the temple. This will be done not by his might but by the spirit of the LORD. These two leaders, the priest and the governor, are the two sons of the oil, the two sons of prosperous return. In their roles as priest and governor, they stand beside the LORD, *the master of the whole earth.* The theme of the LORD as the master of the whole earth will be a recurring theme in the remaining scenes. In the restored temple the LORD will be present and will carry out his role as master of the whole earth. The localized presence of the LORD in the temple in Jerusalem has significance that spills beyond the boundaries of the temple, beyond Jerusalem and beyond Judah.

Zechariah 5.1-6.15
Scenes 6, 7 and 8: A Flying Scroll, an Ephah and Four Chariots

Introductory Remarks

There are three remaining scenes involving Zechariah's interaction with a messenger: scene 6 concerning a 'flying scroll' (5.1-4), scene seven concerning an 'ephah' (5.5-11, NRSV 'basket'), and scene eight concerning 'four chariots' (6.1-8). These three scenes are linked together with the preceding one concerning the golden lampstand by their common setting in the temple in which Zechariah is looking at objects in the temple under construction. A recurring element in each of these scenes is the phrase '*the whole earth*' (4.10, 14; 5.3, 6, 6.6; NRSV translates 'the whole land' in 5.3,6). The symbolism and imagery in these last four scenes concern the LORD and his mastery over *the whole earth*. In scene 5, the golden lampstand symbolizes the eyes of the LORD ranging through 'the whole earth'; it also symbolizes Joshua and Zerubbabel, the two branches of the olive tree, who stand beside the LORD, the master of the whole earth. The flying scroll of scene six symbolizes the curse that will go out over the whole earth (5.3), restoring social order among those who will return. The ephah of scene seven represents the guilt of the whole earth (5.6). The ephah also symbolizes the containment of wickedness; it holds evil, which is to be taken away and deposited in a temple built for it in the land of Shinar. The last scene concerns the LORD's chariots which, after presenting themselves before the LORD of all the earth (6.5), are going out to shake the heavens and the earth so that return from those places will occur. While the scene begins with the images of chariots, it ends by speaking about other figures, 'strong ones' (NRSV translates this word in v. 3 as 'dappled' and as 'steeds' in v. 7) who are eager to go out to patrol the earth. The Hebrew word ('*mṣym*) that I have rendered as 'strong ones' occurs only in Zechariah 7, and its meaning is not clear. I will discuss this word in more detail later in the chapter.

What Zechariah sees in the last three scenes may strike many readers as quite bizarre: a flying scroll, an ephah with a woman in it carried by two women with wings like the wings of a stork, and chariots coming out of mountains of bronze. What Zechariah had seen in the previous scenes—mounted horsemen, four horns, a man with a measuring line, a high priest and a golden lampstand—can be more easily understood as things contemporary readers might expect to see in their world. Of course, a world-view that incorporates messengers who blur the distinction between the human and the divine will strike contemporary 'Western' readers as quite alien. Nevertheless, these appear in Zechariah's world as men (see Zech. 3.7; Hag. 1.13). When these more bizarre images occur in scenes 6, 7 and 8, the question arises, 'What exactly is Zechariah seeing?' The scene involving the lampstand, when associated with the last three scenes, provides us with a clue. Olive trees with ears of corn for branches are bizarre. However, when they are seen as the symbolic adornment of a golden lampstand, the sight becomes less bizarre. It is quite possible that what Zechariah sees is made more bizarre by the way we usually read.

These last three scenes present the messenger in the mentoring role that he began to assume in the previous scene with the lampstand. It is possible that the bizarre imagery Zechariah sees is associated with objects in the temple being constructed to its former splendour, and that the messenger is showing Zechariah the imagery to explain its meaning. Such instruction is necessary for a messenger such as Zechariah, unfamiliar with a new temple, especially one who apparently has not seen the old one in all its grandeur. My reading of the last three scenes is guided by my view of Zechariah, under the tutorship of the messenger, as seeing temple imagery associated with objects in the restored temple.

These scenes are followed by a word of the LORD (6.9-14) as in earlier scenes (see 1.13-17 and 2.6-12) and by Zechariah's word about his own status (6.15), also paralleled in earlier scenes (see 2.8, 9, 11; 4.9). Both the LORD's words and Zechariah's words in this context, however, relate to the last four scenes in particular as well as to everything Zechariah had seen in his interaction with the messenger. Exiles have begun to return, gold and silver are being collected for crowns for the LORD's chosen, and the climactic statement is that when the temple is completed, the people will know that the LORD has sent Zechariah, the messenger, to them.

The Flying Scroll (5.1-4)

This scene, like the preceding one with the golden lampstand, involves only two characters: Zechariah and the messenger who talked with him. The way that the scene opens also suggests that it is a continuation of the last scene: 'Again, I looked up and saw a flying scroll.' (The Hebrew verb wā'āšûḇ translated 'again' here has the sense of doing something 'further' or 'continually'. (See Waltke and O'Connor, p. 656.) Zechariah, after seeing the lampstand, looked again and saw a 'flying scroll'. The impression this gives is that Zechariah turned his attention from one stationary object, a lampstand, to something of a similar kind. The 'flying scroll' is a sacred object like the lampstand rather than an actual scroll hovering between heaven and earth.

The sense of continuity between this scene and the previous one is also evident from the fact that the messenger who spoke with Zechariah is not introduced by the narrator as he was in the previous scene. The messenger continues to be there as he was in the previous scene. The messenger's question to Zechariah, 'What do you see?' can be understood in the sense of 'What are you looking at now?'

Zechariah tells the messenger that he sees a 'flying scroll' and gives its dimensions: twenty cubits in length and ten cubits wide. This object is larger than a normal scroll. In fact it has the exact dimensions of 'the vestibule in front of the nave' in the house of the LORD that Solomon built (1 Kgs 6.3). (See Halpern, p. 179.) What Zechariah sees, then, is an object of temple construction. Perhaps the image of the 'flying scroll' should be understood as an image of an unfurled scroll that is as much a part of the temple Zechariah sees being constructed as was the vestibule in Solomon's temple.

The interaction between Zechariah and the messenger in this scene, the preceding one and the two remaining scenes follows no rigid pattern. Instead, the impression is that an individual is learning about things he has not seen before from someone with more experience.

The first thing that Zechariah learns about this 'flying scroll' is that it is 'the curse that goes out over the face of the whole earth' (NRSV 'the whole land'). As I have been maintaining, Zechariah is presenting us with a picture of *return* and restoration. Therefore, it is reasonable to assume that this scroll also has to do with restoration. The curse associated with the scroll concerns writing about stealing on one side of the scroll and swearing falsely on the other. The association with stealing and swearing falsely suggest crimes against society so that the image of the flying scroll appears to suggest restoration of the social order. The re-establishment of social order, however, is not localized in Jerusalem and its environs but in 'the whole earth' including those 'who live with daughter Babylon' (2.7) and all the nations who will join themselves to the LORD (2.11).

The social infractions of stealing and swearing falsely echo stipulations of the decalogue. The reference to stealing recalls the commandment 'do not steal' (Exod. 20.15; Deut. 5.19), and the reference to swearing falsely by my name seems to conflate the commandments about making a wrongful use of the name of the LORD (Exod. 20.7; Deut. 5.11) and bearing false witness (Exod. 20.16; Deut. 5.20). More importantly, however, these social breaches are clearly related to the failings of the community addressed later in the Twelve. In Malachi 3, the LORD says that he will send his messenger and he will judge 'those who swear falsely' and 'those who oppress the hired workers in their wages'. While the word 'to steal' is not used in Malachi, the text clearly implies that wages are stolen from the hired workers or delayed, as prohibited in Exod. 19.13 and Deut. 24.14-15. Furthermore, the text goes on to say that the community is robbing God by not giving him his 'tithes and offerings'. As a result the community will be 'cursed with a curse'. The social transgressions alluded to in the 'flying scroll' that Zechariah sees are related to the social injustices, including injustices against God, that the messenger in Mal. 3.5, 8-9 speaks about.

The question still to be raised is: in what sense can a scroll be a curse? What could be the meaning of such imagery? While I am not arguing direct influence, the situation portrayed in Deuteronomy 29 can give us insight into how to read this passage. Deuteronomy 29 concerns a covenant, a kind of treaty or pact entered into between God and Israel. Such a covenant includes the blessings and curses that will result from obedience or disobedience of the stipulations of that agreement (cf. Deut. 28). Deuteronomy 29.20-21 speaks about the curses written in a book concerning the calamity that will result from failure to obey the requirements of the covenant. While Zech. 5.1-4 does not mention a covenant, the text can be interpreted to mean that the flying scroll contains the curse that will befall everyone who steals and everyone who swears falsely in the name of the LORD . This meaning is evident in the NRSV translation, 'for everyone who steals *shall be cut off according to the writing on one side,* and everyone who swears falsely *shall be cut off according to the writing on the other side'.* The words that I have italicized are a rather free translation of words in Hebrew that are difficult to render in English. The meaning of the Hebrew implies that the curse has gone out against everyone who steals and against everyone who swears falsely according to the curses on the scroll but who have been left unpunished or exempt from punishment. The word of the LORD in v. 4 makes it clear that this situation will be rectified. The scroll containing the curse will enter the house of everyone who steals and the house of everyone who swears falsely in the LORD's name. It will lodge in the middle of the house, completely destroying the timber and the wood and, by implication, its occupants as well.

An Ephah (5.5-11)

This scene is often seen as one of the most bizarre in Zechariah. It concerns an ephah. NRSV translates this word 'basket'. The Hebrew word however is transliterated as 'ephah' and is usually rendered this way in English translations. An ephah is a measure for grain, and it is precisely in this sense that the imagery should be understood. 'Basket' obscures the importance of an 'ephah' as a 'grain measure'. The ephah symbolizes 'their iniquity' in all the earth. Although the 'their' before 'iniquity' has no clear referent, it apparently refers to that community in all the earth who will return to Jerusalem—the community portrayed in the previous scene. Inside the ephah is a woman identified as 'wickedness', who is thrust back into the ephah. A lead cover is placed on top of the ephah, and the ephah is taken by women with wings like storks to the land of Shinar where a house will be built for it.

There are two active characters in this scene: Zechariah and the messenger who spoke with him. As I will show, I do not see either the woman in the ephah or the women with wings like a stork as characters in the scene. They are objects that Zechariah sees, like the lampstand and the flying scroll.

The scene opens like none of the other scenes in Zechariah. It begins by saying that the messenger who talked with Zechariah 'came forward' or 'came out'. The Hebrew word here refers to the actual movement, the act of coming from somewhere. The situation is similar to scene 3 in which the two messengers come forward to meet one another. This active movement is different from that in the opening of scene four (4.1), which simply notes that the messenger returned and does not specify the actual movement of coming forward or coming out from somewhere.

The messenger coming from somewhere says to Zechariah, 'Lift up your eyes [NRSV 'look'] and see what is this coming out [or coming forward]'. This thing, at which Zechariah is asked to look, is coming forward just as the messenger is coming forward. The same word is used in Hebrew for both. If, as I have argued, we should understand that Zechariah is looking at an object, like the lampstand, then the simultaneous coming forward of both the object and the messenger suggest that they are involved in one and the same activity. The ephah is coming forward because the messenger is coming forward with it.

That the messenger is handling the ephah is suggested by what follows. A leaden cover was lifted from the ephah, presumably by the messenger, to reveal a woman sitting in the ephah. Since an ephah is not

large enough to contain a human being, I think that we must also
assume that this was a figurine of a woman who represents 'wickedness'. The messenger then thrusts the woman back into the basket and
the leaden weight on its mouth, its opening at the top.

Zechariah lifts up his eyes and sees two women with wings like a
stork. Like the messenger and the ephah, they are also coming forward.
Again, we should not think of actual women flying but of decorative
and symbolic imagery associated with the place where the ephah is
deposited. Described in this way, the scene evokes an image like that of
the Ark with two winged cherubim upon it, although this is like a dia-
bolic version of it. These winged creatures, like the ephah, are objects
being brought forward with the messenger, and the winged women are
represented as carrying the ephah.

What does this activity mean? The ephah containing the woman,
called 'wickedness', and the two women with wings like storks can be
understood as cultic objects being put in place as part of the temple
construction. The 'base' envisaged for the support of the ephah in
Shinar (Babylon) referred to in 5.11 gives support to the notion that
cultic objects are being brought forward. This 'base' is a 'stand' used for
supporting sacral objects, and such 'stands' are described in 1 Kgs 7.27-
37 concerning the construction of Solomon's temple.

> He [Solomon] also made the ten *stands* of bronze: each stand was four
> cubits long, four cubits wide, and three cubits high. This was the
> construction of the *stands:* they had borders; the borders were within the
> frames; on the borders that were set in the frames were lions, oxen, and
> cherubim. On the frames, both above and below the lions and oxen, there
> were wreaths of bevelled work. Each *stand* had four bronze wheels and
> axles of bronze; at the four corners were supports for a basin. The sup-
> ports were cast with wreaths at the side of each. Its opening was within
> the crown whose height was one cubit; its opening was round as a
> pedestal is made; it was a cubit and a half wide. At its opening there were
> carvings; its borders were four-sided, not round. The four wheels were
> underneath the borders; the axles of the wheels were in the stands; and
> the height of a wheel was a cubit and a half. The wheels were made like a
> chariot wheel; their hubs were all cast. There were four supports at the
> four corners of each stand; the supports were of one piece with the
> *stands*. On the top of the stand there was a round band half a cubit high;
> on the top of the *stand*, its stays and its borders he carved cherubim,
> lions, and palm trees, where each had a space, with the wreaths all
> around. In this way he made the ten *stands*; all of there were cast alike,
> with the same size and the same form.

The stands described in Solomon's temple also contain, among other
things, winged creatures and wheels, suggesting movement. Clearly, the

imagery associated with the 'stands' or 'bases' in Solomon's temple is described in far more detail and is perhaps more complex than the imagery that Zechariah saw. The decorative features of the stands Solomon had built do not include an ephah and women with wings like a stork. By quoting this text from 1 Kings, however, I am not attempting to show direct influence or exact parallelism. Rather, when this text in 1 Kgs 7.27-37 is read in conjunction with Zech. 5.5-11, it gives us insight into how to interpret what Zechariah saw. He saw a cultic object, an ephah containing a figure of a woman. This was coming forward with the messenger along with a 'stand' or 'base' decorated with the imagery of two women with wings like a stork. When the ephah is placed on the 'base', the women on the base can be seen to be carrying it. The entire image symbolizes taking the guilt and wickedness of the whole earth and depositing it in Shinar. Zechariah speaks of a house and a 'base' being built in Shinar to hold the ephah. Whether this should be under-stood literally or whether the ephah supported by figures of the two women only symbolizes movement out of the temple to Shinar is not made explicit.

To read the scene the way I have—that Zechariah is looking at tangible objects in his world shown to him by the messenger—seems to follow from previous descriptions of Zechariah as lifting up his eyes and seeing things. The activity of 'coming forward' could suggest some sort of ritual activity. As I indicated above, ritual seems to be associated with the previous scenes concerning Joshua and Zerubbabel.

Having looked at the interaction of the characters and the objects they are viewing, I now want to look more closely at the things Zechariah saw and the meaning ascribed to them by the messenger. After Zech-ariah asks the messenger what is coming out, the messenger identifies it as an 'ephah' (5.5) and then proceeds to tell Zechariah that it represents 'iniquity in all the earth'. In the fourth scene, Joshua had been under-stood as taking on the guilt of the land, making prosperity (symbolized by the new wine, the grain and the oil) possible again. The land would become productive and fertile once more. Here the ephah takes on 'the guilt in all the earth', presumably the guilt of those exiles in lands like Babylon (cf. 2.7) and perhaps the nations who will attach themselves to the LORD (cf. 2.11). But in what sense can the ephah be understood to represent guilt? There is no clear indication from the messenger why this is so. In the Twelve (Amos 8.5 and Mic. 6.10) as well as in the larger Hebrew Bible (see Deut. 25.14, 15; Prov. 20.10; Lev. 19.36; and Ezek. 45.10), the ephah as a measure is often presented as being distorted for gain. The ephah, then, could represent guilt because the ephah is often used dishonestly as a measure. This scene then can be understood to be about social transgressions similar to those of stealing and swearing falsely in the last scene. The image of the ephah used for ill-gotten gain can be understood as symbolizing the guilt resulting from dishonesty in social affairs.

The ephah also has other connotations. As I have argued above, the grain, oil and new wine are depleted when the community turns away from the LORD. The ephah empty of grain, which it is normally used to measure, and filled with wickedness is an appropriate symbol of the separation between God and his people. The ephah filled with wickedness symbolizes the lack of grain (prosperity) among the nations because of the LORD's anger which when directed against his own people also resulted in lack of grain (see Hag. 1.11; 2.17-19). For guilt and wickedness to be brought together in the image of an ephah deposited in the middle of one of the nations (Shinar, i.e. Babylon) with whom the LORD is now reported to be angry is rich symbolism. The LORD who is about to overthrow the nations (cf. 1.15, 21; 2.8-9) will make return possible.

But why would a woman represent 'wickedness'? Given the patriarchal ideology of the text of the Hebrew Bible, an association of 'wickedness' with the feminine is hardly surprising. The larger literary context of the Twelve, however, suggests another possibility for such a portrayal. The Twelve opens by portraying a woman, Gomer the wife of Hosea, as representing Israel who had turned away from the LORD. In the second chapter of Hosea it is said of Gomer/Israel,

> She did not know
> > that it was I who gave her *the grain*, the wine and the oil,
> > and who lavished upon her silver and gold that they used for Baal.
> Therefore, I will take back
> > *my grain* in its time
> > and my wine in its season;
> and I will take away my wool and my flax
> > which were to cover her nakedness (Hos. 2.8-9).

For one reading the Twelve as a literary collage, the image of wickedness portrayed as a woman enclosed in an empty grain measure toward the end of the Twelve recalls the portrayal of Gomer at the beginning of the Twelve. Even if the woman in the ephah were seen as representing a goddess, perhaps associated with Baal, the association with Gomer/Israel in Hosea portrayed as going after other lovers, Baal rather than the LORD, is clear.

The physical abuse that follows, 'So he thrust her back into the basket, and pressed the leaden lid down on its mouth' (5.8), perhaps gives us greater insight into Zechariah's world then he himself was able to see. The text of Zechariah is a man's world and when women do appear, even if only representational as 'Wickedness' in the ephah, they are abused as Gomer was (Hos. 2.10).

The women who appear with wings like the wings of a stork reinforce the negative use of women in this passage to represent guilt and wickedness. The stork is one of the 'detestable' birds which is an 'abomination' (Exod. 11.13-19, cf. Deut. 14.11-20). Women with the wings of one of the 'detestable birds' are portrayed as transporting guilt and wickedness. These feminine creatures are unlike the cherubim, winged masculine creatures portrayed on Solomon's stands (1 Kgs 7.29, 36), who are in the inner sanctuary of the temple (1 Kgs 6.23-28), who support the throne of God (Ps. 80.1; 99.1; Isa. 37.16); and who are associated with the ark of the covenant (Exod. 25.18-20; 37.6-9; Num. 7.8-9; 1 Sam. 4.4).

The women with wings like a stork are to take the ephah to the land of Shinar (Babylon, cf., e.g., Gen. 11.1-9) where a house (a temple) will be built for it, and it will be placed on its 'base', the stand on which is placed sacred objects. The guilt and wickedness of the LORD's people, then, are pictured as being transferred from his people—returning to Jerusalem from places like Babylon (2.7)—and placed in a sacred place of one of the nations whom the LORD will terrify and plunder (1.21; 2.9) just as the nations had terrified and plundered Judah (1.21).

Four Chariots (Zech. 6.1-8)

This last scene concludes Zechariah's interaction with the messenger. His conversation with the messenger ends in v. 8. The interaction with the messenger in this scene, however, is rather more complicated than that of the three previous scenes in which the messenger in a mentoring role was explaining imagery to Zechariah in the temple. It is important, therefore, that this interaction in 6.1-8 be examined in close detail. The scene opens with the very same words as in scene 6, '*And again I lifted up my eyes and I saw and there...*' The use of the word 'again' (see the discussion of 5.1) means that there is continuity between this scene and the preceding one, as was the case at the beginning of scene 6. Just as Zechariah turned at the beginning of scene 6 from looking at the 'golden lampstand' and saw a 'flying scroll', so in this scene Zechariah turns from looking at a sacral object, an ephah on a decorated base, and sees another object, four chariots.

Like the previous three scenes, this scene begins with a conversation between Zechariah and the messenger who is explaining things to him. Zechariah looks up and sees four chariots coming out from between two mountains of bronze. Each of these four chariots is drawn by differently coloured horses. Zechariah's question to the messenger who talked with him, 'What are these, my LORD?' is exactly like the first question that Zechariah asked in scene one (1.9), alerting the reader that this last scene is picking up elements of the first scene and forms an *inclusio* with it. The messenger explains to Zechariah that these four chariots are 'the four winds of heaven going out after presenting themselves before the LORD of all the earth' (6.5).

Before continuing the description of the scene, I want to pause and look more closely at some features of the text describing the interaction between Zechariah and the messenger who spoke with him. The text in Hebrew is very difficult. At one point a word seems to intrude (6.3) and at another the words seem to be jumbled and make little sense (6.6). Since in my reading I think the intrusion and jumbled words are important for understanding this text, I offer the following literal translation. I have rendered the problematic passages in italics.

> (1) And I turned and I lifted up my eyes and I saw and behold four chariots coming out from between two mountains and the mountains were mountains of bronze. (2) The horses of the first chariot were red, the horses of the second chariot were black, (3) the horses of the third chariot were white and the horses of the fourth chariot were spotted. *Strong ones.* (4) And I answered and I said to the messenger who spoke with me, 'What are these my lord?' (5) And the messenger answered and he said to me, 'These are the four winds of the heaven going out from positioning themselves before the master of the whole earth (6) *which in it the black horses going forth to the land of the north and the white ones went to after them and the spotted ones went out to the land of the south.*' (7) And the strong ones went out and they sought to go patrol in the earth. And he said, 'Go, patrol in the earth', and they patrolled in the earth. (8) And he cried out to me and he spoke to me, 'See the ones going to the land of the north have put my spirit at ease in the land of the north.'

The very last word in 6.3 does not fit the colour portrayal of the horses Zechariah is describing and seems intrusive. The word occurs only here and in v. 7 in the Hebrew Bible, but is associated with a word root that suggests that it be translated something like 'strong ones'. Some translations such as the NRSV see it as a description of the horses' colouring and translate it 'dappled'. It is in the sense of an intrusive 'strong ones' that I read this word and not as a continuing description of the horses. Shortly after this description of the horses with the intrusive 'strong ones' the messenger's answer to Zechariah's question seems to get a bit muddled in 6.6. In my translation above I have placed the confused words in italics. Immediately after these confused words there is again a reference to the strong ones (6.7, NRSV 'steeds'), and the scene changes. The chariots are mentioned no more; and the strong ones want to get on with patrolling the earth. Furthermore, at this point in the scene, the messenger's attention is diverted from Zechariah's question, 'What are these my lord?' and the messenger says to the strong ones: 'Go, patrol in the earth'. We are then simply told, 'They patrolled in the earth.' The scene ends with the messenger talking to Zechariah not about the four chariots, the four winds of heaven, but about the strong ones who have gone to patrol the north country, 'Lo, those who go toward the north country have set my spirit at rest in the north country' (7.8).

How can one read or make sense of this difficult text? What is happening in the textual portrayal with the intrusive 'strong ones' in v. 3, the muddled answer of the messenger in v. 6, and the movement of the scene from chariots to the strong ones who are now active characters in the scene? Perhaps one can begin to make sense of the text by attending to the end of the scene in which the strong ones are identified through the description of their activities. The strong ones come out, and they are impatient to get off and patrol the earth. And the messenger said, 'Go, patrol the earth'. The strong ones, then, are eager to get on with the activity of the mounted horsemen whom Zechariah first saw in his encounter with the messenger. The mounted horsemen in scene 1 are 'those whom the LORD has sent to patrol the earth' who say, 'We have patrolled the earth, and lo, the whole earth remains at peace' (1.10-11). The end of this scene, which recalls the first scene, makes it clear that the strong ones refers to the mounted riders whose task it is to patrol the whole earth. Their eagerness to get on with patrolling the whole earth can be ascribed to the fact that, as we have learned as readers seeing through the eyes of Zechariah, things have changed. The LORD is now angry with the whole earth which at the beginning 'remained at peace'. The mounted riders, the strong ones, are eager to see the consequence of the LORD's warfare against the nations.

When mounted horsemen (strong ones) first appear in the scene they interrupt the messenger's description of the four chariots going forth like the four winds of heaven. Their sudden intrusion into the scene causes the messenger's somewhat confused response. The interaction between Zechariah and the messenger is coming to an end with this sudden reappearance of the horsemen who appeared at the beginning. This interruption brings a dramatic conclusion to the scenes of Zechariah's encounter with the messenger, an unfolding picture in which the whole world is changing before Zechariah's eyes. The temple is being rebuilt, Jerusalem is being made ready for unbounded habitation, Joshua and Zerubbabel stand in their respective roles alongside the master of all the earth.

Before moving on to consider the word of the LORD to Zechariah that follows this scene, I want to consider in more detail the imagery of the chariots and the very last words that the messenger spoke about the north country. Zechariah sees four chariots coming out from two mountains of bronze. This imagery can be better understood when read in conjunction with other texts describing a temple under construction and referring to the representation of chariots. As with the golden lampstand, the ephah on its base and the flying scroll, the chariots can also be seen as imagery associated with temple furnishings. The instructions David gave to Solomon for temple construction included the 'plan for the golden chariot of the cherubim that spread their wings and covered the ark of the covenant of the LORD' (1 Chron. 28.18). Interestingly, the context of this verse in 1 Chronicles also contains plans for 'golden lampstands' (1 Chron. 28.15) referred to above in the discussion of scene 5. The description of the stand for the ephah in 1 Kings 7 also includes imagery associated with a chariot: 'Each stand had four bronze wheels and axles of bronze... The wheels were made like a chariot wheel; their axles, their rims, their spokes, and their hubs were all cast' (1 Kgs 7.30-33). 'Chariots of the sun' were among the temple objects destroyed by Josiah (2 Kgs 23.11). The point I am making, then, is that to understand the chariots that Zechariah sees as objects in the temple under construction is consistent with the description of chariots as part of the furnishings of a temple encountered in other texts. I am not arguing that any of these texts had any direct bearing on Zech. 6.1-8, nor am I denying the uniqueness of Zechariah's description of what he sees. But when read together, intertextually, they provide a useful perspective on what Zechariah is seeing.

The significance of the two mountains, their construction in bronze, or the horses of different colours is not clear. The image of the four chariots, as the four winds of all the earth going out after having presented themselves to 'the master of the whole earth' is clearly linked to the strong ones.

The scene concerning the four chariots in Zechariah ends with the horsemen, the strong ones, who are impatient to go out to patrol the earth. These are the horsemen who appeared in the first scene and who returned to say that 'the whole earth remains at peace' (1.11). The imagery of the LORD's chariots elicits the horsemen's impatience to patrol the whole earth—to see the results of the actions of the LORD at war.

The last time that this messenger who has been interacting with Zechariah speaks, he calls out loudly to Zechariah, 'The ones going out to the north country have set my spirit at rest in the north country'. The north country as we have learned from scene 3, refers to the land of

Babylon, from which those who dwell with 'daughter Babylon' are called to escape (2.6-7). The situation in the north country is now advantageous for the returnees because the north country has been subdued. The changing world we see through Zechariah's eyes has now, according to the last words of the messenger who spoke with Zechariah, made this escape possible. Indeed, this scene provides a point of transition to a word that came to Zechariah to be addressed to exiles who have indeed come from Babylon (6.9-10).

The LORD's Word (6.9-14) and Zechariah's Words (6.15)

To begin my comments on the word of the LORD in 6.9-14, I want to offer my own translation of vv. 9-10. which differs somewhat from the NRSV. In the translation I give the meaning of the proper names in capital letters rather than transliterate them, as do many translations, since their meanings are significant, such as 'THE LORD IS GOOD' (NRSV 'Tobijah'). All the names in v. 10 end with the divine name Yah (in English transliterations 'iah' or 'jah'), a shortened form of Yahweh, exept for 'MY LIFE' (NRSV 'Heldai'); if a simple 'h' were added to this word the name would be translated something like 'THE LORD IS LIFE' and the list would be a complete list of names using the name of God. I have not emended the text in my reading, and I do not intend to do so here.

> And the word of the LORD came to me, 'Take [NRSV 'Collect silver and gold', but 'silver and gold do not occur in the Hebrew text] from the exiles, from MY LIFE, from THE LORD IS GOOD and from THE LORD KNOWS. And you will go on that day and you will come to the house of THE LORD HAS FAVOURED the son of THE LORD HAS TREASURED; they have come from Babylon.

With this word, Zechariah's unidentified audience, the 'them' without a clear antecedent in 1.3 begins to become a group, although a small one, which is identified. Zechariah, THE LORD HAS REMEMBERED, is surrounded by people whose names also relate them to the LORD, THE LORD IS GOOD, THE LORD KNOWS, THE LORD HAS FAVOURED, son of THE LORD HAS TREASURED and MY LIFE (possibly THE LORD IS MY LIFE). The other character in this scene, the high priest Joshua (THE LORD IS SALVATION) helps identify Zechariah's audience as one for whom the LORD is God. This group contrasts with the community described in Hosea at the beginning of the Twelve, called to *return* to the LORD, unaware that it was the LORD who had given them 'the grain, the new wine and the oil'. The very names of those in Zechariah's community make the LORD's name unforgettable, or, to make a play on Zechariah's name, memorable.

Whether Zechariah's audience consists entirely of those who have come from Babylon is not clear. However, since no other audience has been mentioned, one might suppose that the *returned* exiles comprise the audience. If this is the case, then the call to *'return'* that opens Zechariah also carries the meaning of *return* from exile. The messenger's assertion that the strong ones who go to the north country have set his mind at ease confirms the importance of return from the north country, Babylon for Zechariah's audience. It will be recalled that in scene 3 (6.9-14) the LORD called, 'Flee from the land of the north', and a command was given by Zechariah to those dwelling in Babylon, 'escape' (2.6-7). Apparently those exiles in Zechariah's audience have done just that; they have fled from the north country, escaping from Babylon.

The words of the LORD in scene 3 are significant in another way for understanding the word concerning the exiles who have returned from Babylon. The LORD said that he would plunder the nations so that 'they shall become plunder for their own slaves' (2.9). The reason that the messenger's spirit is at ease about the north country is that he already knows about the north country. The plundering is over and 'the slaves', those who returned from Babylon, have come with Babylonian plunder. In such a context, the opening of this word of the LORD, 'Take from the exiles' becomes more understandable. Zechariah is to take the plunder from the exiles for temple restoration. What has begun to occur is what Haggai had prophesied. Haggai had said that the treasure of silver and gold would come to fill the house of the LORD so that the splendour of the rebuilt temple would be greater than that of the former one (Hag. 2.6-8).

As the word of the LORD continues, Zechariah is specifically told, 'And you will take silver and gold and you will make crowns and you will put [the object of the verb is not given in Hebrew, but a crown or crowns is suggested by the context] on the head of Joshua... (6.11; my own rather literal translation). The specific number of crowns is not given, and the text does not indicate how many crowns are to be placed on Joshua's head. When this is done, Zechariah is to say to Joshua:

> Thus says the LORD of hosts: 'Here is a man whose name is Branch: for he shall branch out in his place, and he shall build the temple of the LORD. It is he that shall build the temple of the LORD; he shall bear royal honour, and shall sit on his throne. And a priest shall be on his [i.e. the priest's] throne [NRSV 'there shall be a priest by his throne'] with peaceful understanding between the two of them' (Zech. 6.12).

Significantly, what Zechariah is saying and doing tells us as much about the role of Zechariah as it does about Joshua and the Branch (Zerubbabel). It will be recalled that in the fourth scene the messenger of the

LORD put clean festal apparel on Joshua and then charged Joshua with stipulations governing his role as priest. During that time the messenger of the LORD only mentions that he is going to bring the Branch (3.9) but nothing more is said about the Branch. In the same scene Zechariah begins to act like a messenger of the LORD and requests that a 'clean turban' be placed on the head of Joshua (3.5). In this scene involving the returnees from Babylon, he is alone and acting as a messenger of the LORD. He makes crowns, puts at least one of them on the head of Joshua, and then speaks to him about the Branch—supplementing the information about the Branch merely referred to by the messenger in 3.8. The high priest and the Branch, the governor Zerubbabel, are to stand side by side in the restored community. This cooperation is consistent with the imagery of the lampstand, on which are represented the two spikes of grain: the master of all the earth is flanked by Joshua, the high priest and Zerubbabel, the governor. The world as seen by Zechariah will have both a priest and a governor who will carry out their roles with mutual understanding.

The act accompanying the making of crowns is not totally clear. Literally the Hebrew of 6.11-13 can be rendered:

> And you will take silver and gold and you will make crowns and you will place on the head of Joshua, son of Jehozadak, the high priest. And you will say to him, 'Thus says the LORD of hosts, 'Here is a man, branch is his name, and from his place he will branch out, and he will build the temple of the LORD. And he will build the temple of the LORD and he will bear honour and he will sit and he will rule an his throne. And a priest will rule on his throne and peaceful counsel will be between them'.

How many crowns are to be made and how many are to be placed on Zechariah's head is not explicitly stated. Also the identify of the man in the phrase, 'Here is a man', is not transparent. Some of the ambiguity of this passage becomes clear, however, if we understand that the 'man' is Zerubbabel. The 'man' will build the temple of the LORD. We know from earlier scenes that Zerubbabel was singled out as the man who will complete the building of the temple (see Zech. 4.8). Since this man will rule and sit on his throne and the priest will rule and sit on his throne, we can understand that this scene is portraying Zerubbabel and Joshua as the two spikes of grain who will rule side by side just as they were portrayed earlier as standing beside the LORD, the master of the whole earth (4.13). If that is the case, then it is not difficult to understand that two crowns were made from the two precious metals collected from the exiles. One was made from silver and the other from gold. While one of the crowns is placed on Joshua's head, the other represents the missing Zerubbabel who is not in this scene. The missing Zerubbabel was represented in his crown, which, when held before Joshua became the basis for the statement, 'Here is the man'. Again this scene involving crowns takes on meaning if it is understood as a ceremony taking place in the temple.

When the temple is completed by Zerubbabel the crowns will be placed in it as a memorial for those who returned with Babylonian plunder. The names of the exiles given in 6.14 have slightly changed by the end of this word. Two appear in shortened form without the divine name, 'Yah', which I have translated as 'the LORD'. They now appear as LIFE, THE LORD IS GOOD, THE LORD KNOWS and FAVOUR. Not only the crowns but also the names of the exiles themselves are a memorial to the LORD.

The word of the LORD about Zerubbabel, the Branch, is the subject of two of the earlier scenes as well (see 3.8 and 4.6-10a). These passages, taken together, undergird the point that Zerubbabel's place in temple construction is that he will complete the construction of the temple. Indeed, in 6.12-13, this point is awkwardly repeated, 'He shall build the temple of the LORD. It is he that shall build the temple of the LORD'. This 'seed of Babel' ('seed of Babylon'), which is the meaning of the name Zerubbabel, is 'the Branch', perhaps better translated 'shoot' or 'sprout'. The seed, shoot or sprout suggests that the very name of this temple builder symbolizes the prosperity promised in these passages resulting from the finalization of temple construction: grain, oil and new wine.

That Zerubbabel is the centre of attention in these texts makes all the more conspicuous the fact that he is never present as a character. Why does Zerubbabel not appear? Why is he spoken about but not spoken to? What does the absence of this person, so often at the centre of spoken words about him, mean?

It is reasonable to assume that the remoteness of Zerubbabel means that he was remote in the day-to-day world of Zechariah. Even his name suggests his difference. It is not a name that includes the divine appellation, Yah (the LORD), as does the name of almost every other character (Zechariah, Joshua, Tobijah, Jedaiah and Josiah). Even fathers' names contain the divine name 'Yah' (Jehozadak and Zephaniah). When Zechariah saw things in his world, what he saw did not include the governor, Zerubbabel. He was in Zechariah's world to be spoken about but not to be spoken to. The governor of Judah was a powerful presence in Zechariah's world as powerful political leaders have been present in the lives of most people everywhere. Their presence is felt in everything that happens (including building projects), but they are almost never actually present. Institutions often depend on the support of these powerful present, yet absent, leaders.

When the scenes involving Zechariah with the messenger opened, the LORD's word was 'my house shall be built' (1.16). However, everything about this world that Zechariah sees makes it clear that the LORD is not able to accomplish anything apart from the governor, Zerubbabel. If the temple is to be completed, it will be Zerubbabel who will accomplish it.

In these scenes Zechariah has claimed a special status for himself. This assertion is stated repeatedly in the following phrase that occurs with some minor variations, 'Then you will know that the LORD of hosts has sent me to you' (2.8, 9, 11; 4.9). Furthermore, this assertion of Zechariah is linked with Zerubbabel's expected completion of the temple (4.9; 6.15), and with the presence of the LORD who will make all this possible (2.8, 9, 11).

It is important to understand, then, that Zechariah's role is not that of the oppressed, the disempowered. Zechariah may not sit at the heart of Persian power, but his world is one in which he is active in powerful institutions (the temple) and is associated with powerful figures: Joshua, the high priest, and wealthy people with 'Yah' names who have returned from Babylon with silver and gold.

Overview and Transition (1.7-6.15)

It will be helpful to review what has taken place between the first and last scene. When Zechariah sees the mounted horsemen a messenger is in his presence to answer his question. This messenger presence was tantamount to the presence of the LORD, who claims that he is 'extremely angry with the nations' (1.15), that he has 'returned to Jerusalem' and that his 'house [temple] shall be rebuilt in it' (1.16). Furthermore, this return and anger with the nations means that Jerusalem and the other cities of Judah will 'overflow with prosperity' (1.17). As the scenes develop, Zechariah is drawn more and more into the action of the scenes of restoration (scene 2, 1.18-21 and scene 3, 2.1-5). This results in Zechariah's claim that many will flee from Babylon (2.7), that the LORD will destroy the nations (2.8-9), and that many nations will join themselves to the LORD. Furthermore, as Zechariah moves into the action he also moves into the temple and participates in the installation of Joshua as high priest (3.1-10). In the temple the messenger explains to Zechariah imagery associated with the temple under construction. That Zechariah is unable to understand what he sees is occasioned by the fact that he had not seen the former temple in all its splendour (cf. Hag. 2.3). He sees a lampstand symbolizing that Joshua the high priest and Zerubbabel the governor stand by 'the master of the whole earth' (4.14). In the next two scenes, he sees imagery suggesting that it will be possible for those 'in the whole earth' to return to Jerusalem: 'a flying scroll' goes out into 'the whole earth' ridding the community of thieves and those who pervert justice by swearing falsely (5.1-4), and an ephah representing 'the guilt of the whole earth' (5.6) contains wickedness and is destined for Shinar (5.11), the place which had held the daughter of Zion captive.

In this last scene the chariots go out from the presence of the LORD in the temple to 'the whole earth'. The LORD, 'the master of all the earth', is in the temple standing beside the two 'spikes of grain', Joshua and Zerubbabel, and from that very centre he is enacting changes in 'the whole earth'. Zechariah is not having a vision of another world, in which the LORD is present. The LORD is present in Zechariah's world. Indeed, the messenger of the LORD, Haggai, put it succinctly: '"I am with you" [i.e. in the sense of 'present with you'] says the LORD' (Hag. 1.13). With that message, work commenced on the LORD's house in which he is present (Hag. 1.14).

The chariots going out symbolize the war that the LORD will wage against the nations already spoken about by Haggai (Hag. 2.6-9 and 2.20-23) and alluded to in Zechariah's experiences (Zech. 1.15, 21; 2.8-9). Chariots, vehicles of warfare in the ancient world associated with the power of kings (see, e.g., 1 Sam. 8.11), are frequently used in the Hebrew Bible to portray the LORD as warrior (see Isa. 66.11 and Jer. 4.13). In the Twelve, among the former prophets, Habakkuk, who waited for the LORD (2.3), offered a prayer for the LORD to return to his actions of the past (3.2) when he 'shook the earth' and 'made the nations tremble' (3.6) when he drove his horses and chariots to victory (3.8). It was just such an action that Haggai announced was soon to happen (Hag. 2.6-9 and 2.20-23) and that is seen as taking place in the imagery of the LORD's horses and chariots (Zech. 6.1-5).

It may be helpful to summarize my observations about the eight scenes in which messengers begin to appear in Zechariah's world advising him on the meaning of what he sees. First, in these scenes, messenger presence is tantamount to divine presence. This is what distinguishes both Zechariah and Haggai—messengers of the LORD—from the former prophets. As Zechariah moves in the world of messengers, he moves into the LORD's presence and establishes himself, like Haggai, as a messenger of the LORD. God's speaking in the Twelve begins with the prophet Hosea and modulates to God speaking by means of his messengers at the time of Haggai and Zechariah. The LORD is present in their world. '"I am with you," says the LORD' (Hag. 1.13).

Secondly, God is present in a particular place—in the midst of Jerusalem in the temple under construction—and is not merely accessible through a vision of another world, as was the case at the time of the former prophets. The power of God, the LORD of the whole earth (cf. 1.11; 4.10, 14; 5.3, 6; 6.5) is localized, and Zechariah and other messengers move around in his presence.

Thirdly, the LORD is now angry with all the nations, making it possible for exiles to return. Nations will be terrified (1.21) and plundered (2.9) so that Jerusalem will be inhabited like a village without walls (2.2-4). Even other nations will join themselves to the LORD (2.11).

Fourthly, the governor, Zerubbabel, whose absence counters the LORD's presence, has a major task to perform in bringing about change. He will complete the temple so that it will exceed its former splendour (4.9-10; 6.12-13, 15). The sharing of power is nowhere more clearly evident than in the image of the lampstand. What is represented there is the LORD of all the earth, standing between the high priest Joshua and the governor of Judah, Zerubbabel.

Fifthly, the claim that Zerubbabel is 'the Branch' is perhaps an attempt to turn him into a Davidic sprout in a world dated by reference to Persian kings. But governors are not kings. And Persian kings are not Davidic. The LORD in Jerusalem relies on the power of a governor of a foreign king to complete the temple's construction. The governor's foreign name incorporates 'Babel' rather than 'Yah', so it is not clear whether 'the LORD' is his god.

Zechariah claims that those from 'far off shall come to help build the temple of the LORD'. They have already come from the north country. When that happens, when the temple is completed, then 'you shall know that the LORD of hosts has sent me to you'. Zechariah is addressing his readers thus, 'This will happen if you diligently obey the voice of the LORD our God' (6.15).

Zechariah 7.1-8.23
Scene 9: A Question from Bethel

Introductory Remarks

Zechariah is divided into three sections (1.1-6; 1.7-6.15 and 7.1-14.21). Each of these sections begins by dating a word of the LORD that came to Zechariah at a particular time during the reign of Darius. In the first short section (1.1-6) Zechariah is introduced as the descendant of Iddo the prophet, and he speaks the word of the LORD, quoting the former prophets, calling on the community to return. In the second longer section (1.7-6.15) Zechariah again is introduced as a descendant of Iddo the prophet. He encounters messengers in his world and emerges as a messenger of the LORD claiming that the LORD has sent him. In this third section (7.1-14.21), in which he speaks as a messenger, his association with a prophetic past has ceased. He is introduced simply as Zechariah (7.1). There is no link to the prophets through his grandfather Iddo.

This section also contrasts with the preceding one in another way. The second section began and ended with Zechariah *asking* questions of the messenger who spoke with him. The third section begins with Zechariah *answering* a question posed to him by representatives from Bethel (7.2-3). His answer as a messenger is a long one and extends from 7.4 to 8.23. This scene, in which Zechariah offers an answer to the representatives from Bethel, is followed by three oracles of the LORD. Such a structure recalls the earlier scenes in which questions answered by messengers were followed by sayings of the LORD. Two of these three oracles occur at the end of Zechariah (9.1-11.17 and 12.1-14.23), and the third is the whole of Malachi. Zechariah is not mentioned by name in any of these oracles. However, my reading suggests that, just as Haggai appeared anonymously in Zechariah (1.11-12 and 3.1, 6) as 'the messenger of the LORD', so Zechariah appears anonymously in the introduction of the last oracle as '*my* messenger' or Malachi (Mal. 1.1). '*My* messenger' corresponds to the 'me' in the repeated claim of Zechariah, 'you shall know that the LORD of hosts has sent *me* to you' (2.8-9, 11; 4.9; 6.15), in the section of the book in which Zechariah emerges as a messenger.

The Date

As indicated above, this section, like the earlier two sections, begins with a date of a word of the LORD that came to Zechariah at a particular time during the reign of Darius. The recurring phrase in each of the sections, 'the word of the LORD came to', not only refers to words of the LORD in what follows but also to the circumstances surrounding how the word of the LORD 'came to' Zechariah. The dates of the first two sections are in the second year of Darius and are separated by three months (the eighth and eleventh months, 1.1 and 1.7). The third date in 7.1 is nearly two years later, in the ninth month of the fourth year of Darius.

This two year gap is significant. Two years have elapsed since work began on the temple of the LORD (Hag. 1.14-15). In fact, it is two years to the month since the foundations were laid for building the temple (Hag. 2.18). This two year gap between what we are told in 6.15 and 7.1 suggests that 'those from far off' have come and helped 'to build the temple of the LORD' so that those in Zechariah's audience 'know that the LORD of hosts has sent' him to them (6.15).

The phrase in 7.1, which dates the word of the LORD that came to Zechariah, varies in two significant ways from 1.1 and 1.7. These variations concern status and reflect the consequence of return. First, Darius is referred to as 'Darius, the King'. Why this change from the designation of him simply as 'Darius' in 1.1 and 1.7? The change represents a return to the way in which Haggai referred to Darius as king (Hag. 1.1 and 2.1). A clue to understanding this change can be found in the fact that Haggai also referred to Zerubbabel as governor (1.1, 14; 2.2, 20). Haggai, therefore, had maintained the division in power between the king, Darius, and the governor, Zerubbabel. Zechariah disguises this distinction by never using the title 'governor' for Zerubbabel and avoiding the use of the title 'king' for Darius until 7.1. It is possible to read the text in such a way as to understand that Zechariah, as he is portrayed in the period of temple construction, was expecting that Zerubbabel's status would become more regal. This 'spike of grain' who was to stand with the high priest Joshua flanking the LORD as master of 'the whole earth' (4.14) may not have attained the expected status as king. Significantly, he disappears, along with Joshua, in the remaining part of the Twelve. Zerubbabel, who never made an appearance in Zechariah, has now vanished altogether at a time when Darius is identified as king. For the first time the reader may be getting a hint that the significance that Zechariah attached to the imagery that he saw in the temple under construction does not match the realities expected as it reaches completion. This will become more evident in the oracles.

The second change is that Zechariah loses his connection with his grandfather, Iddo the prophet. Zechariah now appears without a title and without a genealogy. He is simply Zechariah. This is the last time his name will be mentioned in the Twelve. Similarly, Haggai lost his title and appeared simply as Haggai the last time his name was mentioned (Hag. 2.20). When Haggai appeared again as a character, he was nameless, and was referred to only as 'the messenger of the LORD'. Zechariah, like Haggai, loses his former name identification in his new role as messenger. When he is mentioned in the Twelve again as a character, he will simply appear as Malachi, 'my messenger'.

The reader can assume that in the two years since work began on the temple, it has reached completion. That the temple has been completed is not announced but taken for granted. Since the implied audience is one for whom the fourth year of Darius is already past, the obvious does not need to be stated: the temple has been built. What the reader needs to know is what has been developed in the previous section: that Zechariah has emerged as a messenger of the LORD. As a consequence of Zechariah's status, what follows in 7.1–14.21 can be understood as the LORD's words. When the messenger speaks, the LORD speaks.

The Question (7.2-3)

That the temple has been completed is subtly implied in 7.2-3. We are told that Bethel (read HOUSE OF GOD or HOUSE OF EL) sent representatives to the priests and prophets of the house of the LORD. In other words representatives were sent from one divine dwelling place to another. Being sent from the HOUSE OF EL to the house of the LORD in the Twelve is significant. It will be recalled from the discussion in the Introduction that the only other place a messenger presence is referred to in the Twelve is Hos. 12.4 concerning how the LORD used to speak to Jacob by a messenger at Bethel (HOUSE OF EL). In the time of King Darius the HOUSE OF EL sends representatives to the house of the LORD in Jerusalem to ask a question. It is in the temple in Jerusalem, not Bethel, that the messenger now speaks as he used to speak to Jacob.

One is also reminded of Amos's encounter with Amaziah (Amos 7.10-17). In this episode when Amos attempted to speak in Bethel, Amaziah, the priest, sent him to Judah. The conflict between Bethel and Judah (Jerusalem) evident in Amos 7 can perhaps also be seen in this passage. Bethel, once in a position to send prophets of the LORD away, now comes to Jerusalem to ask a question of the LORD. In Amos 7.13, Bethel is also 'a temple of the kingdom', and can be understood perhaps as a rival religious centre, now sending to ask questions of those in the house of the LORD.

It is significant that these representatives of Bethel do not have 'Yahweh' names like Joshua (THE LORD IS SALVATION), Zechariah (THE LORD HAS REMEMBERED), and those who recently returned from Babylon, THE LORD IS LIFE, THE LORD IS GOOD, THE LORD KNOWS, and THE LORD HAS FAVOURED, the son of THE LORD HAS TREASURED. Those from Bethel are identified as 'Sharezer and Regem-melech and his [NRSV 'their'] men'. They are, however, interested in making an inquiry of the LORD—and such an inquiry cannot be made at Bethel. Not only is the completed temple quietly introduced into the text, but its status, like that of Darius and Zechariah, is indirectly acknowledged. If one wants to inquire of the LORD, one must come to the house of the LORD in Jerusalem.

The phrase used for the way the men of Bethel make their inquiry is translated in the NRSV as 'to entreat the favour of'. The Hebrew phrase can be rendered more literally as 'to appease the face of the LORD'. What the men of Bethel are requesting, then, needs to be done before the 'face of the LORD', that is, in his presence. One must do this at a place where the LORD resides and with an individual who has access to divine presence—in the house of the LORD before priests and prophets. The phrase, 'to appease the face of the LORD' is not uncommon in the Hebrew Bible and always is an appeal to the LORD to prevent some calamity. For example, Moses 'appeases the face of the LORD' to avert the disaster created after the people of Israel had built the golden calf. He does this by posing questions to the LORD (Exod. 32.11-13). The LORD is appeased and changes his mind (Exod. 32.14). The men of Bethel also pose a question, which should be understood as a question intended to avert disaster. What they want to know from the LORD is, 'Should I mourn and practice abstinence in the fifth month, as I have done for so many years' (7.3)? Who the 'I' is in this question is not clear. The text simply tells us that 'Bethel sent' individuals (NRSV has 'the people of Bethel'). Perhaps the 'I' was a representative of the HOUSE OF EL, posing the question. Since the inquiry is addressed to priests and prophets, one might assume that the 'I' was a priest or a prophet. The LORD's initial response is in the form of a question, 'When you fasted and lamented in the fifth month and in the seventh month, for these seventy years, was it for me that you fasted?' When read in the light of the seventy years that the LORD was angry (see 1.12), the implication is that the question concerns appeasing the LORD's anger.

Before turning to analyse the answer to the question from Bethel, however, I want to look at two other issues related to 'entreating the favour of the LORD' by coming before priests and prophets associated with the house of the LORD. First, 'to entreat the favour of the LORD' is envisaged at the end of Zechariah 8 as something that many cities and many strong nations will do (see Zech. 8.20-23 where the phrase occurs twice). What the HOUSE OF EL is doing by sending men with non-Yahweh names is anticipating what many cities and nations will do: they will come to the temple 'to entreat the favour of the LORD'. Secondly, while the individuals from Bethel come to ask questions of priests and prophets, it is Zechariah who gives them an answer. Zechariah as messenger speaks for the priests and the prophets. This is consistent with the suggestion in earlier scenes that prophetic figures are confined to former times and appear in a new guise as messengers. Priests, also, are subordinate to messengers, who admonish them about their priestly duties (see Zech. 3). Furthermore, to anticipate Malachi, the reason why the priests do not answer is that they are, as portrayed at the beginning of Malachi, ones who despise the name of the LORD (1.6). More ominous is that they are described by the LORD as individuals who 'entreat the favour of El' (Mal. 1.9; NRSV 'implore God')—the god El, of Bethel, and not the LORD. El will show no favour to the priestly entreaty: ' "Will he [El] show favour to you?" says the LORD of hosts' (see Mal. 1.9). Zechariah, then, in his new role as messenger pre-empts both prophets and priests. He speaks for prophets who are being confined to former times and for priests who seek to appease the face of El rather than the face of the LORD.

At the beginning of the second section of Zechariah (1.7-6.15), Zechariah asked the messenger a question; at the beginning of the third part, as a messenger himself, he answers a question from the men of Bethel. The prelude to his answer is an imperative from the LORD, 'Say to *all* the people of *the earth* and *the priests* saying...' This phrase, 'all the people of the earth', picks up the recurring phrase, '*the whole earth*' in the previous scenes. In scene 1 the horsemen patrolled *the whole earth* (1.11). In scene 5 the seven lamps with seven lips represented 'the eyes of the LORD, which range through *the whole earth*' (4.10), and the two spikes of grain (Joshua and Zerubbabel) will stand beside 'the master of *the whole earth*' (4.14). This phrase crescendos in the last three scenes with the flying scroll that goes out over 'the face of *the whole earth*' (6.3), the ephah which represents iniquity in '*the whole earth*' (6.6), and the chariots/four winds which present themselves before 'the master of *the whole earth*' (6.5). That Zechariah now speaks to '*all the people of the earth*' is another indication of his change in status. Those who went out to patrol the whole earth in scene 1 and who returned (end of scene 8) suggest that the house of the LORD has implications for the people of *the whole earth*. Zechariah's answer beginning in 7.4 is not just for Bethel but for *the whole earth*. It includes the oracles at the end of Zechariah (chs. 9-14), in which it is said that the LORD will become king over '*the whole earth*'. A messenger who speaks for the LORD speaks to *the whole earth* (14.9). Joshua the high priest and Zerubbabel the governor stand beside 'the master of *the whole earth*'; and the messenger Zechariah speaks to '*all the people of the earth*'. This is another way in which the LORD's speaking changes in the Twelve from its beginning with Hosea (1.2). Even prophets, like the reluctant Jonah, did not have 'all the people of the earth' as their audience. Zechariah's answer, which contains references to the former prophets provides us with further indications of the difference between the way the former prophets spoke and the way Zechariah speaks as a messenger.

This prelude to Zechariah's answer also suggests that it is directed specifically to 'the priests'. In the previous scenes when the high priest Joshua appeared, he had no voice. Instead, messengers of the LORD spoke to him and gave him instructions as in scene 5 (3.6-10) and in scene 8 (6.9-14). Again in this scene the priests do not have a chance to say anything. Silencing the priests (and confining the prophets to former times) has enhanced the verbal authority of Zechariah.

The beginning of scene 9 is important for Zechariah and for the Twelve. The full implications of the narrator's earlier and almost off-handed remark in Haggai that Haggai was the messenger of the LORD (Hag. 1.13) signalled the change from prophets to messengers. The significance of this change now is becoming abundantly clear. In a world where messengers speak, prophets no longer speak. Messengers speak in their stead. Equally, in a world in which messengers speak, priests, even high priests, have no voice—messengers speak to them. The world of restoration in Zechariah, embodied in the construction of the temple where the LORD is present confers the power of that institution upon messengers who speak for the LORD, present when messengers are present. Not only is the LORD 'the master of all the earth', but also his messengers, like Zechariah, speak to 'all the people of the earth'. Temple and messenger are the external expressions of the messenger's message, ' "I am with you," says the LORD' (Hag. 1.13).

The Answer (7.4-8.23): An Overall Perspective

To gain a perspective on Zechariah's answer to the question from Bethel, it will be important to look at the following general contours of the answer as a whole. The most important feature is that the design of Zechariah's answer mirrors that of the first two sections (1.1-6.15), concerning what Zechariah had seen two years earlier. The earlier scenes began with a reference to what the former prophets proclaimed (1.4) and ended with scenes depicting the future with the LORD as 'the master of the whole earth' (scenes 5-8 in 4.1-6.15). Zechariah's answer here also begins by referring to what the former prophets proclaimed (7.6, 12) and ends by depicting the future as a time when all nations and peoples 'of every language' will seek the LORD (8.20-23). Zechariah's answer, then, to 'all the people of the earth' directs them from the former times of the prophets to the future, just as he was earlier directed from what the former prophets had said in the past to a future depicted in what he saw in temple construction during conversations with the messenger.

Even the question posed by Bethel concerns former times, 'Should I mourn and practice abstinence in the fifth month, as I have done for so many years?' (7.3). Zechariah's answer, however, moves the listener into a future orientation: 'The fast of the fourth month, and the fast of the fifth, and the fast of the seventh, and the fast of the tenth, shall be seasons of joy and gladness, and cheerful festivals for the house of Judah: therefore love truth and peace' (8.19). A question about mourning and practising abstinence for one month (the fifth month) has been answered with reference to 'seasons of joy' during four months of the year (the fourth, the fifth, the seventh and the tenth months).

The Answer Begins: Lamenting and Fasting and the Former Prophets (7.4-7)

The answer to the question from Bethel comes in the form of three rhetorical questions from the LORD. The first rhetorical question is: 'When you fasted and lamented in the fifth month and in the seventh month, for these past seventy years, was it for me that you fasted?' (7.5). In light of the fact that it was Bethel (HOUSE OF EL) that raised the question, and in light of the discussion of Mal. 2.9, in which the priests 'appease the face of El,' the implied answer to the rhetorical question must be negative: 'No, we did not mourn and fast for you, we fasted for El.' In the Hebrew text the words in the LORD's rhetorical question, 'fast and lament', are different from those used in the question raised by Bethel, 'mourn and practise abstinence'. The different vocabulary used in the two questions may itself be an indication that what was being done in Bethel was not being done for the LORD. The second rhetorical question is, 'And when you ate and when you drank, were you not the ones who ate and were you not the ones who drank?' (my translation varies slightly from the NRSV). The meaning of this question is not totally clear. But it seems to imply a kind of selfishness. They ate and drank only for themselves. The third rhetorical question concerns the former prophets: 'Were not these the words that the LORD proclaimed by the former prophets, when Jerusalem was inhabited and in prosperity, along with the towns around it, and when the Negeb and the Shephelah were inhabited?' (7.7) This third question suggests that the first two questions had been raised by the former prophets. While it is not possible to point to any passage in the former prophets that contains such questons, passages in Amos relate to the issues raised. Bethel is presented in Amos as a place where the community's actions are not directed to the LORD. For example,

> Seek me and live;
>> But do not seek *Bethel*,
> and do not enter into Gilgal
>> ... or cross over to Beer-sheba;
> for Gilgal shall surely go into exile,
>> and *Bethel* will come to nothing.
> Seek the LORD and live,
>> or he will break out against the house of Joseph like fire,
> and it will devour *Bethel*, with
>> no one to quench it (Amos 5.5-6).

While this passage is not about mourning or fasting, it suggests that cultic activities at Bethel are not directed to the LORD. See also Amos 4.4-5:

> Come to Bethel—and transgress;
>> to Gilgal—and multiply transgression:
> bring your sacrifices every morning.
>> your tithes every three days;
> bring a thank-offering of leavened bread,
>> and proclaim freewill offerings, publish them;
> for so you love to do,
>> O people of Israel!
>> says the LORD, the master (NRSV 'LORD GOD').

The notion of drinking only for themselves resonates with Amos 2.8 (see also Amos 3.14),

> they lay themselves down beside every altar
>> on garments taken in pledge;
> and in the house of their God they drink
>> wine bought with fines they imposed.

When Bethel asks the question about mourning and practising abstinence, the LORD responds with rhetorical questions suggesting that the
practices carried out there were not directed toward him. The reference
to 'seventy years' in the LORD's first rhetorical question recalls the seventy years of the first scene in which the LORD was angry (see 1.12).
The LORD's response to Bethel suggests that the LORD had every right
to be angry for these past seventy years for what was done at Bethel was
not for him. He had every right to be angry for these past seventy years
for he had proclaimed these things—he had raised similar questions—
'by the hand of the former prophets when Jerusalem was inhabited and
in prosperity, along with the towns around it, and when the Negeb and
the Shephalah were inhabited' (7.7). Amos was a former prophet who
had proclaimed such things long before the seventy years of the LORD's
anger.

The Answer Continues: Social Relationships and the Former Prophets (7.8-14)

In the continuation of Zechariah's answer there is again a reference to
the words of the former prophets (v. 12). Whereas the first part of the
answer (7.5-7) had to do with community actions such as fasting and
lamentation concerned with Bethel's relationship to the LORD, this part
of the answer has to do with problems surrounding social relationships.
The community had refused the command the LORD sent by the former
prophets to 'render true judgments', to 'show kindness and mercy to
one another', and not to 'oppress the widow, the orphan, the alien, or
the poor'. All this past mistreatment of others is summarized in the command 'do not devise evil in your hearts against one another' (7.9-11).
This command is identified as 'the law [Torah] and the words that the
LORD had sent by his spirit by the hand of [NRSV has 'through' for 'by
the hand of'] the former prophets' (7.12). But the community refused to
hear; the community made their hearts adamant. This refusal to listen
resulted in the LORD's 'great wrath' that 'scattered the people with a
whirlwind among all the nations' so that 'a pleasant land was made
desolate' (7.13-14).

The answer recalls the beginning of Zechariah. Those who refused to
heed the 'law [Torah] and words' of the former prophets are the fathers
in 1.6 who refused to listen to the 'statutes and words' of the former
prophets. The LORD's 'great wrath', which came as a consequence, also
recalls the beginning of Zechariah, in which Zechariah says, 'The LORD
was very angry with your fathers'. Everything that is reported here about
the past is presented as justification for the LORD's anger that lasted for

these seventy years (1.12; 7.5). The appeal to the past actions of the fathers also serves as a justification of the LORD's past actions in scattering Judah (see scene 2, 1.18-21). The reference to a pleasant land becoming desolate (7.14) relates to the importance of what Zechariah saw in scene 4 concerning Joshua and the removal of 'the guilt of the land' (3.9). As Zechariah's answer develops, then, the present situation is justified by an appeal to 'the former prophets'.

'The law [Torah] and the words that the LORD of hosts had sent by his spirit through the former prophets' sounds familiar to readers of the Twelve. Although Zechariah is not quoting from the former prophets, his allusion to them resonates with what the reader has read in the former prophets, sent by the LORD during the time from Uzziah to Josiah and encountered earlier in the Twelve. For example, the command to render true judgments and to show mercy and kindness recalls Mic. 6.8:

> He has told you, O mortal, what is good;
>> and what does the LORD require of you
> but to do justice, and to love kindness,
>> and to walk humbly with your God?

It also recalls Hos. 4.1-3:

> Hear the word of the LORD.
>> people of Israel;
> for the LORD has an
>> indictment against the inhabitants of the land.
> There is no faithfulness or loyalty,
>> and no knowledge of God in the land,
> Swearing, lying and murder,
>> and stealing and adultery break out;
>> bloodshed follows bloodshed.
> Therefore the land mourns,
>> and all who live in it languish;
> together with the wild animals
>> and the birds of the air,
>> even the fish of the sea are perishing.

The imperative against oppression also echoes passages from the former prophets. One example is Mic. 2.1-2:

> Alas for those who devise wickedness
>> and evil deeds on their beds!
> When the morning dawns, they perform it,
>> because it is in their power.
> They covet fields, and seize them;
>> houses, and take them away;

they oppress householder and house,
>   people and their inheritance.

Another example is Amos 4.1:

Hear this word, you cows of Bashan
>   who are on Mount Samaria,
who oppress the poor, who crush the needy,
>   who say to their husbands, 'Bring something to drink!'

In the first part of his answer, Zechariah is appealing to the former prophets. Such an appeal justifies the LORD's actions. What he did was a consequence of what he had proclaimed through the former prophets to the fathers who refused to listen. The LORD's actions were not arbitrary but a consequence of the actions of the people in turning away from the LORD in their religious practice and against one another in social behaviour. The former prophets, then, both at the beginning of Zechariah and at the beginning of this long answer are important because what they proclaimed is used as a justification of the LORD's wrath for this past seventy years.

Zechariah in appealing to words the former prophets proclaimed, is speaking for the prophets—one of the parties to whom Bethel addressed its question. Prophets do not speak; Zechariah does. Prophets are confined to former times. In order to gain a clearer perspective on how a messenger can speak for the former prophets, I want to look closely at two phrases in this passage associated with the former prophets: (1) 'the words which the LORD *proclaimed by the hand of* the former prophets' (7.7); (2) 'the law [Torah] and words which the LORD *sent* by his spirit *by the hand of* the former prophets' (7.12). What does it mean for the LORD *to proclaim* or *to send* his words *by the hand of* former prophets? Because the answers to these questions are crucial, the discussion will be somewhat extended.

To begin to answer the questions it will be useful to look at other contexts in which someone other than the LORD communicates 'by the hand of'. In 2 Sam. 11.14 it is reported that 'David *wrote* a letter to Joab and *sent* it *by the hand of* Uriah'. In this context 'by the hand of' suggests instrumentality, that is, the means by which the letter was sent. But the phrase also connotes something concrete, a letter, to be carried 'by the hand'. In Est. 3.12-13 scribes of the king were summoned and 'all the king commanded was *written* and letters were *sent by the hand of* runners to all the king's provinces'. (The situation is similar to Hab. 2.2 in which a reader will run with the vision that Habakkuk has written down.) In this passage as well 'in the hand of' connotes both instrumentality, 'by the hand of' and a concrete form, 'in the hand of'. What these two passages suggest about communication 'by the hand of' is that communication is carried out *by means of* a document that is actually carried *in the hand*, which can be read aloud. (For passages in which similar terminology is used see Jer. 29.3; 2 Kgs 19.23 and Isa. 37.24.)

These two passages about communication by means of something 'in the hand' suggests that when the LORD 'proclaims' or 'sends' his law and his words 'by/in the hand of the prophets' he is communicating through something that is written. The prophets, like couriers, are 'sent' carrying 'in the hand' written documents by which the LORD can 'proclaim' his law and his words.

To view the LORD as a god who communicates by sending written documents to be read aloud is a feature of the Twelve that is alien to our world. (See my 'Heard But Not Seen', pp. 55-59). Contemporary texts about the divine construct divinity in more abstract ways. But everything that we have noted about the divine in Zechariah's world is concrete. The LORD's presence is associated with his temple in Jerusalem. The attempt, since the age of romantic idealism, has been to construct the prophets as speakers, making them consonant with Protestant preaching in a more modern world. However, to view prophets as couriers of written words from the LORD is not alien in the textual world of the Hebrew Bible, a world in which the LORD proclaims and sends his words in writing.

A prophet carrying tablets in his hand on which are written words of God is a central feature of the Pentateuch's construction of its world. Moses is ordered in Exodus 34 to cut tablets of stone, to take them 'in his hand' (Exod. 34.1-5) and to write on them just as Habakkuk (Hab. 2.2) was instructed to write down his vision (as was Isaiah, see Isa. 30.8; 8.16). 'The LORD said to Moses, "*Write* these words; in accordance with these words I have made a covenant with you and Israel"' (Exod. 34.27). At the end of the passage, it is reported that 'Moses came down from Mount Sinai...with the two tablets of the covenant *in his hand*' (Exod. 34.29).

From this passage in Exodus 34 we can gain insight into a recurring phrase in the Hebrew Bible, 'the LORD *spoke by the hand* of Moses' (e.g. Exod. 9.35; Lev. 10.11; Num. 27.23). The LORD *speaks* when what was carried *in the hand* of Moses is *read*. Reading written words makes audible the LORD's words. Similarly the frequently recurring phrase 'the LORD *spoke by the hand of a prophet(s)*' (e.g. 1 Kgs 12.15; Isa. 20.2; Jer. 37.2) suggests that written documents carried by the hand become audible as God's spoken words when they are read. Such an interpretation of this phrase is supported by the reference in a prayer of Daniel (9.10), 'We did not listen to the voice of the LORD our God to follow his teachings, which he set before us by the hand of his servants the prophets'. What is 'in the hand of' the prophets makes audible the voice of the LORD. Written words of the prophets are not for the silent perusal of the eye; they are for the ear because they are read aloud. Reading words from God makes God's voice audible. When prophetic words are read, God speaks. The classic example of this is when Baruch reads the words of the LORD that came to Jeremiah, which were written down (see Jer. 36).

All of this has a bearing on what is meant by the LORD who *proclaims* and *sends* his law and words *by the hands of* the former prophets. 'The beginning of the LORD spoke was [with] Hosea' (Hos. 1.2 discussed in the Introduction). Those spoken words occur in the Twelve as writing. When Zechariah speaks for the former prophets, he is recalling what the readers of the Twelve have just read—the written words of the former prophets by which they proclaimed the words the LORD spoke.

The Answer Continues: The Present (8.1-8)

As Zechariah's answer develops, it moves from the time of the former prophets to the present in 8.2-3. This present is not based on what was 'proclaimed' or 'sent by the hand of former prophets' but what is happening in Zechariah's world, which we are seeing through his eyes. The LORD says, 'I am jealous for Zion with great jealousy, and I am jealous for her with great wrath' (8.2). This word of the LORD has the basic tenor of the word of the LORD that followed scene 1 (although it is not directly quoted), 'I am very jealous for Jerusalem and for Zion. And I am extremely angry with the nations that are at ease; for while I was only a little angry, they made the disaster worse' (1.14b-15). His anger against Jerusalem has become jealousy or zeal for Zion/Jerusalem.

Zechariah's answer, in which he is speaking the LORD's words, continues: 'I have returned (NRSV 'I will return') to Zion, and I am dwelling (NRSV 'will dwell') in the midst of Jerusalem; Jerusalem is called (NRSV 'will be called') the faithful city and the mountain of the LORD of hosts, the holy mountain' (8.3). Again we know from what Zechariah saw that these things have occurred. In the word of the LORD associated with scene 1, the LORD said, 'I have returned to Jerusalem' (1.6). In the words of the LORD accompanying scene 3 the LORD said, 'I am about to come and I am about to dwell in your midst' (2.9). The 'about to' has become a reality. This is evident not only from the call to silence when 'the LORD roused himself from his holy dwelling' (2.13), but also from the subsequent scene in which Joshua appears before the LORD in the temple (3.1-10). Although nowhere in the previous scenes is Jerusalem called 'a faithful city' or 'the mountain of God', 'the holy mountain', nevertheless 'the faithful city' and 'the holy mountain' resonate with the scenes concerning what Zechariah saw. 'Holy mountain' recalls the 'holy dwelling' mentioned in 2.13. 'The faithful city' represents the present in contrast with the past, in which there was a failure to render 'faithful judgments' (7.9; NRSV 'true judgments'), and anticipates the imperative to speak 'faithfully [NRSV 'the truth'] to one another' in 8.16.

The answer moves in 8.4-5 from the present to the imminent future. It refers to things that are about to occur as a consequence of changes that have taken place. Very old men and women, who need staffs to support themselves, and young boys and girls, like young children at play, will fill the 'open places' (NRSV 'streets') of Jerusalem. The reference here to the young and the old suggest the totality of the population. The open spaces of Jerusalem filled with a total population, from the very young to the very old, recall the similar description of Jerusalem in scene three in which Jerusalem will be inhabited like 'open country' or like 'villages without walls' (2.4).

Zechariah addresses the community concerning what is about to occur. The community that had been addressed as 'a remnant of the people' by Haggai (Hag. 1.12, 14; 2.2) is first identified as 'a remnant of this people' in Zech. 8.6. The issue raised concerns the insignificance of the present compared with the magnificence of the future. This has been a recurring theme in Haggai and Zechariah (see Hag. 2.3-9 and Zech. 4.8-10a). In the earlier references, however, the contrast was drawn between the present state of temple construction and the anticipated magnificence of the completed temple. The gap between the present and future in 8.6 is different. It envisages the vast population of Jerusalem in a city without walls. Although this may seem an impossibility to the present remnant, Zechariah is asking his audience to believe that it will not be too difficult for the LORD, whom he has seen in temple imagery to be the 'the master of the whole earth' (see Zech. 4.14; 6.5).

Although, as we have seen, the riders have gone out to patrol 'the whole earth' (see 1.11 and 6.7), 'the remnant' has returned only from the north country (see discussion of 6.8, cf. 2.6). While the LORD is 'master of all the earth' there has been no 'return' from any other part of the world. However, a return is anticipated from 'the east country' and 'the west country' in 8.7-8. The LORD says, 'I am about to save [NRSV 'will save'] my people from the east country and the west country; and I will bring them to Jerusalem. They shall be my people and I will be their God, in faithfulness and righteousness'. The detail of this envisaged return of the east country and the west country—and as we shall see, the south country also—is a subject that is taken up in the oracle in ch. 9.

The Answer Continues: The Contrast between the Past and the Present (8.9-17)

This passage also concerns 'the prophets' (8.9) and 'the former days' (8.11) of the 'fathers' (8.14). It therefore has links with the opening of Zechariah (1.1-6) and the opening of the answer to the men from Bethel (7.1-14), both of which concern 'the fathers' and 'the former prophets'. The passage is significant because it suggests that the former prophets are written words in the sense that they are read out during the commencement of temple construction. This reading of 'the former prophets' occurs at the time of Haggai, which itself provides the setting for the beginning of Zechariah. The reference to 'the former prophets' at the beginning of Zechariah was occasioned by the reading of past prophetic words at the beginning of temple construction initiated by Haggai. (The opening of the Persian section of the Twelve, like the beginning of the Persian section of Isaiah, is occasioned by reading written prophetic words from the past. See my *Reading Isaiah*, pp. 130-53.)

In order to make my reading clear, it will be necessary to begin by offering a rather literal and somewhat awkward translation of 8.9, which differs from the NRSV in the following significant ways: (1) I translate 'mouth' in the singular to reflect the singular noun in Hebrew (NRSV has 'mouths'); (2) I translate the relative 'which' referring to the words 'which' were present when the foundation of the temple was laid; NRSV translates the relative 'who' suggesting that it was the prophets 'who' were present.

> Thus says the LORD of hosts, 'Let your hands be strong, the ones who are hearing in these days these words from the mouth of the prophets which were in the day the foundation of the house of the LORD of hosts was laid to rebuild the temple.

The phrase in this passage, 'from the mouth of the prophets' is a phrase having to do with written words, not with spoken words. As mentioned in the Introduction, it is an idiomatic expression for dictation; the same phrase is used in Jer. 36.4, 6, 17, 18, 27 and 32 with reference to the production of the scroll Jeremiah dictated to Baruch (see also Jer. 45.1). In Zech. 8.9, then, 'from the mouth of' suggests words written from dictation (as it does in Ezra 1.1) and much later read out 'on the day the foundation of the house of the LORD was laid'. The former prophets are portrayed as being present in the Persian period in the Twelve as they are present for the reader of the book—in the form of written words.

Such a presence, however, does not suggest a silent reader (like a contemporary reader of the Twelve); these words are for the ear—or 'the ones hearing...these words'. Prophetic words from the past are made audible by reading them aloud to later communities (see my *Heard But Not Seen*, pp. 45-59).

The time when the words of the former prophets were read aloud, that is, when 'the foundation of the house of the LORD of hosts was laid to rebuild the temple', can be linked with the time of Haggai as portrayed in the Twelve. Language in the larger context of Zech. 8.9-13 is reminiscent of the language of Haggai:

1.   [T]he day the foundation of the house of the LORD of hosts was laid to rebuild the temple' is reminiscent of Hag. 2.18, which concerns 'the day that the foundation of the LORD's temple was laid'. Indeed, the opening of Haggai emphasizes that the time has come 'to rebuild the LORD's house' (Hag. 1.2). These two phrases in Haggai pick up all the words of the phrase in Zechariah.

2.   The phrase 'let your hands be strong' (Zech. 8.9, 13) echoes the thrice repeated 'take courage' uttered to Zerubbabel, Joshua and the remnant of the people (Hag. 2.4). The same Hebrew verb is used in Hebrew for 'be strong' and for 'take courage'.

3.   The comforting 'Do not be afraid' (Zech. 8.13, cf. 8.16) is the same phrase used to comfort Zerubbabel, Joshua and the remnant of the people in Hag. 2.5.

4.   The reference to the community as 'the remnant of this people' (Zech. 8.11, 12, cf. 8.6) echoes the address of Haggai to 'the remnant of the people' (Hag. 1.11, 14, 2.2).

5.   The phrase 'you will be a blessing' in Zech. 8.13 is paralleled by the similar phrase, 'I will bless you' in Hag. 2.19.

6.   The description of the days before the foundation of the temple was laid as a time when there 'were no wages for people or for animals;' recalls similar language about those who earn wages in Hag. 1.6 and the deprivation of both humans and animals in Hag. 1.11.

7.   The envisaged change in prosperity, '[T]here shall be a strong sowing of peace; the vine shall yield its fruit, the ground shall give its produce, and the skies shall give their dew' recalls similar language in Haggai about things withheld in the past

(Hag. 1.10-11) as well as the envisaged prosperity now that the foundation of the temple has been laid (Hag. 2.18-19).

In the Twelve, then, the prophets are from former times. They appear in Zechariah's (and Haggai's) world as written words and as law or Torah. The beginning of temple construction, the time when the foundation of the temple of the LORD was laid, marks the occasion for reading these prophetic words. In many ways the words of the prophets are a written justification of the LORD's actions in the past. The appearance of messengers in the Twelve marks the end of prophecy. Prophets proclaim the LORD's word in a world in which the LORD is absent, and this is reflected in the lack of fertility and prosperity. Messengers are associated with the LORD's presence in the rebuilt temple and with a marked contrast to the past.

According to the passage under consideration, there will be wages for people and for animals (8.10); there will be safety from the foe; there will be 'a sowing of peace' (8.10) so that the vine will produce its fruit, the ground will give its produce, and the skies will give their due (8.12). The remnant of the people will now possess all these things (8.12). It is a time to be strong and not to fear for although the house of Judah and the house of Israel had been 'a cursing among the nations', the LORD will now save them and they will become a blessing (8.13). The language 'be strong' and 'do not be afraid' is used to comfort a warrior before battle (see my *Fear Not Warrior*). Such language recalls the LORD's warfare against the nations—a recurring theme in the earlier part of the book (see Zech. 1.21; 2.9; 6.1-6). It also anticipates the final chapter of Zechariah.

The other language used here raises interesting questions. What is meant by 'the house of Judah' and 'the house of Israel' (8.13)? And what does it mean that those who have been a curse among the nations will now be a blessing? While 'house' may be used in the sense of a dynasty, the phrases 'the house of Israel' and 'the house of Judah' in the present context can only refer to temples. Temple construction has been the subject of the immediate context (8.9), and the references to houses also draw us back to the beginning of Zechariah's long answer to the question posed by men from THE HOUSE OF EL (Bethel) who came to ask questions of the house of the LORD (7.2-3). Given the larger literary context, the house of Israel refers to 'the house of El' and 'the house of Judah' to 'the house of the LORD', the temple in Jerusalem. The house of Israel and the house of Judah will be changed from a curse to a blessing (8.13). It is significant, however, that the remaining part of the answer focuses only on the house of Judah (8.15, 29). Although the LORD used

to speak through his messenger to Jacob at Bethel, the status of the the
house of Israel (Hos. 12.4) has changed. The men of THE HOUSE OF EL
must come to the house of the LORD to enquire of the priests and
prophets. From the beginning of Zechariah's answer, Bethel, 'the house
of Israel', is given a secondary standing to the house of the LORD.

What does it mean to be 'a cursing [or curse] among the nations?'
(8.13). The answer can best be seen when this passage is read in light of
Jer. 29.22-23.

> On account of them [Ahab and Zedekiah] this curse [or cursing] shall be
> used by all the exiles from Judah in Babylon: 'The LORD make you like
> Zedekiah and Ahab, whom the king roasted in the fire.'

This passage suggests that Ahab and Zedekiah have been used in a
formula for making curses. In the same way it is possible to understand
that the house of Israel and the house of Judah have been used by the
nations in formulas of cursing—The LORD make you like the house of
Judah [or, the house of Israel] whom the LORD...' The calamities that
befell these two houses made them the subject of cursing formulas. In
the future, however, they would be used in formulas of blessing.

As this part of Zechariah's answer comes to a close, it is important to
see, as indicated above, that it centres only on the house of Judah which
the LORD will now treat with mercy instead of anger. The LORD had
planned to bring disaster on the house of Judah because the 'fathers
provoked the LORD to wrath' by failing to heed the words of the former
prophets. This theme has been encountered since the beginning of
Zechariah (see 1.2; 7.12). Now, however, the LORD plans 'to do good to
Jerusalem and to the house of Judah' (8.15). The members of the remnant of the community are charged to do the things their fathers refused
to do.

> 'Speak the truth to one another, render in your gates judgments that are
> true and make peace, do not devise evil in your hearts against one another,
> and love no false oath; for these are things that I hate,' says the LORD
> (Zech. 8.16-17).

These instructions mirror what the earlier words of the former prophets
had proclaimed to the fathers (7.9-10), although they are not identical in
detail. This link with what the former prophets had proclaimed is suggestive of how the words of the former prophets can become Torah or
teaching for the community. The reference to 'false oath' uses similar
vocabulary to the 'swearing falsely' in scene 6 (Zech. 5.4). Indeed, these
instructions about living in the present, the time when the temple has
been rebuilt, resonates with scenes 6 and 7 concerning the restoration
of the social order.

The Answer Continues: The Future (8.18-23)

The answer now turns from the present to the future. In doing this, it returns to the issue of fasting (8.18-19) with which it began (7.5). The focus is on fasts to be held in the fourth, fifth, seventh and tenth months. In the beginning of his answer Zechariah turned Bethel's question from 'mourning and practising abstinence' to 'fasting and lamenting' (compare 7.3 with 7.5) and at the end of his answer he turns the issue of fasting and lamentation to 'seasons of joy and gladness and cheerful festivals'. The emphasis in this part of the answer is on the house of Judah, the house of the LORD. In the course of the response to the question from Bethel the focus has come to centre on this house, giving it superior status although both 'the house of Judah and the house of Israel' had been a cursing among the nations (8.13).

The future envisaged in 8.20-23 is no longer centred on 'the remnant of the people' but on 'the nations', reminding the reader that the LORD is 'the master of the whole earth'. Like the suggestions of the imagery Zechariah had seen in the temple (4.14; 5.3, 6; 6.5), the close of Zechariah's answer focuses on 'the whole earth'. The 'peoples' and the 'inhabitants of many cities' will invite each other 'to appease the face of the LORD' and 'to seek the LORD of hosts' (8.20-21). This nicely rounds off the first part of Zechariah's answer. It indicates that what the men of Bethel had done when they came 'to appease the face of the LORD' will be enacted by peoples everywhere. As if to underscore the point in 8.22 'peoples' becomes 'many peoples' and 'inhabitants of many cities' becomes 'strong nations'. They will come 'to seek the LORD of hosts and to entreat the favour of the LORD'. The house of the LORD in Jerusalem will become the focus of the entire world of peoples, cities and nations.

The universal theme builds even to the very last verse (8.23). We are told, '[T]en men from nations of every language shall take hold of a Jew, grasping his garment and saying, "Let us go with you, for we have heard that God is with you"'. These words, addressed to 'the remnant from Babel' (see 1.7 and 6.10), resonate with the story of the Tower of Babel (Gen. 11.1-9), highlighting the universality of what is pictured here. More importantly, what 'the men from nations of every language' say they have heard, 'God is with you', recalls the very first words the messenger of the LORD, Haggai, spoke, ' "I am with you," says the LORD' (Hag. 1.13). Even the use of *God* by the nations—'we have heard that God is with you'—recalls Haggai 1.13. In the two verses bracketing the first time the messenger spoke (1.12 and 1.14), it is said of Zerubbabel,

Joshua and the remnant of the people that the LORD is *'their God'*. When the nations come to Jerusalem grasping the garment of a Jew, the LORD will also be *'their God'* (8.23), the God of the nations.

The whole of Haggai and Zechariah thus far has presented a world in which 'the LORD is with you', that is, present with you in the temple in Jerusalem. Haggai and Zechariah are his messengers. There is a strong monotheism in the unfolding picture of the LORD who is 'the master of all the earth', comparable to the monotheism in the Persian section of Isaiah (see, e.g., 43.11-13)—and there is an emphasis on God's presence in Jerusalem. The image of ten men grasping the garment of a single Jew suggests how numerous will be the people coming to Jerusalem.

Summary

This chapter began with a question from the men from Bethel. It was addressed to 'the prophets and the priests of the house of the LORD'. It was answered by neither a prophet nor a priest, but by Zechariah who, as the messenger of the LORD, speaks for prophets portrayed as former prophets whose words are available in writing. Zechariah speaks as a messenger of the LORD who is present in the temple in Jerusalem.

The answer began with the question from one locale, Bethel, which sent representatives to appease the face of the LORD. It ended by envisaging that this sort of inquiry will be made world-wide when people from nations of every language will come to inquire of the LORD because they have heard that God is present with the inhabitants of Judah. As was suggested by the temple imagery Zechariah saw, the LORD is 'the master of the whole earth'.

The oracles that follow are part of Zechariah's continuing answer as a messenger. The oracles lack the euphoric tone characteristic of the first part of Zechariah in which the temple was seen as the centre of the LORD's power extending over the whole earth. The oracles address the disparity between the meanings symbolized by the imagery Zechariah saw in the temple under construction and the reality when one looks beyond Jerusalem.

Zechariah 9-11
Oracle 1: All the Tribes of Israel Belong to the LORD

Reading the Oracles

Zechariah's answer to the question from Bethel (Zech. 7-8) is followed by three oracles, two in Zechariah (9.1-11.17; 12.1-14.21) and one in Malachi (1.1-4.6). It has become conventional in biblical studies to understand the two oracles in Zechariah to be secondarily related to Zechariah 1-8 and to be read as an independent unit often referred to as Deutero-Zechariah. Sometimes the two oracles at the end of Zechariah are grouped together with the oracle in Malachi which follows, and the three oracles are understood as a unit. Since I read the oracles in Zechariah and Malachi as a continuation of Zechariah 1-8, not as an independent Deutero-Zechariah, it will be important to indicate how the oracles are related to the earlier part of Zechariah.

I have read Zechariah 1-6 primarily as scenes associated with the temple under construction. Their setting was established in Haggai, in which the foundation of the temple of the LORD was laid (Hag. 2.18). The scenes involving Zechariah's interaction with messengers portray a movement from the outside world into the temple. In the temple Zechariah participates in the installation of Joshua as high priest and sees in temple imagery that the LORD is the master of the whole earth and that temple construction has consequences for the whole earth over which the LORD exercises his power. The scenes end with 'the strong ones', those who patrol the whole earth, eager to move out from the temple.

After the scenes come to a close at the end of Zechariah 6, the theme of the LORD as the master of the whole earth is sustained, but the focus is on the land surrounding Jerusalem and the cities of Judah. This land includes, of course, the area that the biblical text describes as having been Israel, before the exile. When Zechariah begins to speak as a messenger in Zechariah 7, it is significant that the question Zechariah is asked comes from Bethel (7.2-3) in Israel.

The oracles maintain this focus on the north. Indeed, all the oracles concern Israel. The first oracle makes the point that all the tribes of Israel belong to the LORD (9.1); the second oracle is 'the word of the LORD concerning Israel' (Zech. 12.1); and the third oracle is 'the word of the LORD to Israel in the hand of Malachi' (NRSV has 'by' for 'in the hand of').

Since the oracles are given no date, I read them as being associated with Zechariah's answer to the question from Bethel. Each of these oracles is a 'word of the LORD' concerning Israel, the locale of Bethel. The oracles are attached to the last scene involving the question from Bethel, just as sayings of the LORD are attached to earlier scenes (1.14-17; 2.6-12; 6.9-14).

I understand these oracles to be written texts. That the oracles are written helps explain how 'the word of the LORD' can be 'in Hadrach', a city in the north. Because it is written, it can be carried there. In the other two places in which oracles occur in the Twelve (Nahum and Habakkuk), oracles are clearly written words. In Nahum, the 'oracle concerning Nineveh' is understood as 'the book of the vision of Nahum of Elkosh' (Nah. 1.1). Secondly, the oracle that Habakkuk the prophet saw (Hab. 1.1) is to be written down on tablets so that a reader may run with it (Hab. 2.2). That the oracles at the end of the Twelve can also be understood as written documents is evident from Mal. 1.1 where the oracle is understood as 'the word of the LORD to Israel in the hand of my messenger'. As I noted in scene 9, 'in the hand of' signifies something written and carried in the hand.

The Oracles in Zechariah (9.1-11.17 and 12.1-14.21): Their Setting

How do the oracles in Zechariah relate to Zechariah's answer to the question posed from Bethel? I understand the backdrop of the oracles to be the question the LORD poses in 8.6 about the future. What the LORD has been saying about the future in his answer to the question from Bethel does not reflect present realities. (The disparity between present realities and expectations is indicated elsewhere in Haggai and Zechariah; see Hag. 2.1 and Zech. 4.10.) The oracles, therefore, are an attempt to provide an answer to a question such as, 'How can these things be?' Indeed, even as a contemporary reader of Zechariah, I would wish to raise a question like this. The promised future does not appear to match the existing situation. Riders have gone out to patrol the four corners of the earth (1.11; 6.7), but one wonders whether 'the whole earth [still] remains at peace' (1.11) and whether the LORD is 'master of the whole earth' (4.14; 6.5). Why can the spirit of the messenger be at ease about the north country (6.8)? Some may have escaped from Babylon, but it is only 'the remnant of this people' (8.6, 11, 12), of which only four are identified by name (6.10, 14), and one wonders whether

Jerusalem will ever be 'inhabited like villages without walls' (2.4, 8.5). Joshua, the high priest and Zerubbabel, the governor, may be imaged in the lampstand as spikes of grain, that is, as religious and political leaders associated with temple construction 'standing beside the master of all the earth' (4.14). But since they are never given a voice in Zechariah, one also wonders whether this envisaged role of religious and political leadership associated with the temple is hyperbole. Why does Joshua the high priest not speak when the men from Bethel come to inquire of the priests and prophets (7.3)? How can a governor, in a world where Darius is king, have the power envisaged for Zerubbabel by both Haggai and Zechariah (see Hag. 2.20-23; Zech. 4.6; 6.12-13)? These are only several of a myriad of similar questions that might be posed. The LORD's own question raises the issue of plausibility. The oracles are an attempt to address that question of the difference between current circumstances and the envisaged future. Ironically, although the time of the prophets was presented as a time of waiting (see Hab. 2.3), it may still be necessary to wait even after the time of temple completion when the LORD was to have been the master of the whole earth. Things are not what they were expected to be. The outcomes expected to arise from temple construction are yet to eventuate.

To read the oracles which address the disparity between present realities and future expectations is a problem for those modern readers, so far removed from the world in which the text of Zechariah originated. The author(s)/compiler(s) of Zechariah clearly shared with the intended readers/audience an understanding of their world that now eludes us. Details are sometimes given, as in the beginning of the first oracle, about specific places (9.1-8), but the significance of these places is now obscure. Particular individuals, such as the 'worthless shepherd' in 11.17 seem to be highlighted in some passages. While an original reader may not have had trouble understanding the significance of these specific places and this particular individual, contemporary readers lack the information brought to the text by its intended audience. References to those persons, places and events may have played a prominent part in generating the rhetorical power of these oracles, but it is problematic to look behind these oracles to find specific persons, places and events. My strategy for interpreting the oracles, therefore, will be to read them in relation to the preceding literary context. How do the oracles address questions about the seeming implausibility of the restored world that we have seen through the eyes of Zechariah and heard in the words of the LORD accompanying what Zechariah has seen?

The whole of Zechariah has been constructed with question and answer. The LORD posed questions in 1.1-6 to the community, and the

answers could be found in what the former prophets proclaimed. The
questions Zechariah poses in 1.7-6.15 are answered by the messenger
of the LORD. In 7.2-3 a question is posed to the messenger Zechariah,
and this last question is answered in part by an appeal to what the
former prophets had proclaimed (7.4-14). In 8.1-23 the LORD begins to
speak about the present and future. The two oracles at the end of
Zechariah, to which we now turn, answer the question raised by the
LORD himself in 8.6: ' "Even though it seems impossible *in the eyes of*
the remnant of this people *in those days* [NRSV 'these days'], should it
also seem impossible *in my eyes*", says the LORD of hosts?' (The NRSV
does not translate the phrase 'in the eyes of' referring to the remnant
community, nor 'in my eyes' referring to the LORD, but I think that
translation of the phrase is important, since it indicates a transition in
the text from Zechariah lifting up his eyes and seeing to the LORD's
eyes.)

The LORD is raising the question about the difficulty of the remnant
people in understanding in '*those days*'. But to what do 'those days'
refer? I interpret the phrase to refer to the future described in 8.4-5, just
as 'those days' refers to the future in 8.23, '*In those days* ten men, from
nations of every language shall take hold of a Jew, grasping his garment
and saying, "Let us go with you, for we have heard that God is with
you" '. 'Those days' are contrasted with 'these days' (8.15), the present,
when the LORD is purposing 'to do good to Jerusalem' and are also contrasted with the '*former days*' of the prophets (8.11). Those future days
are discussed in the oracles with increasing frequency (9.16; 12.3, 6, 8,
11; 13.1 4; 14.1, 4, 6, 8, 9, 20). The oracles speak about the future as a
series of days to come ('those days'): '*that day*' (9.16, cf. 9.14-15) when
the LORD will appear over them and his arrow will go forth like lightning; '*that day*' when the LORD will make Jerusalem a cup of reeling or
staggering (12.3, 4, 6, 8, 9, cf. 12.2); '*that day*' when the LORD will
pour out a spirit of compassion on the house of David (12.11; 13.1, 2);
'*that day*' when the plunder of the nations will be divided and the
nations gathered for battle in Jerusalem (14.4, 6, 8, 9, cf. 14.1); and '*that
day*' when the nations who survive shall come to worship in Jerusalem
(14.20; cf. 14.16-19). The oracles, then, are about 'those days' to come,
which seem impossible 'in the eyes of' the present remnant community.
These things are not too difficult to visualize 'in the eyes of the LORD'.
As the oracles unfold, the future—'those days'—described in more and
more detail, with fantastic sights of the future attempting to address and
compensate for discrepancies between promise and present realities.
What is seen about the future is not seen through Zechariah's eyes,
though this was a key theme in his viewing of temple imagery

(1.7-6.15); nor is it seen 'in the eyes of' the remnant community for whom seeing these things is impossibly difficult (8.6). Rather the future is seen 'in the eyes of the LORD' (8.6), a central theme of temple imagery (see 4.10).

The First Oracle (9.1-11.17): An Overview

Before considering this oracle in detail, it will be useful to look at it as a whole. This oracle concerns the return of those who were exiled from the northern kingdom, referred to as Ephraim (9.10, 13; 10.7) or as the house of Joseph (10.6). Both of these terms can be used to refer to the northern kingdom as a whole, but they may also refer to more localized areas of the north. (Ephraim refers to the northern kingdom in Isa. 7.2 and Ezek 37.16, 19, and the house of Joseph is used for the northern kingdom in 1 Kgs 11.28, Obad. 18, cf. Amos 6.6.) Ephraim is one of the twelve tribes of Israel, which together with Manasseh makes up the tribe or house of Joseph. Since Bethel is in the tribal area of Ephraim, the oracle recalls those who had come from Bethel and who had raised a question at the house of the LORD (Zech. 7.2-3), to which Zechariah responded in 7.4-8.23. (See Amos 5.6 in which Bethel is used in poetic parallelism with 'house of Joseph'.)

The oracle begins by noting that 'all the tribes of Israel' belong to the LORD (9.1). The concern is with the future in which the LORD will destroy Tyre and also the Philistine cities, some of which will attach themselves to the LORD (9.1-7). This will take place from a base in Zion/Jerusalem where the LORD will encamp to protect daughter Zion/Jerusalem (9.8). There a future king will come humbly, riding on a donkey, commanding peace among the nations (9.10). The envisaged future appears to involve the restoration of the old empire of David and Solomon, as it is portrayed in the Hebrew Bible, with its centre in Jerusalem. The emphasis is on the LORD, as warrior rather than king. In 9.11-10.12 the overarching theme is of the LORD as warrior making it possible for those exiled from Ephraim to return. Metaphorically, Judah and Ephraim are presented as the implements of the LORD's warfare against the nations.

The consequence of the LORD's military activity will be the return of those who had been exiled from Ephraim. They too will become like triumphant warriors when they return (10.7-12). The image of Gilead and Lebanon as being too small to contain them recalls the earlier scene in which Jerusalem is described as receiving returnees who will inhabit it like a city without walls (2.4-5).

At the end of the oracle, the issue of why these things have not come about is finally addressed. The problem is that the shepherds have failed to tend the flock (10.2). The language of the long prose account concerning the shepherds (11.4-17) is cryptic and offers no easy answer for readers, such as ourselves, who are not part of the original audience. The identity of the shepherds and much else about this passage is obscure. A modern reading of that passage, while acknowledging conflict between present realities and the envisaged restoration, will not be able to fill in the details of that conflict with any certainty.

The Master of the Whole Earth (9.1-8)

Because my literal translation of the Hebrew text of 9.1 varies from the NRSV, it will be useful to give my own translation of that verse. The significant differences from the NRSV are indicated by italics.

> An Oracle.
> The word of the LORD is *in* the land of Hadrach
>   and Damascus *is its resting place*.
> Because to the LORD belongs *a human eye*
>   and all the tribes of Israel.

The NRSV translates the beginning of the oracle 'The word of the LORD is *against* the land of Hadrach'. 'In' is by far the most common translation of this preposition although it can mean 'against' when it is used with verbs of hostility as, for example, in Exod. 1.10. There is no verb of hostility used in association with Hadrach or Damascus.

That the word of the LORD is *in* Hadrach and that Damascus is its *resting place* supports the notion of the portability of the LORD's word, that the oracles can be carried in the hand by readers to be read out to an audience elsewhere. The opening of this oracle is consistent with the movement out of the temple to the whole earth that characterized the end of the scenes in the temple. This is the only place where Hadrach is mentioned in the Hebrew Bible, and its association with Damascus suggests that it was in Syria (see Holladay, p. 96).

The NRSV, reasonably assuming a scribal error, emends the Hebrew word *'ādām* (human) to *'ārām* (Aram) and translates 'eye' as 'capital' (i.e. capital city). It may be, however, that the text is not in error. There are several possible meanings of the 'human eye' belonging to the LORD. There may be a play on words here. The Hebrew for 'human', *'ādām*, sounds very much like the Hebrew word for 'Aram', *'ārām,* and the text through a kind of pun may be suggesting both meanings: human eye and eye (capital) of Aram. The LORD's eye is a motif of earlier scenes. For example, in 4.10 the seven lamps with the seven lips are understood as 'the eyes of the LORD, which range through the whole earth'. In 8.6 'the eyes of the LORD' can see what is too difficult for 'the eyes of the remnant community. The pervasiveness of 'eye' imagery may impel the double use of the eye as the source of vision and as the capital of Aram. The 'eye', the capital of Aram, would be a reference to Damascus, which belongs to the LORD.

However, not only Damascus but also 'the tribes of Israel' as well as Hamath, Tyre and Sidon belong to the LORD. With the mention of the 'tribes of Israel' the oracle is turning to Israel as its central focus. Israel and Damascus are coupled here, and the connection, while it may have resonated with the original readers, eludes me. The intriguing aspect of this connection is that Damascus and Israel in other places in the Hebrew Bible are normally portrayed as being in conflict. The mention of Hamath in conjunction with the 'tribes of Israel' may be explicable in that it was one of the cities given to the tribe of Naphtali by Joshua (see Josh. 21.32) and is also a city at the traditional border of Israel to the north.

When the poem moves to the cities of Tyre and Sidon, which also belong to the LORD, it is also moving geographically from the northeast to the northwest, that is, from the perspective of Jerusalem. When the LORD's word moves to Tyre and Sidon, it becomes bellicose. This changed situation is signalled by the phrase, 'though they are very wise' (9.2), suggesting that the wisdom of Tyre and Sidon cannot save them from the LORD. Tyre's wisdom is described in 9.3 in terms of building defences (a rampart) and building up possessions (silver and gold). Silver is heaped up like dust and gold like dirt (literally 'wet clay' or 'mud'). The reference to building a rampart is alliterative in Hebrew. Ṣôr (Hebrew for Tyre) has built a māṣôr (NRSV, 'rampart'). But the word māṣôr also has other connotations. It is sometimes used in poetic texts as a word for Egypt (see Isa. 19.6; 37.25; Mic. 7.12; 2 Kgs 19.24). The significance of the allusion to Egypt will become apparent shortly.

The next verse (9.4) describes how the 'master', the LORD, is about to take possession of Tyre. Again, since my translation differs from the NRSV, I offer my own.

> Now my master is about to take possession of it,
>> and he will hurl its army into the sea
>> and it will be consumed by fire.

This verse describes the imminent destruction of Tyre. The reference to the LORD as 'my master' recalls the earlier scenes in which the LORD is identified as 'the master of the whole earth' (4.14; 6.5). As 'the master of the whole earth' the LORD is beginning to bring about what was described in the earlier scenes—plundering of the nations (2.9; cf. 6.6). He will take possession of 'silver and gold' from Tyre, recalling Haggai's reference to silver and gold filling the temple (Hag. 2.6-9) and Zechariah's collection of gold and silver from the exiles to make crowns (Zech. 6.9-14). Because silver and gold are important in the restoration, it is difficult to translate the next line as does the NRSV, 'and hurl its wealth into the sea'. The word translated 'wealth' can also mean 'army' as it does in Exod. 14.4 and 15.4. I, therefore, prefer to read this line 'and hurl its army into the sea'. Such a reading is supported by the play on words, alluded to above, in which the Hebrew word translated 'rampart', *māṣôr*, is the same as a Hebrew word for 'Egypt'. That the LORD will cast the army of Tyre into the sea resonates for the reader with the famous hymn about Egypt in Exod. 15.4, describing how the LORD cast Pharaoh's 'army into the sea'. The allusion to Egypt in the reference to rampart (*māṣôr*) now should become clear. The LORD will do to Tyre just as he had done to Egypt. The final destruction of Tyre by fire recalls Amos's earlier mention of the destruction of Tyre by fire (Amos 1.10).

With Tyre, then, the LORD as 'the master of the whole earth' begins to carry out his destruction of the nations. Why Tyre is singled out for destruction is not clear. But this lack of clarity is inevitable when we read old and alien texts such as Zechariah. The authors are (author is) unknown; the original audience is unknown; and as a result much of the knowledge shared by individuals in the world of its inception is gone forever. We can attempt to live in the literary world of a text like Zechariah, but we are always made aware that the words of the text conceal as much as they reveal about the absent world out of which they have come.

In 9.5-7 the oracle moves south to speak about Philistine cities and the LORD's actions against them. The destruction of these cities is portrayed as incomplete, and it is envisaged that a remnant of these Philistine cities will attach itself to Judah (9.7). There is a modulation from the third person to first person in these verses. Whereas the LORD is spoken about in the third person in 9.1-4, he begins to speak in the first person in 9.7. This modulation of speaking voices is characteristic of messenger speech (see, e.g., 2.5-12).

Ashkelon, Gaza and Ekron are portrayed as being terrified by what they see happening in Tyre. This language (9.5) recalls the scene involving the artisans who will cast down the horns (symbolizing the nations) 'terrifying' them (1.18-21). The calamities befalling these cities are specific: a king shall perish from Gaza, Ashkelon shall be uninhabited, and a 'bastard' (NRSV translates 'mongrel people' but see Deut. 23.3) shall settle in Ashdod. Again one senses that an original reader would have seen more in this list of specific adversities than we can know. Why are these three mentioned in particular? Why has Ashdod replaced Ekron when the list of calamities to befall these cities is presented? Part of the answer to the last question appears to be that Ekron is destined to be like a clan of Judah (9.7). But why only Ekron?

All these specific disasters to befall the Philistine cities are summarized generally as the LORD making an end to 'the pride of Philistia' (9.6), that is, an end to its wealth and its power. Similarly Tyre will be stripped of its possessions and its military power, but Philistia (or at least a remnant of Philistia) is envisaged as having a future whereas Tyre will be burned with fire. Apparently, since Philistia is prepared to become a remnant for Judah, as one of the nations who will attach themselves to Judah (2.11; 8.20-23), unclean food will be taken away: 'I will take away its blood from its mouth, and its abominations from between its teeth.' The Hebrew word translated abominations, while it can be used to refer to a foreign god (see 1 Kgs 11.5, 7, 2 Kgs 23.13, 24), is also used for unclean foods (see Lev. 7.21; 11.10, 12, 13, 20, 23, 41). The cleansed Philistia will be a remnant for 'our *God*'. The language here recalls that of Zech. 8.23. The verses having to do with Jebusite cities conclude with the notion that Ekron will be like the Jebusites, that is, the people who inhabited Jerusalem when it was taken over by David (see 2 Sam. 5.6-10; 1 Chron. 11.4-9).

The first part of the oracle concludes in 9.8 with the use of military imagery to portray the LORD as he brings to a close his warrior activities against Tyre and the Philistine cities. This part of the oracle provides a transition to the depiction of the LORD's activities to enforce peace in 9.9-17. The LORD will, like a military leader, 'encamp' (see Judg. 9.50) at his house, the temple. The encampment is for protection. An oppressor will never again overrun 'them', apparently the conquered areas that have now become 'a remnant for our God'. The last line in 9.8 'for my own eyes have seen them' recalls the 'human eye' at the opening of the oracle. That the LORD has seen what is going on in the earth, at least in Damascus and down along the Mediterranean coast, also recalls the imagery of the lampstand, which in part symbolizes 'the eyes of the LORD which range through the whole earth' (4.10)—eyes which see what is too difficult for the remnant people to see (8.6).

Commanding Peace from Zion/Jerusalem (Zech. 9.9-10)

While the opening of the oracle concerns the consequences of the LORD's military prowess against Tyre and the Philistine cities (9.1-8), these verses describe the LORD at war. This section of the oracle opens by calling on 'daughter Zion', also referred to in the poetic parallelism as 'daughter Jerusalem', to 'rejoice greatly' and to 'sing aloud'. The language here recalls the earlier words associated with scene 3, in which 'daughter Zion' was to 'sing and rejoice' because the LORD dwelt in her midst (2.10-11), and many nations would join themselves to the LORD. The present call to 'rejoice' and 'shout aloud' has to do with victory in the LORD's battle against the nations and assumes the LORD's encampment in the temple at Zion. In 9.9 the reason for celebration is suggested: 'your king will come [NRSV 'comes'] to you', a king who will be 'triumphant and victorious'. In the earlier scenes in Zechariah, Zerubbabel is depicted as a king 'who will rule on his throne' (6.13). The king's rule is characterized in 9.10, the last lines of which are almost a word-for-word quotation of Ps. 72.8:

> his dominion shall be from sea to sea,
>   and from the River to the ends of the earth.

That the LORD's dominion shall be to 'the ends of the earth' and that 'he shall command peace to the nations' (9.10) recalls earlier language about the LORD as 'the master of the whole earth' (see 1.11, 4.10, 14; 5.3, 6; 6.5). A universal role for Zerubbabel was imagined by Haggai (2.20-23) and is here suggested also; but it is the LORD, not the king, who will usher in peace to the nations,

> I [the LORD] will cut off the chariot from Ephraim
>   and the war horse from Jerusalem
> and the battle bow shall be cut off,
>   and he [the king, Zerubbabel?] shall command peace to the nations
>   (Zech. 9.10).

When the king comes, 'riding on a donkey//on a colt, the foal of a donkey' (9.9), he will be 'humble' because, recalling scene 5, Zerubbabel's victories will have been won 'not by might, nor by power, but by my spirit' (4.6).

That the king is yet to come is consistent with my earlier observations about Zerubbabel. He is mentioned increasingly frequently as the scenes come to a conclusion in Zechariah, but he is never present as a character. The oracle, which is explaining the disparity between the present and the future, suggests that his coming as king with dominion over the whole earth may have something to do with the victories forecast to take place over Tyre and the cities of Philistia. Zerubbabel is not mentioned again in this oracle. However, one can speculate that the second oracle (12.1-14.20) addresses the situation of his demise (see 12.10-14, especially v. 10).

Setting the Prisoners Free (9.11-17)

Who is the addressee in 9.11-12 is not obvious. The problem concerns the referent of the pronoun 'you', a problem compounded in the Hebrew text because the gender of the second person varies as I have indicated in the following:

> (11) As for you (fem. sing.), because of the blood of my covenant
> with you (fem. sing.),
> I will set your (fem. sing.) prisoners free from the waterless pit.
> (12) Return (masc. pl.) to your stronghold, O prisoners of hope:
> today I declare that I will restore to you (fem. sing.) double.

The pronouns 'you' and 'your' in 9.11 are feminine singular. The command to 'return' in 9.12 is masculine plural, and the 'you' in the phrase 'to you' (9.12) is again feminine singular.

One possible solution is that the feminine singular pronouns refer to a place addressed in the second person as 'daughter Zion/daughter Jerusalem' in 9.9. The masculine plural command to return is addressed to the potential inhabitants of that place, identified in these verses as 'prisoners'. However, if 9.9 is read as I have chosen to read it, that is, as a continuation of Zechariah 1-8, then the reference to 'daughter Zion/Jerusalem' is redundant. In the earlier chapters in Zechariah, the community in Judah has already heeded the command, 'return' (1.3, 6), and exiles have already escaped from Babylon (2.7, 10; 6.9-10). The larger literary context of the oracle suggests the referent to be 'the house of Joseph' (see 10.6), which will return from the nations among whom it has been scattered (10.9). The problem is, of course, that neither 'house of Joseph' nor 'Ephraim' is feminine.

One possible way of interpreting the feminine singular 'you' in 9.11 is to understand its referent not as a place but as the inhabitants identified as the 'sheep' or 'flock', a feminine singular noun in Hebrew. The 'flock' at the end of this unit (9.16) is the third person referent for the second person feminine pronoun that opens the unit (9.11). It is this community with which the Zech. 9.10 made a covenant, whose prisoners will be freed from the waterless pit, and whose prisoners of hope are summoned to return. Just as the house of Judah is understood as the Zech. 9.10's flock (10.3), so also the house of Joseph is the Zech. 9.10's flock. It is this northern flock, scattered among the nations, not the house of Judah, that is the subject of this oracle. Indeed, this flock, deserted by its shepherds (10.2) and sold and doomed to slaughter (11.1-17), will become the major focus at the end of this oracle.

Zechariah 9.11 represents a transition from a focus on Judah/-Jerusalem to a focus on the flock of the house of Joseph. It is important to reiterate here that, whereas in the scenes involving Zechariah's interaction with a messenger we saw the restoration of Zion/Jerusalem, the oracles envisage restoration of the northern kingdom. 'The blood of my covenant with you' recalls the covenant that the LORD made with all Israel and closely resembles Exod. 24.8:

> Moses took the blood and dashed it on the people, and said, 'See the blood of the covenant that the LORD has made with you in accordance with all these words.'

Because of this covenant the prisoners will be freed from 'the waterless pit'. Since the oracle refers to the northern kingdom as 'house of Joseph' later in 10.6, perhaps this is an allusion to the time when Joseph was thrown into 'the waterless pit' by his brothers (Gen. 37.24) after which he was sold to the Ishmaelites for twenty pieces of silver (37.28). Such an allusion to the story about the ancestor Joseph, may have something to do with the imagery of the shepherds who sell the flock in Zech. 11.4-17, but the relationship to that story seems to be more peripheral than central, although highly allusive.

In the oracle the call to the northern kingdom to return (9.12) matches the earlier call for those in Judah to return (1.2). In the earlier passage, the LORD had promised that if the community returned, he would return (1.2) and in response to the community's decision to return (1.6), he does return to Jerusalem (1.16). In this passage he does not promise to return (he has already returned to Jerusalem) but to 'restore' or 'cause the community to return' in numbers that will be twice what they had previously been (9.12). The word translated 'stronghold' is found only this one place in the Hebrew Bible. It seems to be used for an inaccessible place so that a translation like 'stronghold' or 'fortress' is appropriate. The peculiar use of this word may be explained because in Hebrew it is related alliteratively with Zion. Hence, the LORD encamps in Zion to protect it (9.8), and the house of Joseph is to return to its own Zionlike stronghold (9.12).

The subsequent verse (9.13) suggests how the LORD will cause this return. He will do the fighting. He has already bent Judah, a bow with which he is using the arrow, Ephraim. The imagery is important. The arrow will not be shot out from Ephraim but from Judah. The locus of power is Judah and particularly Zion, suggested by the associated imagery of the sons of Zion being wielded like a warrior's sword. Why Greece is mentioned here is not clear. What references such as this might have meant to early readers escapes present readers of the text.

The next verse (9.14) continues to present the LORD as a warrior, but here there is a change from the first person address of the LORD in the preceding verses (9.6-13) to the third person. The use of the third person matches the use of the third person at the beginning of the oracle concerning the defeat of Tyre and Sidon and the Philistine cities (9.1-5). The reference to the LORD as 'my master' (NRSV, 'LORD God', 9.14) recalls the use of 'my master' in the earlier third person account (9.4). Both parts of this oracle, then, in which the LORD is portrayed in the third person as warrior, echo the language of the earlier scenes in which the LORD is 'the master of all the earth' (4.14; 6.5).

In 9.14, the LORD is presented in the image of the storm, an image not uncommon in other Old Testament texts (see 2 Sam. 22.8-13; Hab. 3.11). While in the previous verse the LORD is pictured as shooting Ephraim his arrow from his bow Judah, in this verse his arrow is like lightning. As other commentators have pointed out, the image of the LORD sounding the trumpet (*shophar*) is unique in the Hebrew Bible. However, given the imagery of the storm, the thunder may be seen as the sounding of the trumpet—a kind of military signal (cf. Ps. 29, esp. v. 3). That the LORD will march forth in the whirlwinds of the *south* also uses imagery found elsewhere about how he will march forth from the *south* (see Hab. 3.3-4; cf. Judg. 5.4 and Deut. 33.2).

The LORD, then, as warrior, will fight to set free his flock, the prisoners of hope, from the waterless pit. He will 'protect them', literally 'fence or hedge them in'. The imagery in 9.15, suggesting that the returnees 'will devour and tread down the slingers' and 'drink their blood like wine', is gruesome, as is other imagery in the Hebrew Bible that portrays the LORD as a warrior against the nations (see, for example, Isa. 63.1-6). The literary significance of this, however, becomes clear in relation to the earlier personification of Judah, Ephraim and the sons of Zion as implements of war (bows and arrows and swords). Other texts personify arrows and swords as drinking blood and devouring flesh. For example,

> I will make my arrows drunk with blood,
> and my sword shall devour flesh (Deut. 32.42).

(See also Isa. 34.5; Jer. 46.10; Ezek. 39.17-19.) That those who drink the blood will 'be full like a bowl' and 'drenched like the corners of an altar' adds to the grotesquerie. The enemies (apparently the sons of Greece) are portrayed as sacrificial victims whose blood fills the bowls designed to collect the blood of the sacrifice (see Exod. 27.3; 38.3; Num. 4.14). The drenched corners of the altar refer to the practice of throwing the blood against the sides of the altar (see Lev. 1.5). The depiction of the

LORD's slaughter in these verses is like the behaviour of the shepherds who sell the flock doomed to slaughter (11.4-17).

This LORD's warfare will happen 'on that day' in the future when the LORD will save 'his people like a flock'. What is being pictured in the opening of this oracle is one of 'those days' to come in the future, a future that is not impossible 'in the eyes of the LORD'. This flock is, as I have indicated, the 'house of Joseph' (cf. 10.6). The identification of the people as a 'flock' or as 'sheep' anticipates a motif that will appear again in the oracle (10.2) and that will dominate the end of the oracle (11.4-17).

The LORD is designated as 'their God' on that day of return. This recalls the same designation of the remnant of the people in Judah, including Zerubbabel and Joshua, when they returned and began work on the temple (see Hag. 1.12, 14). It is important to reiterate that this oracle envisages the return of the *northern* kingdom. While Zechariah's interpretation of temple imagery in earlier scenes allowed us to see the restoration of *Judah*, this oracle focuses on the future return of *Ephraim*/the *house of Joseph*. The inherent worth of this flock is clear from the image of the people as jewels of a crown that will shine on his land.

The imagery in v. 17 concerning the grain and new wine, imagery associated with the prosperity that will be a consequence of return, recurs throughout the Twelve as indicated above in the discussion of scenes 4 and 5 in the earlier part of Zechariah. The opening phrase in the last verse of the chapter 'For what goodness and beauty are his!'—is quite ambiguous in Hebrew. Does goodness and beauty refer to what proceeds— 'the flock' as good and 'the jewels of the crown' as beauty— or to what follows, 'the grain' and 'the new wine'? Like so much that is ambiguous, especially in poetry, the verse should perhaps be understood in both senses.

Asking for Rain (10.1-2)

As a continuation of ch. 9, the command to 'ask for rain from the LORD', is addressed to Ephraim or the house of Joseph (10.6). It picks up the theme of the preceding verse (9.17), that in that day 'grain' and 'new wine' will evince fertility. Prosperity and well-being are associated with fertility that comes from the LORD, who is portrayed throughout the Twelve as providing the grain, the new wine and the oil (see Hag. 1.10-11; 2.18-19; and the imagery associated with scenes 4 and 5, Zech. 3-4). Later on in this chapter it is said that 'the LORD will answer them'. The imagery of fertility combined with the notion that the LORD will answer recalls Israel portrayed in the beginning of Hosea as Gomer, 'parched' and threatened with 'thirst' (2.3) because she did not know it was the LORD who had given her the 'the grain, the wine and the oil' (2.8). The former prophet Hosea looked to 'that day' when the LORD would say 'I will answer them' and replenish the land with grain, wine and oil (2.21-22). This oracle anticipates the imminence of 'that day' when the LORD will answer Israel, the house of Joseph.

According to the oracle, requests for rain were made by means of 'the teraphim' who 'utter nonsense', 'the diviners' who 'see lies' and 'the dreamers' who 'tell false dreams and give empty consolation'. The word 'teraphim' sometimes refers to idols (see Gen. 31.19, 34-35 and 1 Sam. 19.13, 19) but in Ezek. 21.21 is associated with divination.

> For the king of Babylon stands at the parting of the way, at the fork in the two roads, to use divination; he shakes the arrows he consults the teraphim, he inspects the liver (Ezek. 21.21; see also Hos. 3-5).

Divination is often viewed negatively in the Hebrew Bible (see, for example, Deut. 18.9-14). Dreams, understood as 'visions of the night', are understood to be bereft of any substance in other passages in the Hebrew Bible (see Isa. 29.7; cf. Job 20.8 and 33.15). Requests for rain through these means—teraphim, (divination) or dreams—will be useless because the LORD provides rain. In the presence of these sources of false hope, 'the people wander like sheep//they suffer for lack of a shepherd'. There is no-one to give them the LORD's answer or to direct them to the means by which the LORD can answer them. The teraphim, the diviners and the dreamers do not answer for the LORD. Because the community lack a shepherd, seeking answers from unreliable sources, the people wander like sheep. They have no equivalent to Zechariah in the temple in Jerusalem who is the messenger of the LORD. Even Bethel must send to the house of the LORD in Jerusalem to make requests of the LORD (7.2-3).

The shepherds who allow the sheep to wander or who shepherd a flock doomed to slaughter can be understood to be the leaders of the people, referred to both in a general sense in Zechariah and also more specifically as a particular person (11.17; 13.7). Zechariah himself is also understood to be a shepherd (11.4, 7). The passages are too cryptic to allow identification of the shepherds. While the implied author(s) and the implied audience may have understood who was meant by the shepherds, we are too far removed from the text to read it as its original audience did. What we have is a community's construction of a world in which unidentified leaders are understood as shepherds who have angered the LORD. There is also a specific reference to one of these shepherds. While the text emerges out of a real world, we are distanced from it in two ways: (1) We receive a particular construction of a state of affairs; and (2) the specific world out of which the text emerged is dimly known. What is clear, however, is that the shepherds have made it impossible for the LORD to answer the returned community (see 10.6; 13.9).

The way the LORD speaks and answers was the major concern in the earlier scenes involving Zechariah's interaction with a messenger. Those scenes established Zechariah as one sent from the LORD who could speak as a messenger. In the capacity of messenger Zechariah began to answer the representatives from Bethel, and it is in that capacity that he delivers the oracles.

The House of Judah Shall Be Like Warriors (10.3-5)

Because the shepherds have caused the people to wander like sheep, consulting teraphim, diviners and dreamers who speak 'utter nonsense', divine 'lies' and give 'empty consolation' (10.2), the LORD's 'anger is hot against the shepherds', and he 'will punish the leaders'. The word for 'leaders' in Hebrew is literally 'rams' or 'he-goats' and is used in the sense of 'leaders of the flock' (see Jer. 50.8). In some passages it can be used figuratively as it is in this passage to refer to 'leaders' (see, e.g., Isa. 14.9). The LORD's ire against the shepherds will manifest itself in making the house of Judah warriors, recalling the earlier imagery in 9.13. These three verses (10.3-5) concern strengthening the house of Judah (see 10.6) so that the LORD will save the house of Joseph (10.6-7), gathering the wandering sheep (the house of Joseph) and bringing them home from places such as Assyria and Egypt (10.8-12). Here again, then, the house of Judah is presented as playing a key role in the restoration of the north (Ephraim or the house of Joseph).

It will be helpful to make some more specific comments on 10.3-5. The LORD has already 'mustered' (NRSV 'cares for') his flock, the house of Judah. The use of the verb in the past tense makes it clear that this is a completed action. Unlike the house of Joseph, the house of Judah cannot be seen as wandering sheep. Perhaps in order to emphasise this point the Hebrew text uses a word meaning flock for the house of Judah ('*ēder*) to distinguish it from the house of Joseph referred to as 'sheep' (*ṣō'n*). This distinction is mostly preserved by the NRSV. However, the NRSV in 9.16 uses 'flock' (a different Hebrew word from the one translated 'flock' in 10.3) to translate a Hebrew word which it elsewhere translates in this oracle as 'sheep'.

In 10.4 there is a change from pastoral to military imagery. Just as military action was launched from Judah, the bow (9.13), so Judah will be made 'a proud war horse' (NRSV has 'war horses' but the Hebrew word is singular) and out of it will come 'the cornerstone', 'the tent peg' and 'the battle bow'. The word translated 'cornerstone' can be used figuratively to mean a leader (see Judg. 20.2; 1 Sam. 14.38 and Isa. 19.13), as can 'tent peg' (Isa. 22.23), and the association here of 'battle bow' with 'cornerstone' and 'tent peg' suggests that it, too, is used in this sense. Indeed the last line in 10.4 reinforces this figurative meaning: 'every commander will come out together'. Judah is again the origin of his military onslaught.

Notice that those who come out from Judah 'shall be like warriors', as the text continues to use the simile of warfare in 10.3. The image of trampling the enemy 'in the mud of the streets' is used elsewhere (see, e.g., Mic. 7.10 and 2 Sam. 22.43). That the warriors will fight because 'the LORD is with them' emphasizes the motif of divine presence that has appeared since the messenger Haggai spoke the LORD's message, ' "I am with you," says the LORD' (Hag. 1.13; cf. Zech. 8.23). Because the LORD is with the warriors, they will shame those mounted on horses.

Before closing the discussion of these verses, it will be helpful to say a few words about the change between a third and first person voice. The preceding verses (10.1-2) spoke about the LORD in the third person, continuing the third person reference to the LORD beginning in 9.14. However, at the beginning of 10.3, there is a first person speaker. This poses the question of the speaker's identity, especially since the LORD is again referred to in the middle of v. 3 in the third person and will not speak again in the first person until 10.6. This modulation between first and third person is also typical of the previous chapter, which is part of this same oracle (see, e.g., 9.7). The alteration between first and third person address is indicative of the language of oracle, particularly an oracle delivered by a messenger so closely identified with the LORD (see the discussion above concerning 8.3); when the messenger speaks, the LORD speaks. (See also the discussion above on Zech. 2.6-12). In such a situation there obviously can be a modulation from language that speaks about the LORD in the third person to language in which the LORD is speaking in the first person. It is the LORD, then, who speaks in the first person in 10.3.

Saving the House of Joseph (10.6-7)

A running motif of the oracle has been that the LORD will use Judah as a weapon in his military arsenal to effect the restoration of Ephraim. Whereas the previous verses spoke about the issuing of the LORD's warlike activity from Judah, vv. 6-7 concern how the LORD 'will bring back' Ephraim (10.6). A more literal translation of these words is 'will cause [Ephraim] to return'. (The Hebrew word is difficult because it seems to combine the spelling for two Hebrew words: one meaning 'to cause to return' and the other 'to cause to dwell.' I have followed the NRSV in understanding the word to mean 'to cause to return', since this word clearly occurs in 10.10. However, since returning and dwelling are such closely related ideas in Zechariah, the word may indeed be interpreted to carry both meanings.) In the opening of Zechariah the remnant community made an active decision to return, a decision which resulted in the LORD's return to the temple. But the point of the oracle is that the LORD will actively bring about the return of Ephraim. What seems to be hindering this restoration is Ephraim's 'lack of a shepherd' so that the people 'wander like sheep' (10.2).

The distinction between the house of Judah and the house of Joseph is clear in 10.6, which can be translated,

> I will make the house of Judah strong [or mighty],
>   and will bring the house of Joseph victory.

The word translated 'make strong' is the verbal form of a noun that has the meaning of 'warrior' (see 10.7) The verb, then, has the connotation of making someone like a warrior, and the house of Judah is described in just this way in the preceding verses in which it is said that the LORD will make the house of Judah 'like his proud war horse' (10.3). The whole of the oracle up to this point has been to suggest that Judah's power will bring victory to the house of Joseph.

The strengthening of the house of Judah and giving victory to the house of Joseph will eventuate in the return or restoration of Ephraim (or house of Joseph), envisaged in these verses and in the rest of ch. 10. The reasons that are given for the LORD's restoration of the house of Joseph echo the words of the LORD in the first scene concerning the return of Judah. The LORD's positive statement in ch. 10, 'I have compassion on them', resonates with the question the messenger of the LORD asked in 1.12, 'How long will you withhold compassion (NRSV 'mercy') from Jerusalem and the cities of Judah?' The LORD's further remark that 'they will be like I had not rejected them' (10.6) mitigates the situation in much the same way as his 'I was only a little angry' in 1.15. More significant, however, is the LORD's remark that 'I will answer them' (10.6), which highlights an issue implied by the oracle. Immediately after the first scene, when it becomes clear that the LORD does have compassion on Jerusalem and the cities of Judah, we are told that 'the LORD answered the messenger who talked with him with gracious and comforting words' (1.12). But in relation to the impending restoration of the house of Joseph, how will this promise of an answer be fulfilled? Who will answer Ephraim (the house of Joseph)? Clearly not the teraphim, the diviners or the dreamers whose words deceive. Ephraim wanders like sheep without a shepherd. In the context of the larger whole of Zechariah, the answer can only be when the LORD speaks through a messenger—a shepherd like Zechariah.

Upon returning, Ephraim will be like a warrior, recalling the portrayal of the house of Judah as a warrior (10.3-5), and the hearts of the people 'shall be glad as with wine, their children shall see it and rejoice, their hearts shall exult in the LORD'. The language here recalls language from the earlier scenes that typify the return of daughter Zion; return from Babylon also calls for rejoicing (see 2.6-12, esp. v. 10).

Ephraim Returning (10.8-12)

This unit envisages the return of Ephraim. At the end of the envisaged return in 10.12, the LORD, referring to himself in the first person, says, 'I will make them [Ephraim] strong in the LORD'. A similar thing was said earlier about the house of Judah that had already returned or, to use the language of the oracle, that the LORD 'had mustered' (see the discussion of 10.3 above). In 10.6 the LORD says, 'I will make strong the house of Judah', and this is repeated in 10.12. (The same word is used in Hebrew although the NRSV translates it 'strengthen' in 10.6 and 'make strong' in 10.12.) The oracle makes clear that what Zechariah saw in the restoration of Judah is also envisaged for Ephraim. Both will be made strong when they have returned.

The word that the NRSV translates 'I will signal' (10.8), seems, in most of its uses, to have the notion of making a hissing noise as an expression of derision. See, for example, 1 Kgs 9.8; Zeph. 2.15; Mic. 6.16; Ezek. 27.36 and Lam. 2.15-16. In two places in Isaiah, it is used in the sense of 'to whistle' (Isa. 5.26; 7.18); the LORD whistles 'to the ends of the earth' (5.26) or to Assyria and Egypt (7.18) as a signal to come and bring destruction on his people. Here, however, the LORD is whistling to far away countries (10.9), to Egypt and Assyria (10.10-11)—not to call enemies from those places but to signal his people to return.

To 'gather them' (10.8) reintroduces the imagery of vegetation and agriculture. The word 'gather' is associated with gathering grain (see Gen. 41.35, 48) and fits the present context in which the LORD says, 'I have scattered them among the nations' (10.9) because the Hebrew word translated 'scattered' is often used in the sense of 'scattering or sowing seed' (see, for example, Gen. 47.23). The image suggests that what will be gathered are the children of those whom the LORD had scattered and who had taken root in far countries (10.9). That this scattered seed will return (10.9) resonates with the return to Judah of the fathers and the offspring who constituted the remnant of the community (see Zech. 1.1-6). The claim that 'they will remember me' not only recalls Zechariah's name, THE LORD HAS REMEMBERED, but also suggests that when they do remember and return (10.9), the former prophets will be important for remembering the past. We are reminded again that Zechariah's answer to this northern community in chs. 7-8 made references to what the former prophets had proclaimed. The oracle about the restoration of Ephraim, then, achieves clarity when it is read in the context of the earlier part of Zechariah, which speaks about the restoration of Judah.

Ephraim has been 'scattered' among the nations (10.9) just as the LORD had scattered Judah (see 1.21), but the LORD will redeem Ephraim (10.8). This imagery recalls how the LORD redeemed Israel when he delivered the people from slavery in Egypt (Deut. 7.8), and the description of that redemption in 10.11 clearly recalls Israel's liberation at the sea (10.11). When the LORD causes Ephraim to return from the land of Egypt and gathers the people from Assyria, there will be no room for them in the land (10.10). Again we are reminded of Judah's restoration; the city of Jerusalem would not be able to contain the people, and would be like a village without walls (2.4). The new land that will accommodate the people is suggested by the reference to Gilead and Lebanon (10.10). While the land of Gilead in the transjordan had, according to the Pentateuchal story, been allotted to the tribes of Gad and Reuben and half of the tribe of Manesseh (Num. 32.33), Lebanon was never inhabited by Israelites. Ephraim will burst out from its traditional boundaries just as Judah was envisaged to do.

The return in 10.11 is described in language that is reminiscent of the exodus from Egypt. Such imagery is used elsewhere to speak about return (e.g. Isa. 43.2, 16-17). But the language also recalls the reference to the destruction of Tyre and the Philistine cities with which the oracle opened. First, in the phrase, 'they will pass through the sea of distress', the Hebrew word for 'distress', ṣārâ, is related alliteratively with Tyre, ṣôr and rampart (Egypt), māṣôr in 9.3. Secondly, while not so clear in English translation, the phrase translated by the NRSV, 'and the waves of the sea shall be struck down' is a near repetition of the phrase in 9.3 translated by the NRSV, '[the LORD] will hurl its army into the sea'. In both places the phrase contains three words in Hebrew, the first two of which are identical, 'He will cast [or throw] into the sea'. The object of the verb in 9.3 is 'army' (NRSV, 'wealth') and in 10.11 'waves', or possibly 'a heap of stones'. The word can have both meanings in Hebrew. Thirdly, the verb in the phrase 'all the depths of the Nile are dried up' is the same as the verb in the phrase 'and Ekron because its hope is dried up' (9.5).

Such a link with the beginning of the oracle suggests that return from distant lands such as Assyria and Egypt will be made possible when the returnees return or pass into the land on the return to Gilead and Lebanon. At any rate 'the pride', that is, the arrogance of Assyria will be laid low and the 'sceptre', that is the 'authority' of Egypt will depart.

As I have indicated above, when the house of Joseph returns, the LORD will strengthen them (10.12) just as he strengthened the house of Judah (10.6). To summarize this chapter, then, the LORD has mustered his flock, the house of Judah. He will strengthen the house of Judah (10.6) and in so doing make the house of Joseph victorious and make its return possible. When the house of Joseph returns, the LORD will strengthen the people. They will then 'walk in the name of the LORD'. In Hebrew, the form of the verb 'to walk'—also used in the patriarchal stories to connote walking throughout the land (see Gen. 13.17)—seems to indicate here that the house of Joseph will move freely in the land.

The Mighty Have Fallen (11.1-3)

These three verses give dramatic expression to the theme of the LORD's strengthening of the house of Joseph through the destruction of the powerful. The LORD orders the doors of Lebanon to open so that fire will enter and destroy the cedars. The phrase 'cedars of Lebanon' is used elsewhere to stand for the proud and lofty, often powerful kings (2.13; 14.7; Ps. 29.5); here it represents the haughty, the mighty nations and their leaders. However, the reference to Lebanon in Zechariah 11 has a second purpose—to locate the place of return. Lebanon is ordered to open its doors so that the powerful 'cedars' will be destroyed, but also so that the returnees can come in (cf. 10.10 in which the LORD promises to bring the scattered people to Lebanon). The imperatives to the 'cypress' and the 'oaks of Bashan' to wail sustains the image of the trees as symbols of ruling power (see Isa. 2.13 and Judg. 9.8-15) and communicates the grievous ruin of what the NRSV renders as 'glorious trees' (11.2). The word used to refer to trees here metaphorically suggests majestic kings (cf. Ps. 136.18), powerful nations (cf. Ezek. 32.18), and in one instance, leaders who are also called shepherds of the people (cf. Jer. 25.34-36).

The relationship between 11.2 and 11.3 is interesting. The twofold

command, 'wail' in v. 2 is matched by the twofold 'listen' in v. 3. It is as
if the command to wail has been followed immediately by the sound of
wailing. The wailing of the shepherds (the leaders) is because their
'glory' is despoiled. 'Glory' translates a word in Hebrew that can mean
'cloak or mantle' and is sometimes used as a symbol of royal power (see
Josh. 7.24 and Jon. 3.6). 'Lions' can be used for kings or princes (Nah.
2.12 and Ezek. 19.5-6), and in Prov. 19.12 and 20.2 it is said that the
anger of a king is like the roaring of a lion. The lions, then, also represent the leaders who roar because 'the pride of the Jordan is destroyed'.
The word for 'pride' is the same word used in 10.11 in the phrase 'the
pride of Assyria' and should be understood here also to indicate the
arrogance or the pride of leaders.

The Worthless Shepherd (11.4-14)

I have already indicated that this passage concerning the shepherds is
rather cryptic. In fact, from v. 4 to the end of the chapter, metaphors
abound, and the text is richly allusive—but the import of the metaphors
and also the reference points for the allusions are virtually inaccessible
to a contemporary reader. The grim development of events suggests a
peculiar logic now impenetrable. The baleful humour is recognizable as
sarcasm but is difficult to appreciate.

In this chapter, the LORD orders Zechariah to become a shepherd
to the doomed sheep of uncaring shepherds. In his role as shepherd,
Zechariah destroys three other shepherds—but then he turns against the
sheep themselves, abandoning them to certain death. After breaking one
of his two staffs—each of which has explicitly symbolic meaning—he
asks for a shepherd's wages from the traders in sheep. He is offered an
insulting amount that he casts to the 'potter' or 'artisan' (NRSV 'treasury') in the temple, then breaks the second staff. The chapter closes
with indications of complete destruction, first the image of a shepherd
who will devour his own sheep and then a curse on the worthless
shepherd. Who and what is 'the worthless shepherd'? There are no satis-
factory answers for the contemporary reader. Nevertheless, an explora-
tion of the imagery, symbolism and tenor of the oracle suggests the
sharpness of the contrast between the anger and disappointment represented by this oracle and the earlier joy and confidence in the presence
of the LORD in the rebuilt temple.

Chapter 11.4-14 begins with Zechariah speaking in the first person,
'Thus says the LORD my God'. What the LORD says is a command to
Zechariah, 'Be a shepherd of the sheep doomed to slaughter' (11.4). The
oracle here is a variation on the theme of the people wandering like

sheep because they lack a shepherd (10.1-2). The sheep (people) are described as being purchased for slaughter.

The passage implies that purchasing sheep is an offence that should incur guilt but instead goes unpunished (11.5). The same sort of punishable offence is implied by those selling the sheep who say, 'Blessed be the LORD, for I have become rich' (11.5). The reference to the wealth made from selling the sheep anticipates and is in contrast with the reference to the paltry sum that Zechariah was paid for his services as a shepherd (11.12-13).

These sheep do have shepherds, but their shepherds have no pity on them (11.5), that is, the sheep (people) have no shepherd who is carrying out the duties expected of a shepherd. The call for Zechariah to be a shepherd of the sheep who have incompetent shepherds recalls the earlier passage (10.2-3) in which the shepherds are portrayed as remiss in their responsibilities.

It is probably not possible to see a direct analogy between the LORD's imperative to Zechariah to become the shepherd of the doomed flock, accompanied by his condemnation of the traders and shepherds in vv. 4-5, and the words of the LORD in v. 6, in which the association is evoked by the final clause only: 'and their own shepherds have no pity on them'. The first person words of the LORD in 11.6 are: 'I will not again have pity on the inhabitants of the land.' (NRSV translates 'earth' not 'land'. The word can mean both the earth in general or land, i.e. a specific region or area. The larger context of the oracle suggests the translation 'land'). The opening of the oracle (9.1-8) concentrates on the land around Judah and Israel. Even when passages speak about subduing mighty powers such as Assyria and Egypt, the goal is to bring the exiles back to the land of Gilead and Lebanon (10.10). The sheep are associated here with the 'inhabitants of the land'. Again in the first person, the words of the LORD are a threat of overwhelming proportions: 'I [the LORD] will cause each human being to fall into the hand of his neighbour and into the hand of his king and they will devastate [literally, 'beat', or hammer into pieces'] the land, and I will not rescue anyone from their hand' (11.6). To cause someone to 'fall into someone else's hand' suggests handing someone over to the enemy (see 2 Sam. 3.8). Buying and selling 'sheep' may suggest gaining wealth by delivering up individuals into the hands of the enemy. The crimes that go unpunished are like those outlined at the beginning of Amos, which concern this same land although portrayed at an earlier period of time (Amos 1.2–2.3).

In 11.7 Zechariah carries out the command given in 11.1. He says, 'I became the shepherd of the sheep doomed to slaughter'. The phrase

translated in the NRSV, 'on behalf of the sheep merchants [or traders]'
results from an emendation of the Hebrew text. A more literal translation of the Hebrew text would be, 'therefore, the poor ones of the
sheep'. (See the TANAKH translation, 'for those poor men of the sheep'
and KJV, 'verily the poor of the flock'.) The emendation is not a difficult
one. It simply requires the compression of two Hebrew words. But the
simplicity of the emendation may suggest another way of understanding
this text. For those who read the text in Hebrew, especially an un-
pointed or unvocalized text, as its original readers did, both meanings
are there in this play on words. In the following reading I want to
preserve this ambiguity.

The phrase, 'therefore [or 'for'] the poor ones of the sheep' is a link
back to the first time the sheep lacking a shepherd are mentioned in the
oracle (10.2). The verb 'suffer' in the phrase, 'they suffer for lack of a
shepherd' (10.2) uses the same word root as the word translated 'poor
ones' in 11.7. The ones who have 'become poor' or are 'bowed down'
for lack of a shepherd in 10.2 are those for whom Zechariah has become
a shepherd in 11.7. The phrase 'sheep merchants' or 'sheep traders'
points forward to the very last verse in Zechariah (14.21) which says
that there will no longer be 'traders' or 'merchants' in the house of the
LORD. The phrase carries the double meaning that Zechariah became
the shepherd of the sheep on behalf of the sheep merchants and
therefore became the shepherd of the poor ones of the flock.

Acting in his role as shepherd, Zechariah tells us that he took two
staffs to tend the sheep: one he named Favour and the other Unity. The
image created here is of a shepherd who is dealing with two different
flocks requiring a staff in each hand. My own mental picture of this,
given the discord outlined in 11.6, is of a shepherd of flocks out of control. In the next verse (11.8) Zechariah tells us he disposed of three
shepherds in one month. What does it mean that the shepherds were
disposed of? The word can mean 'to cut off' in the sense of 'destroying
from the face of the earth' (1 Kgs 13.34, cf. Ps. 83.4). Interestingly, this
verb, which is not used frequently in Hebrew, is used in two verses to
indicate actions involving a 'messenger of the LORD': 2 Chron. 32.21
speaks about how the LORD sent a messenger to 'dispose of' or 'cut off'
'the mighty warriors, and commanders and officers in the camp of the
king of Assyria', and in Exod. 23.23 it is reported that when the messenger of the LORD goes in front of Israel the LORD will 'blot out' the
Amorites, the Hittites and the Perizzites (among others). How the shepherds were disposed is not clear, but it is interesting that Zechariah is
acting in a capacity not unlike that of other messengers in the Hebrew
Bible. The identity of these three shepherds is unknown, and there is no

clue as to why there are three shepherds. The only other place where shepherds are mentioned in this oracle is in 10.3, in which the LORD says, 'my anger is hot against the shepherds' and in 11.4 where it is reported that even the shepherds have no pity on the sheep.

In 11.8 it becomes clear that the problem is not just with the shepherds, as might have appeared to be the case in 10.2. Now Zechariah says of the sheep, 'I had become impatient with them, and they also detested me'. The strife between shepherd and sheep may explain why the previous shepherds had 'no pity for the sheep' (11.5). The impression one gains is that Zechariah's shepherding involves both hopeless shepherds and hopeless sheep. It is at this point that Zechariah takes the staff Favour and breaks it, annulling the covenant he had made with all the peoples (11.10). There is the same play on words in 11.11 as in 11.7. Those watching, 'the sheep merchants/poor ones of the sheep' knew that it was the word of the LORD. The breaking of the staff Favour raises three questions: (1) What is the covenant that was annulled? (2) Who are 'all the peoples'? and (3) What is the word of the LORD? The first two questions can be answered together. Since 'peoples' can refer to nations or states, in the context of this oracle 'peoples' may refer to those peoples spoken about in the beginning of the oracle, Damascus, Tyre and Sidon and the cities of Philistia as well as Ephraim (house of Joseph). The covenant or treaty must refer to an agreement involving all these peoples, although details of that agreement are missing. The word of the LORD is what Zechariah spoke in 11.9.

> So I said, 'I will not be your shepherd. What is to die, let it die; what is to be destroyed, let it be destroyed; and let those that are left devour the flesh of one another.'

In this verse the messenger's 'I' is also the LORD's 'I'. The LORD has mustered his flock Judah (10.3), but Zechariah will not be the shepherd of these peoples.

The act of shepherding, requiring a shepherd with two staffs, is beginning to come undone. The shepherd who had become impatient with his sheep now asks for his wages. Thirty pieces of silver are weighed out for him. Zechariah then follows the LORD's directive to take the thirty pieces of silver and throw them to the 'potter' or 'artisan' in the house of the LORD. (NRSV translates 'treasury' not 'potter' or 'artisan'. But the Hebrew word, as indicated in the NRSV footnote, means 'potter' or 'craftsman' and here can perhaps refer to someone who works with silver.) The sarcastic phrase, 'this lordly price at which I was valued by them' (11.13) suggests that this was a grossly inadequate wage. It has often been remarked that the amount is equivalent to the price offered for a slave (Exod. 21.32). Perhaps one can gain perspective if one relates this to an earlier section of Zechariah. In 8.1, Zechariah indicated that the building of the temple foundation resulted in higher wages. Throughout Haggai and Zechariah, temple construction is associated with increased wealth. Perhaps, it is in this context that the sarcasm is to be understood. The LORD, responsible for the production of wealth, was only given 30 pieces of silver, the price of a slave. The notion that this was thrown to the 'artisan' achieves some clarity when read in the light of the passage concerning the exiles who returned from Babylon (6.9-14). Gold and silver were collected from them to make crowns. Perhaps the wages (30 pieces of silver) collected from those in the north were to be used for fashioning items for the temple.

As a consequence of this insulting payment of wages, Zechariah takes his second staff, 'Unity', and breaks it. This action symbolizes the breaking down of the family ties between Judah and Israel.

The opening verses of this extended passage on the shepherds gave Zechariah a directive, 'shepherd the flock' (11.4). This directive is matched at the end by a second directive to Zechariah (11.15). He is to take up the implements of a worthless shepherd. This action is apparently symbolic, like the breaking of the two staffs. What the implements are is not specified. The symbolic action signals that the LORD is raising up a worthless shepherd. He will not care for the flock. Not only will he desert the 'poor ones of the flock' (the perishing, the wandering, or the maimed) but also he will feed on 'the flesh of the fat ones, even tearing off their hoofs'. The meaning of 'tearing off their hoofs' is not clear but seems to imply that they will be totally consumed.

The oracle ends with a curse placed on this worthless shepherd. The curse is that a sword should strike his arm and right eye so that the arm is completely withered and the eye utterly blinded. The use of a sword suggests warfare and the blinding of the right eye and the withering of the arm suggest that he be made defenceless—unable to wield a sword or properly see his target.

The Shepherds and the Sheep in the Context of the Oracle

Any contemporary reader of this passage will come away knowing that there is more to this passage than can be understood. The author and the original audience must have brought to their reading a shared view of the world that would have provided answers to a number of questions: Why are three shepherds mentioned? Who are they? How did Zechariah dispose of them? Who is the worthless shepherd?

The beginning of the oracle has envisaged a future in which the house of Judah would play a major role in the return of exiles to Ephraim (also referred to as the house of Joseph). This envisaged return was seen as overflowing into the lands of Gilead and Lebanon and the surrounding areas of Syria, Tyre and Sidon and the Philistine cities. The close of the oracle presents a far different world. The covenant with all the peoples has been annulled and the family ties between Judah and Israel have been broken. The symbolic breaking of the staffs represents a shattering of what had been envisaged. One is reminded again of the rhetorical question in 8.6, 'Even though it seems impossible in the eyes of the remnant of this people in those days, should it also seem impossible in the eyes of the LORD of hosts?' Readers see through Zechariah's eyes the restoration of Jerusalem and the surrounding areas of Judah, the rebuilding of the temple, and the establishment of Joshua the high priest and Zerubbabel the governor as leaders standing beside the LORD, the master of all the earth. In answer to the question of the representatives from Bethel, Zechariah's view of restoration in 1.7–6.15 was heightened in 7–8 to the hyperbolic: the view that ten men from every nation of every language grasp the garment of a Jew and say, 'Let us go with you, for we have heard that God is with you' (8.23).

By the time the reader has finished the first oracle it is clear that this grand view of the future has been called into question by leaders in the community, the shepherds, who stand in opposition to 'the master of all the earth' present in the temple in Jerusalem. What the temple has gained was thirty pieces of silver, not the envisaged wealth that comes from being at the centre of power. The passages about the sheep doomed to slaughter are in conflict with the notion of restoration. The response to the failed attempt to extend the power of the temple is a second oracle that ends with language which becomes even more exaggerated and embellished. Indeed, it moves to the fantastic.

Zechariah 12-14
Oracle 2: Jerusalem and the Nations

The Second Oracle: An Overview

The close of the oracle in ch. 11 suggested that the motif of the LORD as 'the master of the whole earth' has been challenged. The LORD is no longer the 'master of the whole earth'; the restoration and union with the land surrounding Jerusalem, especially with Ephraim/the house of Joseph have broken down. The actions of both shepherds and sheep undermine the hyperbolic claims about the centrality of power in the temple in Jerusalem that were made in Zechariah's answer about the future in ch. 8 (see especially, 8.22-23). Indeed, it is precisely this issue, Jerusalem as the centre of the whole earth, that is the primary theme of the second oracle. This second oracle, however, betrays an acceptance of the current unreality of Jerusalem as the centre of power by grounding such claims in the future—in 'those days'. Claims about the days to come develop into fantastic depictions of the LORD's power as the oracle draws to a close in ch. 14.

Chapter 12 speaks about the invincibility of Jerusalem. But even this chapter suggests the wistfulness of such a world-view because it ends in mourning and grief for one who has been pierced (or stabbed). Again this passage is cryptic for it is not clear who the individual is or whether the person has been killed. Chapter 13 concerns the end of prophecy, perhaps implying that the opposition to the notion of Jerusalem as the centre of power is associated with prophecy. This passage suggests why prophecy in Zechariah is confined to former times and is seen as coming to an end. The section on prophecy (13.2-6) followed by the passage on the shepherd (13.7-9) indicate that prophets are affiliated in some way with the leaders (the shepherds) who lead the flock astray. The concluding chapter of the oracle (ch. 14) speaks about a final purging of Jerusalem, suggesting that opposition to Jerusalem as the centre of power lies not only outside (as is the case with the first oracle) but within Jerusalem itself. This final chapter in Zechariah, then, provides another perspective on the remnant community surrounding Haggai and Zechariah. After half the city is forced to go into exile (14.2), fantastic claims are made about the LORD and Jerusalem's status in the days to come.

Introducing the Oracle (12.1-2)

I read these first two verses as the introduction to the oracle, which concerns both Israel (12.1) and Judah (12.2), mentioned toward the end of the first oracle (see 11.14). Interestingly, what concerns both Israel and Judah are not internal matters but is the centrality of Jerusalem in the days to come. What will take place in Jerusalem will concern both Israel and Judah, and furthermore, Jerusalem will play a central role in the destiny of the whole earth.

Since I do not read the oracle as being '*against*' Judah (as does the NRSV, 12.2), but '*concerning*' Judah, I will offer my translation of the beginning of the oracle.

> An oracle, the word of the Lord concerning Israel, a saying of the Lord who stretched out the heavens and founded the earth and formed the human spirit within:
> 'Behold I am about to make Jerusalem a cup of reeling for all the surrounding peoples.'
> And also *concerning* Judah,
> 'It will be in the siege against Jerusalem.'

Notice how the oracle concerning both Israel and Judah involves Jerusalem. In the case of Israel, this means that Israel will drink from Jerusalem imagined as a cup of reeling to be drunk by the surrounding nations. The imagery here appears to indicate that Jerusalem will cause the nations to stagger like someone intoxicated. The intoxicant in the cup, however, is not wine but the LORD's wrath (see Isa. 51.17, 22). The surrounding peoples, including Israel, will stagger, having drunk of the LORD's wrath. A similar image occurs in the well known passage concerning 'the cup of the wine of wrath' in Jeremiah (see Jer. 25.15-16).

The oracle also concerns Judah, but in a different way. It will be in the '*siege*' against Jerusalem. The Hebrew word translated 'siege' is the same word in Hebrew as the word translated 'rampart' encountered earlier in 9.3 in the clause 'Tyre built a rampart [*māṣôr*]'. Understood as 'rampart' the word suggests how Judah will be involved. It will be a rampart around Jerusalem, that is, as a kind of defence.

To understand the introduction of the oracle this way suggests its relationship to the first oracle. The first oracle opened with a view of the future in a day to come (9.16) when surrounding peoples would attach themselves to Jerusalem (9.7-8). It ended with imagery about a worthless shepherd and worthless sheep, which was in sharp contrast to the earlier expectation of restoration and return. The image of the broken staffs annulling the covenant with these surrounding peoples is associated with breaking family ties between Israel and Judah. Israel, as one of the surrounding peoples, will drink from the 'cup of reeling'; Judah will be a rampart in the fortification of Jerusalem.

Before concluding the discussion of the opening of this oracle, I want to look at two phrases in more detail. First, the LORD is described as the one 'who stretched out the heavens and founded the earth and formed the human spirit within'. Such descriptions often identify the LORD in hymns of praise (see Ps. 104.2, 5; cf. Amos 9.6). More importantly, however, these descriptions of the LORD as creator of heaven and earth resonate with the restoration of Jerusalem and the building of the temple. Just as he 'stretched out the heavens' (12.1) so he will 'stretch out' the measuring line over Jerusalem (1.16). And just as he 'founded the earth' so the foundations of the temple were laid (Zech. 8.9, cf. 4.9; Hag. 2.18). The LORD 'who stretched out the heavens and founded the earth' is the same LORD who stretched out Jerusalem and laid the foundations of the temple in it.

Secondly, I want to point out the double meaning in the phrase the NRSV has translated as 'cup of reeling'. This phrase can also mean a 'shaking threshold or door-frame'. The same spelling is used in Hebrew for a word meaning 'cup' and another word meaning 'threshold or door-frame'. In a context of judgment on nations or peoples, both meanings make sense. The image of the LORD's cup of wrath making the nations stagger is found in Jer. 25.15-17, as I indicated above. (The Hebrew words for 'cup' and 'reeling or staggering' are different in Jeremiah, but the image is the same. For a similar image see Hab. 2.16.) On the image of the shaking threshold as a manifestation of the LORD's anger, see Amos 9.1. The combined imagery here suggests that those who attack Jerusalem will taste the cup of the LORD's wrath, causing them to reel and their own thresholds to shake and collapse. Such a phrase is indicative of the richness of meaning in Zechariah.

Attacking Jerusalem (Zech. 12.3)

As I have already indicated, the invincibility of Jerusalem is a central motif in this oracle. This unconquerability will be demonstrated in the future when the LORD will make 'Jerusalem a cup of reeling for all the surrounding peoples'. 'On that day' the LORD will make Jerusalem 'a heavy stone for all the peoples'. The phrase translated by the NRSV 'all who lift it will grievously hurt themselves', has the sense that 'all who lift it will seriously lacerate themselves'. The verb suggests 'cutting' or 'scratching'. The question this poses is: How can a heavy stone cause lacerations? There is no obvious answer to this question. The verb 'to lacerate' is rare and is found outside of Zechariah only in Lev. 19.28 and 21.5 where it is used in the sense of making gashes in the flesh in a context that also concerns itself with tattooing.

Distinguishing Judah (12.4-9)

The day when Jerusalem will become 'a cup of reeling' is further described, and in this description it becomes clear how Judah will be treated differently from Israel and the surrounding nations. On that day, the LORD will intervene militarily against the horse and rider (cf. Exod. 15.1) and 'strike every horse with panic, and its rider with madness'. This action will take place presumably among all the surrounding peoples. But concerning Judah (not Israel and not the peoples), 'the LORD will open his eyes' when he strikes 'every horse of the peoples with blindness'. Here again the theme of the 'LORD's eyes' reappears as it did in the first oracle (9.8, cf. 9.1) and in the temple imagery (4.10). One is reminded that what seems impossible 'in the eyes of this remnant people in those days' is not impossible 'in the eyes of the LORD' (8.16). Judah will receive the protection of the LORD who is present in the temple. His eyes symbolized in the lampstand (4.10) will protect Judah; nothing is impossible in his eyes (8.16).

Furthermore, on that day, 'the leaders of Judah will say to themselves' (literally, 'say in their heart', or 'think') that 'the inhabitants of Jerusalem have strength through the LORD of hosts, their God'. Here the oracle is picking up the theme of 'leaders' (or 'shepherds') that was important in the first oracle. (The NRSV translates 'clans', since the consonantal spelling can mean both 'clans' and 'leaders', but the vowel pointing of the MT indicates that it understands the word to mean 'leaders', and because both oracles are concerned with 'shepherds' or 'leaders' of the people, I prefer to follow the MT and translate the word as 'leaders'; the word occurs in the singular in 9.7.)

The way in which the 'leaders' of Judah are contrasted with the shepherds in the first oracle also explains how Judah is distinguished from Israel and the surrounding peoples. Judah recognizes that the inhabitants have strength through the LORD of hosts and also knows that the LORD is 'their God'. The reference to the LORD as 'their God' recalls the first time that the messenger Haggai spoke the message that the LORD was with the remnant community in Jerusalem. The narrator reminded the reader that the LORD was 'their God' (Hag. 1.13).

That day when the LORD will be 'a cup of reeling for all the surrounding peoples' is further described in 12.6. Here again the distinctiveness of Judah appears. The LORD will make the 'leaders of Judah like a blazing pot . . . and they shall devour . . . all the surrounding peoples'. This image is extended to describe how Judah will be a 'rampart' (NRSV 'siege') around Jerusalem (12.2). When Jerusalem becomes 'a cup of reeling', the leaders of Judah will be like a 'blazing pot' and a 'flaming torch'. While all the surrounding peoples are being destroyed by fire, Jerusalem will again (or perhaps better 'still') be inhabited in 'its place'. Here imagery of a fiery Judah recalls the saying of the LORD in the scene involving the restoration of Jerusalem in 2.1-5 where the LORD says that he will be 'a wall of fire' around Jerusalem. The fiery wall is Judah in a destructive blaze consuming the surrounding peoples. It is in this sense that Judah will be a rampart around Jerusalem.

Judah's special status is reflected in the next verses (12.7-9), which continue to describe that day when the LORD will become 'a cup of reeling for the surrounding peoples'. The LORD will give victory initially to the tents of Judah so that 'the glory of the inhabitants of Jerusalem may not be exalted over that of Judah' (12.7). The phrase 'tents of Judah' does not occur elsewhere in the Hebrew Bible, but it appears to be used here as a way of speaking about the inhabitants of Judah. (See Ps. 83.6-7, in which the phrase the 'tents of Edom' appears to refer to the 'inhabitants of Edom'.) Again one is reminded of the earlier scene of the young man measuring Jerusalem (2.1-5). The inhabitants of Jerusalem were seen as spilling beyond the boundaries of Jerusalem like a village without walls. In that scene the LORD spoke of himself as 'the glory' within Jerusalem. That presence however is not to be understood as exalting 'the glory of Jerusalem' over 'the glory of Judah'.

In 12.8 Judah disappears from the oracle. There is no further reference to Judah apart from a mention of Uzziah who had been king in Judah (14.5). The focus in the remainder of the oracle is on Jerusalem. The LORD 'will shield the inhabitants of Jerusalem' (12.10). While the verb translated 'shield' does mean 'to protect', it also carries the related meanings of 'to enclose, fence in, hedge in' (see Holladay, p. 63). Hence this remaining part of the oracle, especially ch. 14, is concerned with a 'fenced in' Jerusalem, protected from the outside world—the very opposite of a village without walls (2.1-5). What one is seeing on that day envisaged for the future is a city retreating behind its walls. (See 2.5, 'I will be a wall of fire all around it'.)

I read with some scepticism the promise that on that day the feeblest will be like the house of David, the house of David like God—like the messenger of the LORD—at their head. What are these similes suggesting? Is everyone's status enhanced here? The weak will be like David, and the house of David, that is the Davidic dynasty, will be like God.

Furthermore, the messenger of the LORD is equated with God himself. If, as I have argued, Zechariah is portrayed as a messenger, then his own status and the power of the house of the LORD have grown exponentially. In reading the oracles one begins to see a different picture from that seen through Zechariah's eyes in earlier scenes. One is meeting fantastic images; and the more fantastic the claims, the more unbelievable 'those days' come to appear. The oracle is beginning to emerge as a retreat from the world. Everything about what Zechariah had seen (Zech. 1-6) indicated movement outward; the LORD is 'the master of the whole earth' and the strong ones at the end of the scenes depicting temple imagery were eager to patrol the whole earth. This oracle, however, is painting a different picture. As if to withdraw from the bolder promises that he was about to plunder the nations (2.9), the LORD now says that on that day 'I will seek [or, 'try'] to destroy all the nations that come against Jerusalem' (12.9). Perhaps more was said in this phrase than was intended. We can never know. But the verse does undermine the earlier confidence expressed so consistently about the LORD's power that was associated with temple imagery.

Mourning the Deceased (12.10-14)

The next part of the oracle is quite opaque. Like the text associated with the sheep merchants (11.4-17), it moves the focus away from the future to recall an event portrayed as having taken place in the past. The passage seems to be associated with information, unavailable to contemporary readers, that both the author and the original audience brought to the text. In a future day, the LORD, according to the NRSV translation, 'will pour out a spirit of compassion and supplication on the house of David and the inhabitants of Jerusalem, so that, when they look on the one whom they have pierced [that is, one thrust through by a spear or a sword], they shall mourn for him' (12.10). It is not clear who was pierced nor when the piercing occurred. The Hebrew is even more obscure than the NRSV translation since the reference to the one pierced is in the first person (not the third person): 'when they look at me whom they have pierced' (see NEB and NIV). But what would it mean for the LORD to be stabbed by a spear or a sword? Could it have some metaphorical significance? I think that this passage will need to remain obscure. However, whatever it might mean, it is referring to some situation that stands in the way of future promise. Could there be an allusion here to the death of a figure like Zerubbabel, the person whom Haggai and Zechariah associated with restoration (see Hag. 2.20-23; Zech. 4.8-9)? Whatever the case may be, in the future 'the house of

David' and 'the inhabitants of Jerusalem' will look back in mourning.

The word for mourning here is used in contexts associated with death (BDB, p. 704), and the intensity of the mourning is indicated by the analogy of mourning for 'an only child' or a 'firstborn'. The extent of the mourning in Jerusalem is also likened to the mourning 'for Hadad-rimmon in the plain of Megiddo'. But who or what is Hadad-rimmon and why the association with the plain of Megiddo? Is Hadad-rimmon a deity? A place? Much else about this passage remains obscure. The extent of the mourning is suggested in the notion that the land will mourn family by family. But why will they mourn as separate families? Why will the women mourn by themselves? Does this refer to some special group skilled in mourning (see Jer. 9.17, 20)? Why are the four families of David, Nathan, Levi, and the Shemeites singled out? The house of David and the house of Levi appear to refer to royal and priestly families, but who exactly is meant by Nathan and the Shemeites? Nathan was a son of David (1 Chron. 14.4) and Shemei was a grandson of Levi (1 Chron. 6.16-17) but are these the individuals referred to? Does Nathan suggest the prophet in David's time? The very last line in the verse refers to all the families that are left. Four families and the others who are left does not sound like a great multitude of people inhabiting Jerusalem like a city without walls. The reader is reminded again of a remnant community (see Hag. 1.12, 14; 2.2; Zech. 8.11). The passage also suggests that expectations do not match present realities.

Cleansing Impurity and Cutting Off Idols (13.1-2a)

Not only will the LORD pour out a spirit of compassion and supplication on the house of David and the inhabitants of Jerusalem so that they will mourn the one whom they have pierced (12.12), but also on that day the LORD will open a fountain to cleanse the house of David and the inhabitants from their sin and impurity. While the word for 'sin' can be used generally for human misbehaviour, the word translated 'impurity' is interesting here, especially in its use with 'fountain'. While impurity can be understood more broadly, it can also be used for the defilement associated with contact with a dead corpse, as it is in Numbers 19. In this chapter of Numbers the word is used in the phrase 'waters of impurity' (see Num. 19.9, 13, 20, 21, cf. Num. 31.23) in the sense of waters that remove impurity. In this sense the verse rounds off the section associated with one who was slain (12.10-14) by speaking about the LORD as opening a fountain of waters to cleanse those who have been in contact with a corpse, the one whom they have slain (12.10).

But the word translated 'impurity' can also be used for 'idolatry', as it is in 2 Chron. 29.5 and Ezra 9.11. In that sense the verse marks a transition to the subsequent verse which continues to describe that day as a time when the names of the idols will be cut off so that they will be remembered no more. 'Impurity' in the sense of 'idolatry' makes one rethink the literal translation of the phrase in 13.10, 'they will look on me whom they have pierced'. Could the impurity mean that the LORD himself has been slain or wounded, at least metaphorically, by the idolatry of the land that requires cleansing? One cannot be clear about these matters. However, such a reading is in line with the undermining of divine power reflected in the oracles.

The End of Prophecy (13.2b-6)

On that day not only will there be the removal of the names of the idols, but also prophecy will end. This passage is significant for understanding the larger context of Zechariah because it helps give clarity to the confinement of prophets to former times—a feature of the earlier part of the book (see 1.4; 7.7, 12; 8.9). I have argued above that 'the former prophets' were seen in a positive light in Zechariah because from the perspective of the Persian period they meet the criterion of the true prophet as it is outlined in Deut. 18.22. What the prophets had proclaimed about the future has come about. However, such a criterion is difficult to apply to contemporary prophets, and the Twelve confines prophecy to the former times from Uzziah to Josiah. In the time of Darius, a change takes place in the way the LORD speaks. The LORD *first* spoke through the prophet Hosea (1.2), but with Haggai the LORD came to speak through messengers. This change has taken place because the LORD is now present in the temple in Jerusalem. Access is direct, and there is no waiting for confirmation.

Deuteronomy 18 also helps to clarify why prophecy is envisaged as coming to an end on that day in the future when the LORD will cleanse Jerusalem of its idolatry. While Deuteronomy outlines a criterion for identifying true prophets (Deut. 18.22), it also suggests that 'any prophet who speaks in the *name* of other gods, or who presumes to speak in my *name* a word that I have not commanded the prophet to speak— that prophet shall die' (Deut. 18.20, cf. 13.1, 5). The possibility of a prophet's speaking in the name of another god helps explain why the LORD 'will cut off the *names* of the idols from the land' (13.2). Prophets cannot speak in the *names* of other gods if the *names* of other gods are banished. Future prophets cannot speak in the names of idols because the names of idols will be cut off from the land. However, if prophets do appear, 'their fathers and mothers who bore them will say to them "You shall not live, because you speak lies in the *name* of the LORD"' (13.3). But how will these fathers and mothers know that their sons are not speaking in the name of the LORD? The only answer to this question from the perspective of Zechariah is that the LORD has ceased to speak through prophets. He now speaks through messengers, the way it used to be in the days of Jacob when a messenger met Jacob at Bethel. The LORD now speaks through his messengers in the temple in Jerusalem. In the history of the LORD's speaking in the Twelve, prophecy has come to an end and is confined to the written words of the prophets from former times. When the Twelve ends, the LORD speaks through his messenger, Malachi (MY MESSENGER). All prophets will be ashamed of their visions, and unlike Amos (Amos 7.14), they will know no ambiguity concerning their status as prophet. They will simply say, 'I am no prophet' (Zech. 13.5). In the light of this passage, the reader gains a clearer perspective on the question raised earlier about the prophets in 1.5, 'And the prophets, do they live forever?' The answer is clearly 'No'. The prophets belong to former times, and any new prophet will not live. The prophet's parents will stab him when he prophecies. The language of this denial of prophecy's validity in the future is violent and hyperbolic—and may be related to the violence directed against the one who was pierced (see the discussion below).

When this passage is read in connection with the first oracle, especially in association with the teraphim (or idols) who utter nonsense, the diviners who see lies and the dreamers whose false dreams give empty consolation (10.2), other matters achieve some clarity. Both passages (13.2-6 and 10.2) concern religious leaders and appear prior to the passages concerning a shepherd (13.7 and 10.2-3). One can begin to see that the shepherds may be diviners, dreamers and prophets. These are the ones who speak lies (10.2 and 13.3), tell false dreams (10.2) and should be ashamed of their visions (13.4). As I have been arguing, Zechariah is presenting an alternative to these ways of speaking. The LORD is present in the temple in Jerusalem where he will speak by means of his messenger. In such a situation of divine presence, the message and the messenger have become one. When the messenger speaks, the LORD speaks. The disparaging of visions or dreams (visions of the night), coupled with the appearance of messengers who appear with the construction of the temple, suggests that Zechariah is not a prophet who has visions of the night. He is a messenger speaking for the LORD, who is present with him in the temple in Jerusalem.

Having spoken generally about this passage, I now want to look more specifically at some other features in more detail. That the *names* of the idols will not be *remembered* recalls the name Zechariah, THE LORD

HAS REMEMBERED. Zechariah's name not only means that the LORD's name is remembered in Zechariah's own name, but also suggests that the LORD himself has remembered and has returned. But the LORD's name will be remembered not only in the name of Zechariah but also in the names of Joshua, THE LORD IS SALVATION and the exiles who have returned (THE LORD IS GOOD, THE LORD KNOWS, THE LORD HAS FAVOURED, THE LORD HAS TREASURED, THE LORD IS MY LIFE, 6.10, 14).

The verse concerning the prophets who will be pierced (or stabbed) if they prophecy (13.3) has links with the earlier passage (12.10) about the one who was pierced (or stabbed). One wonders whether it was the prophets who were responsible for the one who was pierced. As I pointed out earlier, the fountain that will cleanse the house of David and the inhabitants possibly concerns the impurity associated with contact with a corpse. The 'unclean spirit' refers also to ritual uncleanness (see, e.g., Lev. 5.3; 15.26). The removal of the 'unclean spirit' (along with the removal of the prophets) suggests the elimination of impurity arising from contact with a corpse and stands in contrast to another kind of spirit—the spirit of compassion and supplication that the LORD will pour out on the house of David and the inhabitants of Jerusalem (12.10).

Although the oracle will focus on Jerusalem in the last chapter (Zech. 14), the removal of the prophets is from 'the land' (13.2), that is, from the land beyond the borders of Jerusalem as spoken about in the first oracle. One is reminded again that the oracles are a continuation of Zechariah's answer to the question from Bethel addressed to the prophets and priests (7.3). This passage about the end of prophecy helps explain why it is that the prophets were given no voice in answer to the question posed.

The phrase 'hairy mantle' occurs in only one other place in the Hebrew Bible. It is used in Gen. 25.25 to refer to Esau whose entire body at birth was 'like a hairy mantle'. The allusion in Zech. 13.4 seems to be to the incident in Genesis 27 in which Jacob donned the skins of kids in order to deceive his father into thinking he was Esau (see especially, 27.1, 23). Such deception led to his stealing the birthright. The prophets, then, are described in Zech. 13.4 as acting with Jacob's deceit.

The allusion to Jacob's deceit is significant in this passage about the end of prophecy for it recalls Hosea 12 in which there is a reference to how Jacob tried to supplant his brother in the womb (12.3). This passage is the other place in the Twelve in which a messenger is mentioned, a messenger who used to speak to Jacob at Bethel (12.4). The implications of these two passages when read together are that the

LORD no longer speaks with his messenger at Bethel but at the temple in Jerusalem. To speak to a messenger of the LORD, Bethel must now send to the house of the LORD in Jerusalem. Furthermore, the LORD no longer speaks through prophets for they are as deceitful as Jacob.

The last verse (Zech. 13.6) concerns a hypothetical prophet. When he is asked on that day, 'What are these wounds between your hands', he will respond, 'the wounds I received in the house of my friends'. The phrase 'between your hands' is an idiom for chest (see 2 Kgs 9.24) and is reflected in the NRSV translation, 'wounds on your chest'. The word translated 'friends' here is regularly used in the Hebrew Bible in the sense of 'illicit lovers' and is frequently used to speak of pursuing foreign gods or idols as lovers. It is used this way in Hosea at the beginning of the Twelve (Hos. 2.5, 7, 10, 12, 13; see also Ezek. 16.33, 36, 37; 23.5, 9, 22; Jer. 22.20, 22; 30.14 and Lam. 1.19). The wounding, then, does not refer to the stabbing by the parents of their offspring who deign to prophecy on that day (13.3). Because the wounds were received before the LORD cut off the names of the idols (13.2), the wounds on the chest may suggest the wounds sustained by prophets lacerating their flesh in pursuing their 'lovers', the idols (for such a practice see 1 Kgs 18.28).

One finds in these verses, then, a persistent attack on prophets. Not only will prophecy come to an end, but anyone who dares to prophesy will be put to death by his parents. Prophets are no longer seen as speaking for the LORD but for the idols whose names will be cut off from the land. When read in the light of the earlier passages about former prophets (1.4; 7.7, 12), prophecy is understood as an outmoded way in which the LORD spoke, implying an illicit origin of any further prophesying. He now speaks through his messengers with whom he is present in the temple in Jerusalem. Any future prophet who speaks will be like Jacob, who put on a hairy mantle in order to deceive.

Striking the Shepherd (13.7-9)

This passage begins with the notion of arousing a personified sword against the shepherd. It picks up the themes of violence already present (12.10 and 13.3). The identity of the shepherd remains unclear although he is identified as a powerful man and, in the context, promotes what according to Zechariah are deception and lies. The shepherd's powerful status is in contrast to that of the sheep who are understood as 'little ones', a word in Hebrew connoting someone or something which is trifling or insignificant. The word is sometimes used to refer to the young and helpless in a flock (see Jer. 49.20; 50.45). What 'my associate' refers to here is not clear. The word appears elsewhere only in Leviticus (6.2;

18.20; 19.11, 15, 17; 24.19 and 25.14, 15, 17) in which it is used in the sense of 'neighbour' or 'fellow human being' in passages about proper social behaviour. Two of the passages in Leviticus (6.2 and 19.11) are concerned with deception against the 'neighbour'. The same verb in Zechariah is used as in the passage about the prophet who 'put on a hairy mantle in order to deceive' (13.4). Although it is possible to over-interpret on the basis of few examples of usage, the shepherd who is Zechariah's associate (13.7) may suggest a prophet who is acting against the LORD in a deceptive manner, as one practises deception against his neighbour.

The consequence of the shepherd being struck by the sword is that the flock will be scattered. The death of the strong one will affect the little ones. Notice here that this will take place in 'the whole land' (13.8). This phrase could also be translated 'the whole earth' (as I under-stood it in 4.14; 5.3, 6 and 6.5). The phrase is ambiguous, but here it seems to refer to Jerusalem and the surrounding land that is the subject of the oracles. Clearly again the more expansive world-view concerning 'the whole earth' in the early part of Zechariah is being displaced by the more modest notion of 'the whole land' in the oracles, that is, to Jeru-salem and all the surrounding peoples. Indeed, in the second oracle the focus has been primarily on Israel and Judah which surround Jerusalem.

When the LORD scatters the little ones only one-third will be left—evoking the idea of the remnant associated earlier with Haggai and Zechariah (Hag. 1.12, 14; 2.2; Zech. 8.6). The remaining one-third will be refined like silver and tested like gold, suggesting that what is left will be rare and precious like these precious metals. (The notion of refining and testing the people is found elsewhere. See Mal. 3.2-4; Isa. 1.25-26; Jer. 9.7; Pss. 17.3; 26.2; 66.10.) The image is similar to the 'jewels of a crown' characterizing the rescued flock in 9.16. This precious remnant community will call on 'the *name* of the LORD' (13.9). No longer will the community call on the *names* of the idols (13.2). Reference to this community refined like silver and gold is in the singular in the last verse. While the NRSV translates, '*They* will call on my name, and I will answer *them*', the Hebrew text reads '*he* will call on my name, and I will answer *him*'. What is envisaged here is that the broken communities symbolized by the broken staffs in 11.10, 14 will become a unified com-munity, although only one-third of that community is left in the land. Notice that the LORD will *answer* (cf. 10.6). The way the LORD answers in Zechariah is not through the deceptive diviners, dreamers and proph-ets but through his messenger. The LORD will say 'He is my people' and the community, understood as a singular 'he', will say 'The LORD is our God' (13.9). Thus the community alluded to earlier in Zechariah—about whom the LORD said 'they shall be people and I will be their God', 8.8—will be established. This remnant community, like the remnant community addressed by Haggai, is one for whom the LORD is 'their God' (Hag. 1.13).

The shepherd referred to in this passage is a recurring motif in the oracles (see 10.2-3 and 11.1-17). In 10.2-3 the theme of the shepherd followed a passage concerned with the equivocation of the diviners and dreamers—just as the references to the shepherd in 13.7 follow a section concerned with the deceit of the prophets. Shepherd passages, then, recur in contexts concerned with those who, rather than speak for the LORD, tell lies and offer empty consolation. The shepherds, there-fore, represent leaders who do not speak for the LORD and consequently lead the people astray. That the sword is to be wielded against the shepherd, 'Awake, O sword, against my shepherd', picks up the theme at the end of the shepherd passage in 11.17, 'May the sword strike his arm and his right eye'.

The bellicose images indicate that the world-view of the LORD's mastery over the whole earth, seen in temple imagery by Zechariah, is put in jeopardy by circumstances that call the LORD's domination into question. How can the LORD be master when the shepherds can thwart the LORD's power? Zechariah's notion that men from nations of every language will come to Jerusalem (8.23) is challenged by the scattering of the flock. Rather than finding a centre in Jerusalem, the flock is led astray by the shepherds. This section on the shepherd (13.7-9) serves as a transition to the final chapter (ch. 14). In that chapter, there is a defensive retreat behind the walls of Jerusalem. The limitation of the LORD's power over the whole earth is suggested by the fantastic and outlandish descriptions of the days to come at the end of this oracle, the last chapter in Zechariah.

Overview and Transition (Zech. 14)

As the oracles develop, the view of the world the reader has seen through Zechariah's eyes in the opening scenes (Zech. 1-8) is increas-ingly undermined. The contrast between the opening scenes and the oracles is most clearly evident in the final chapter (Zech. 14). Whereas earlier scenes are concerned with *return* from exile (1.1-6; 6.6), Zech-ariah 14 speaks about half the city *going* into exile (14.2). The scenes earlier in Zechariah are concerned with the LORD, who has already returned to Jerusalem (1.16) and is present in it (8.23; cf. Hag. 1.13), Zechariah 14 speaks about the LORD coming to Jerusalem (14.5) in the future. The consequence of the return of the people and the LORD to

Jerusalem in the earlier scenes is a movement outward to the world of nations. The riders go out to the four corners of the earth (1.11; 6.7), and the last four temple scenes concern 'the whole earth' (4.13; 5.3, 6; 6.5). Return to Jerusalem precedes, metaphorically speaking, an explosion bursting outward toward the whole world. Zechariah 14, on the other hand, reads more like an implosion—a withdrawal from the world to the city of Jerusalem. The earlier scenes envisage a population explosion beyond the walls of Jerusalem (2.4, cf. 8.4-5), but Zechariah 14 speaks about shrinkage by one half (14.2; cf. 13.8-9). The earlier scenes picture the nations as coming and attaching themselves openly and with enthusiasm to Jerusalem (2.11-12), while Zechariah 14 speaks about the LORD gathering the nations to Jerusalem for battle. The earlier scenes speak about the LORD protecting Jerusalem (1.16-17; 2.8-9), while Zechariah 14 speaks about the nations who will attack Jerusalem so that 'the city will be taken and the houses looted and the women raped' (14.2).

How does one account for this contrast? Why do the oracles, especially Zechariah 14, give such a different view of the world? The worldview with the temple in Jerusalem as the centre of the LORD's power is challenged by the opposition to that ideology in cryptic references to the 'other' in the oracles. As indicated in the first oracle, the surrounding peoples as well as Israel (Ephraim/the house of Joseph) see things differently so that what was understood as unifying 'the whole land' is called into question.

The oracular defence of the LORD in his temple as 'the master of the whole earth' exposes its weakness. Just how powerful is the LORD whose mastery of the whole earth can be called into question by the thrust of a sword (12.1)? What kind of control does the LORD have, when others can so easily lead the flock astray? These limits to the LORD's power are further suggested by Zechariah 14 which reflects a retreat from 'the whole world' to Jerusalem where apparently that half of the people who do not support Zechariah's world-view will go into exile. Finally, however, the LORD in defence of Jerusalem will rout the nations.

Perhaps because of the strained credibility of the claim that the LORD, present in Jerusalem, is the centre of power over the whole earth, this last chapter speaks of a coming day of triumph in a fantastic manner. The LORD standing with his feet on the Mount of Olives creating a valley, 'on that day', the notion of a continuous day, and the whole land being turned into a plain while Jerusalem stands aloft—all are in the language of hyperbole.

The Nation's Battle against Jerusalem (14.1-11)

This passage is a description of a day which is 'about to come' (14.1). The construction in Hebrew suggests something that is about to take place. It is more imminent than is suggested by the NRSV's 'a day is coming'. It is addressed to a second person 'you'. This 'you' is masculine singular in Hebrew, apparently continuing the masculine singular portrayal of the community in 13.9 ('He will call on my name...I will answer him...and he will say, "The LORD is our God"'). It can be assumed also that this 'you' is the half of the city that will not go into exile (14.2).

The reader is little prepared for the beginning of this verse of the LORD's battle against Jerusalem in which the nations will divide the plunder taken from them in their midst. The city will be taken, the houses looted and the women raped. The LORD appears to be turning against the city and the people he promised to protect (see 2.8). I suggested in the discussion of 1.3 that Zechariah's audience, addressed as an unidentified 'them', was 'the remnant of the people' referred to by Haggai (Hag. 1.12, 14; 2.2; see Zech. 8.6). This 'remnant of the people', given a voice in only one sentence (Zech. 1.6), is part of a larger whole that has no voice whatsoever. What emerges into view for the first time in Zechariah 14 are those others (the half of the people who will go into exile) over against which Zechariah's community is defined as a remnant. The factional differences that are beginning to appear in Zechariah, the two-thirds in the land that will perish and the one-third that will be refined (13.9), the half who will go into exile and the remainder who will not be cut off from the city (14.2), expose the division in Zechariah's community. The existence of a remnant (the one-third to be refined suggests a minority) means that not everyone has seen the world in Zechariah's time as the reader has seen it through Zechariah's eyes. There is a rift between Zechariah's view of restoration and the outlook of others.

After allowing the heinous behaviour of warfare, the LORD will quite literally make his stand on the Mount of Olives. It will happen 'on that day' when the nations will come to fight against Jerusalem. Only after the atrocities of warfare have been carried out will the LORD come forth in combat 'and fight against those nations as when he fights on a day of battle'. When I read about the LORD standing on the Mount of Olives pushing it apart with his feet to form a valley, it conjures up pictures of the Colossus of Rhodes. The valley created by splitting the Mount of Olives will be a means of escape, apparently for the community left in

Jerusalem after the other half has been taken into exile. Later verses concerning a plague (14.12-15) and the references to Egypt (14.18-19) may suggest that the mountain will be divided as a means of escape just as the waters were divided allowing the Israelites to escape at the sea (Exod. 14.21). The Hebrew verb for splitting the mountain in Zech. 14.4 is the same as the verb used for dividing the sea in Exod. 14.21. The meaning of Azal, the place to which the valley will reach, is not clear. Actually, there is much about 14.5 in particular that is unclear in the Hebrew and creates a number of problems for translators.

Interestingly, flight through the valley is likened to the flight from the earthquake at the time of Uzziah. The earthquake is also mentioned at the beginning of Amos, who is dated in the days of Uzziah, two years before the earthquake. Furthermore the community fleeing the splitting of the Mount of Olives is linked to the community who fled in the days of Uzziah. As the Twelve is coming to an end there is a link with the beginning of the Twelve, a suggestion of solidarity between the community in the days of Uzziah, (the time of the former prophets) and the community in the days of Darius (the time of the reappearance of messengers).

At the time of flight through the valley, Zechariah says, 'the LORD my God will come and the holy ones with him'. 'Holy ones' is used in other texts in the Hebrew Bible to speak of the LORD's army when he does battle (see Deut. 33.2-3; cf. Ps. 89.5, 7). But 'holy ones' also suggests the remnant community in Zion. Isaiah 4.3 speaks about those left in Zion as 'holy ones'. In the light of the larger context of Zechariah, the remnant community is set apart, with special status. We have seen that Jerusalem will make the land holy (2.12) and in 14.20-21 everything in Zion is understood as being holy.

The fantastic imagery used to characterize what will happen continues with a further description in 14.6-7 of the day in which the LORD will manifest his power in Jerusalem. The Hebrew text is obscure, with v. 6 being translated literally, 'And on that day, there will be no light, precious things will congeal'. The NRSV translation, 'On that day there shall not be either cold or frost' follows ancient versions. Whatever the meaning of the Hebrew, it seems to refer to an extraordinary day. The NRSV's translation of v. 7, 'and there shall be a continuous day' could be translated 'and it will be day one' recalling the phrase used in Gen. 1.5 at the close of the first day of creation. However the phrase 'it is known to the LORD, not day and not night' conjures up images of that day when the LORD made the sun stand still so that it 'did not set for about a whole day' (Josh. 10.12-14); hence, 'at evening time there shall be light'.

A further description of that day is given in v. 8. Living waters will flow out of Jerusalem, half to the eastern sea and half toward the western sea. This water shall flow throughout the year so that there will be no seasonal variation. It is possible that these fresh waters will be the source of the agricultural abundance which is viewed in both Haggai and Zechariah as a sign of future prosperity (Hag. 1.10-11; 2.19; and Zech. 8.12, cf. 13.5). Commentators have attempted in the past to relate this text to Ezek. 47.1-20; Joel 3.18 or Gen. 2.10-14.

The series of descriptions of that day to come continues in 14.9. The LORD will become king over 'the whole earth'. This phrase recalls the LORD as imaged in the earlier scenes as 'the master of the whole earth'. 'Master' is a title that can be used for a king (see Jer. 22.19; 34.5; Gen. 40.1; Judg. 3.25). That the LORD is one and that his name is one uses language similar to Deut. 6.4. One recalls the previous chapter in which it is envisaged that 'the names of the idols will be cut off' (13.1) so that the community will call only on the name of the LORD (13.9; cf. 10.12).

The description of that day continues in Zech. 14.10-11. The elevation of Jerusalem created by turning the surrounding land into a plain climaxes what has been a running description of dramatic change on that day. The Mount of Olives will be split in half when the LORD arrives with his holy ones at a time when there will be no day or night. Living waters shall flow out of Jerusalem making the surrounding land fecund in both summer and winter. Then the LORD will be king over the whole earth—one LORD and one name. But what is the significance of Jerusalem being turned into a mountain so that the surrounding land will be literally 'like the Arabah'? Since much of the Arabah was below sea level, the unusual lowness of the surrounding land indicates the extraordinary elevation of Jerusalem. What may be suggested here, in the image of an elevated Jerusalem to which the LORD comes as king, is that Jerusalem as the dwelling place of God will be turned into a holy mountain. Jerusalem will be like Sinai where Moses came to meet the LORD who claimed that 'the whole earth is mine' (Exod. 19.5); and the LORD in Jerusalem will be king of 'the whole earth' (14.9). This possible link with Sinai is suggested when the elevated Jerusalem is read alongside the envisaged restoration of Jerusalem in an earlier scene (Zech. 2.4-5). There it was said that Jerusalem would be inhabited like a village without walls and that the LORD 'will be a wall of fire around it'. When the LORD came down upon Mount Sinai, it is said that he descended upon it in fire (Exod. 19.18).

The presence of the LORD in a mountain-like Jerusalem conjures up images of that other mountain, Sinai, in which the LORD was present when he spoke with Moses and the people. The appearance of the LORD at Sinai (Exod. 19) was associated with Israel's experience in

Egypt and the plagues that fell on the Egyptians. It is interesting, therefore, that the arrival of the LORD as king over all the earth from an elevated Jerusalem is also followed by the mention of a plague and a panic
that will befall any nation that comes against Jerusalem (14.12-16).

The image of the ground sinking around Jerusalem, while seemingly
fantastic, is associated with details of topography and the layout of Jerusalem. It has been suggested that the phrase 'from Geba to Rimmon
south of Jerusalem' refers to the extreme northern and southern limits
of Judah. If this is the case, then Jerusalem would stand elevated in
Judah with the surrounding land sunken below sea level. The specific
sites of the city are important because they suggest a hint of the real in
what is otherwise a bizarre picture of the future.

Verse 11 says that 'they will dwell in it' (NRSV, 'it shall be inhabited').
Who are 'they?' Perhaps we should understand them to be those left
in the city (14.2), the 'holy ones' who will come with the LORD (14.5).
What is envisaged here is what was said at the beginning of the oracle
about that day which is coming: Jerusalem will be inhabited again
(12.6), 'the inhabitants of Jerusalem' will be seen to have strength
through the LORD of hosts, their God (12.5), and 'the LORD will shield
the inhabitants of Jerusalem so that the feeblest among them will be like
David' (12.8). These inhabitants of Jerusalem, then, will be elevated in
status just as the city is elevated. On that day, they will abide 'in secu-
rity' and never again 'be doomed to destruction' (14.11). The phrase
'doomed to destruction', actually one word in Hebrew, is used for total
destruction in warfare in which everything that breathes is killed (see
Deut. 20.16-17), and every destructible thing is eliminated (see Deut.
7.25-26).

A Plague on Peoples Who Wage War (14.12-15)

The previous verses (14.1-11) concerned a time when the LORD will
gather the nations together to fight against Jerusalem so that it will be
ravaged and half the population taken into exile. On that day or 'in that
time' the LORD will fight for Jerusalem with the consequences that the
LORD will be king over all the earth and Jerusalem will be elevated as an
impregnable city. When that happens the LORD will strike the peoples
who have waged war against Jerusalem with a plague (14.12). Furthermore, the LORD will send a panic so that the peoples will fight among
themselves. In that time even Judah will fight at Jerusalem. Here there
are links with what has come earlier in both Haggai and Zechariah. That
Judah will fight at Jerusalem picks up the notion of cooperation
between Judah and Jerusalem mentioned earlier in the oracle (12.4-7).

The wealth of the surrounding nations will be collected (14.14). The collection of wealth echoes both the earlier scene about the wealth of the nations becoming plunder for their slaves (2.9) and also Haggai's envisaging of treasure pouring into the temple (Hag. 2.6-9). The last comment—that the animals of the nations will also be struck down by plague—seems to be an explanation of why the livestock is not mentioned as part of the wealth to be gathered.

The plague (14.12, 15) highlights the Exodus imagery that has been flickering in the background. Not only will the LORD divide a mountain as a means of escape as he divided the sea (14.5), and not only will he be king of 'the whole earth' in an elevated Jerusalem (14.9-10) as he was the owner of 'the whole earth' speaking to his people at Sinai (Exod. 19), but also he will send a plague in the defence of his people as he did in the case of the Egyptians (Exod. 7–11). Even the 'panic' that he sends among the peoples (14.13) recalls the panic he caused the Egyptians (see Deut. 7.17-26, esp. v. 23). The horror of plague shows that Zechariah at the end of the book looks to a future time that is as excruciatingly repugnant as the future envisaged at the end of Isaiah (see Isa. 66.24).

Those Who Survive (14.16-20)

This passage concerns a subsequent time in the future when those who have survived the previous devastation will worship in the very city they had fought against—Jerusalem. Just as the LORD had allowed only half of the population to survive in Jerusalem (14.2), so he is also allowing only some people within each nation to survive (14.6). Every year the survivors will go up to pay homage to their king, the LORD of hosts. They are to keep the festival of booths. But why the festival of booths? It may have to do with the fact that this festival is celebrated in the autumn at the end of the agricultural year. One does homage to the LORD because it was the LORD who made the harvest possible. Indeed, according to Haggai (1.10-11; 2.18-19) and implied in the imagery of the rebuilt temple, the temple ensures agricultural prosperity. The LORD as king of the whole earth is the source of fertility and productivity. If a nation does not go up to pay homage, the LORD will withhold rain, causing drought (14.17).

Among the nations only Egypt is identified by name. If Egypt does not make homage to him at the time of the festival of booths, then the LORD will plague it not with drought but with a different kind of plague. The Hebrew says this in a roundabout way. Literally translated v. 18 reads, 'If the family of Egypt does not go up and does not come, then the plague which the LORD places on the nations who do not come up to celebrate the festival of booths will not be against them'. This verse seems to imply that a different kind of plague will come on the Egyptians. What that plague will be is not described. Egypt may be singled out because of the exodus imagery recurring in the text. More significantly, however, Egypt may be singled out because it is a country that will not suffer lack of productivity from drought; its crops are watered by the overflowing of the Nile.

Of course, Egypt may be mentioned separately for a quite different reason for which historical evidence is missing. Perhaps Egypt represents the place where a different temple community makes claims about the presence of the LORD with its people. It is possible that Egypt may, like the north represented by Bethel, pose a threat to power located in the temple in Jerusalem.

Zechariah closes by describing what will happen on that day, or perhaps better, in those times, when the nations go up to celebrate the festival of booths. Not only will the remnant of the people who inhabit Jerusalem be holy (see 14.5), everything in Jerusalem will be holy (14.20-21). On the bells of the horses will be inscribed, 'Holy to the LORD'. The elevation of Jerusalem mentioned earlier in the oracle (14.10-11) is matched by the radical way in which Jerusalem is set apart by a pervasive sacredness. Cooking pots in the house of the LORD will be as holy as the bowls in front of the altar (14.20). Indeed, every cooking pot in Jerusalem will be able to be used for sacrifice (14.21). It will not only be the priests in the temple who will benefit from the produce brought from 'the whole earth' to the temple but apparently every one of the holy ones in Jerusalem who owns a cooking pot, 'so that all who sacrifice may come and use them to boil the flesh of the sacrifice'.

Except for the final sentence, vv. 20-21, the picture is one of complete holiness, even touching the bells of the horses and cooking pots. However, the closing sentence is in the negative—indicating what will *not* be in that day. In the future, there will no longer be 'traders' (or Canaanites) in the house of the LORD. The implication is that 'traders' are now in the house of the LORD. One is able to see what stands in the way of the implementation of what is envisaged for the temple community in Jerusalem. Jerusalem is not elevated, the LORD is not king because the sheep merchants, 'traders' (11.7, 11) are still in the temple. The grandiose view of the future is deflated by a suggestion of the present reality. Perhaps we should understand Canaanite to refer to 'the other', those who share an alien world-view (see Lemche, p. 167).

Afterword

In my reading of Zechariah in the Twelve, I have encountered a literary world in which prophecy comes to an end. Prophets are confined to 'former times', and their words are encountered in writing. Prophets in a new guise, like Haggai, begin to speak as messengers of the LORD. This change in speaking, from the way it used to be when the LORD first spoke to the prophet Hosea in the Twelve, coincides with the construction of the temple. It is a time of return: the people have *returned*, and the LORD has *returned* to them. It is also a return to the way it used to be when the LORD spoke to Jacob through a messenger at Bethel. At such a time of return, Zechariah emerges as a messenger and sees the implications of the changed world in temple imagery. The central message of this new time of return is that the LORD is 'with you'. Such a radical localization of divine presence is manifested in temple symbolism portraying the LORD as 'the master of the whole earth' dwelling in the temple in Jerusalem, where the wealth of the plundered nations will come pouring in.

Zechariah's name, meaning 'the LORD has remembered', should not be associated with nostalgia. While the LORD remembers the former times, things have changed. The LORD is present in Jerusalem, not in Bethel as he was in the days when a messenger used to speak to Jacob. Royalty is Persian; Judaean and Israelite kings have passed from the scene. Those taking their stance beside the LORD of the whole earth are a Persian governor and a high priest.

When Zechariah answers the question from the representatives from Bethel, the universal implications of the LORD's presence in Jerusalem persist in his answer. He understands that in the future ten men from nations of every language will come to Jerusalem because they acknowledge that the LORD is present there. The oracles that accompany Zechariah's answer to Bethel's question, however, suggest that such a glorious picture of the future is questionable. The family ties binding Israel and Judah, as they did in the days of David, have been broken. Jerusalem stands alone. The imagery of Jerusalem as the centre of the whole earth is exaggerated. This exaggeration suggests that the temple images in which Zechariah saw the LORD's power earlier in the book may not be believable in the eyes of others.

Within the Twelve, then, Zechariah is portraying a changed world in which unique status is given to Jerusalem, where the LORD is present in the temple. Messengers, like Zechariah, also gain status as individuals sent by the LORD. The oracles, part of Zechariah's answer to the question raised by Bethel, while defending the LORD's supremacy over the whole earth, unwittingly allow the opposition to Zechariah's world-view to surface. There are those who stand in opposition to Jerusalem as the centre of power.

The Twelve, then, creates a literary world. But the cryptic allusions in the oracles to the shepherds, for example, suggest that the text relates to the world out of which it came in ways that are unavailable to contemporary readers, even as they want to know more. While it is impossible to date the text with any precision in time, and while it is impossible to know if any of the individuals mentioned in the Twelve from Hosea to Malachi were historical figures, the text can disclose something about its world. This disclosure will arise, however, by asking critical questions about how the literary world is constructed, not by reading the text as a reflection of the past.

When read as a whole, the Twelve portrays a world in which there is a sharp break with the past. Formally, this rupture is evident in dating. As was indicated in the Introduction, Haggai breaks the earlier convention of the Twelve by referencing dates to Persian kings rather than Judaean kings. (Hos. 1.1 and Amos 1.1, of course, also refer to King Jeroboam of Israel.) The split with the past is evident in other ways: in the rise of messengers beginning with Haggai; in the view that prophecy has come to an end and belongs to 'former' times; and in the commencement of temple construction.

This fracture with the past raises the question, 'Who is served by this construction of the world?' The broad answer is that it is the community associated with the construction of the temple as the centre of power and authority, and particularly with messengers like Zechariah, whose claim about his own status is associated with temple construction. To gain further insight into who is empowered and who is disempowered in Zechariah, it is important to see who has a voice and who has not.

There are a number of characters who are given no voice. The satan appears primarily to take the blame for Joshua's shocking condition. The exiles, Heldai, Tobijah, Jedaiah, as well as Josiah son of Zephaniah, appear as those from whom silver and gold are to be collected for making crowns. However, these figures have a marginal, non-speaking role in Zechariah. More significant is the silencing of the voices of the opponents. One does not hear any words from the nations who are to be plundered or from the shepherds who stand in opposition to the

LORD's plan for the north. This is to be expected because it is typical to deny a voice to the 'other'. The silence of the 'other' should alert the reader that there is undoubtedly an*other* way of constructing the world.

Joshua the high priest and Zerubbabel the governor are characters who stand more clearly at the centre of the construction of Zechariah's world. Yet, these two individuals are silenced (although differently) throughout Zechariah. Joshua never speaks. Although he is the central focus of the one scene in which he appears, he is placed in a subordinate position; the messenger of the LORD (Haggai) and Zechariah have authority over him. They dress him in new garb and charge him to carry out specific requirements. He is spoken to, but he does not have an opportunity to speak. Not only the high priest Joshua is silenced but also other priests. In Haggai, the priests can speak only to give simple answers to technical questions put to them (see Hag. 2.12, 13). When Bethel sends representatives to Jerusalem to ask a question of the priests and prophets of the house of the LORD, the priests do not answer. Rather, Zechariah answers the question. Furthermore, the priests come in for harsh judgment in Malachi, where their only words are questions that are quoted purely to be rebuked. The priests are not given an opportunity to reply. In the literary world of Zechariah, the power of the priests is subordinated to the power of the messengers who charge them with responsibility.

Zerubbabel the governor is also given no voice. Unlike Joshua, he is never present in the scenes, and this gives an entirely different impression of his silence. He is mentioned as one who has a central role in temple construction, which is metaphorically in his hands: 'The hands of Zerubbabel have laid the foundations of this house; his hands shall complete it' (4.9). When Zerubbabel completes temple construction, Zechariah will gain authority: 'Then you will know that the LORD of hosts has sent me to you' (4.9). Zerubbabel, therefore, can be seen as significant for authorizing those, including the LORD, for whom the temple is crucial. His absence underscores the temple community's dependence on him. As is the case in many societies, communities needing support for major development must go to the source of power; the source of power does not come to them.

Messengers situate themselves between two leaders of unequal power. The messengers themselves are empowered by the role of Zerubbabel in temple construction. They in turn empower Joshua by instructing him in his role as high priest. The power claimed from Zerubbabel gives the messengers power over the priests, including the high priest Joshua, whom they instruct in the LORD's ways and in the LORD's requirements.

Prophets do not speak in Zechariah. Their words appear in uniform summary statements spoken by Zechariah reducing the plurality of what the prophets had to say, denying them individuality and specificity. The prophets are confined to former times and need messengers such as Zechariah to speak for them. The prophets, then, are also effectively silenced in Zechariah. When the question is posed by Bethel to the priests and the prophets, the prophets, like the priests, are given no voice, Zechariah speaks for them. The only words that the prophets will be imagined to speak in the future are words of denial: 'I am no prophet, I am a tiller of the soil for the land has been my possession since my youth' (13.5). In 13.6 the prophets are predicted to have a voice in the future when they will identify the source of wounds they have received, but this is hardly an authoritative voice.

In Zechariah the literary world portrays a situation in which messengers such as Zechariah are claiming power over the prophets and the priests. That power is associated with temple construction and with Zerubbabel the temple builder. What prophets and priests have to say about this view of the world cannot be known because they are not given a chance to express their point of view. The opposition met in the north, centring on the shepherds, is also denied a voice. The shepherds do not speak, and even their identity is concealed. How the shepherds and the people of the north feel about the centralization of the LORD's power in Jerusalem is unexpressed.

A few characters are given speaking roles, but what they say does not represent a point of view. Rather, their words are descriptive and functional in the unfolding of the scenes. In the first scene, a voice answers Zechariah's question about the identity of the mounted horsemen. It identifies them as those who go out to patrol the earth. Those who patrol the earth also speak, reporting that the whole earth remains at peace. The man with the measuring line in his hand answers Zechariah's question about what he is doing. The men from Bethel ask a question, but they do not get a chance to respond to Zechariah's answer; hence we learn nothing from them about what they think of Zechariah's answer. All of these individuals when they speak lack the opportunity to put a point of view—to speak of things as they see them. Even when the community addressed by Zechariah speaks, the voice is one; there are not differentiated voices, 'The LORD has dealt with us according to our ways and deeds, just as he planned to do' (1.6). Similarly, the nations who will speak in the future will proclaim with a uniform voice that 'God is with you' in Jerusalem (8.23).

The only characters who are allowed to present a view of the world are the LORD and his messengers. Messengers, like Zechariah, speak primarily to claim authority from the LORD whose words they speak. The voices of the LORD and his messengers meld, merging in a single view of the world. The claim in the opening scenes in the temple in Zechariah 1–6 is that the LORD is the master of the whole earth, and this claim is reiterated in the last chapter in Zechariah, which looks at the world in the days to come.

To read this one-sided portrayal of the world without considering the other possible views of the voiceless ones—the individual voices of those who agreed to return, Zerubbabel, Joshua, the returned exiles, the nations, the shepherds, the representatives from Bethel—is to hear only in part. To read the account of the days to come as an expression of universal bliss when Jerusalem will become the centre for the gathering of nations to celebrate the festival of booths, is to forget about all the anger. To remember the LORD's anger in reading Zechariah is as necessary as to recognize his pornographic portrayal at the beginning of Hosea.

The call to return, in order for Jerusalem to become the centre of power, is presented with much emotion, and the overwhelming passion is anger. Throughout 1.1-17, which depicts a change through 'returning', the LORD remains angry; but the object of that anger changes. In 1.2 the LORD is 'very angry', and that anger was directed at the fathers. In 1.12 the anger is with Jerusalem and the cities of Jerusalem and presumably its present inhabitants. In 1.16 the LORD is still 'extremely angry' but the anger is now directed against the nations. The LORD's contention that I 'was very jealous [in the sense of 'zealous'] for Zion and Jerusalem' (1.14) is in tension with that extreme anger. There is a clear discontinuity between the LORD's announced return with 'compassion' (1.16) and his withheld mercy for a long period of seventy years (1.12). Indeed, the LORD's suggestion that things are changing lacks credibility, given the emotional chasm between his anger and compassion. The LORD attempts to defend his past anger by redirecting the blame for the anger elsewhere. The LORD says in effect, 'It wasn't I; it was the nations'—after all, 'I was only a little angry'. In the scene involving Joshua, as I indicated above, the LORD seeks to blame the lamentable state of Joshua on the satan. In the context of continual anger for seventy years, and the diverting of blame to others, claims that he will be compassionate lack persuasiveness. Perhaps for that reason, the audience is not very clearly identified and has a feeble voice, resigned to its fate at the hands of the LORD. Resignation suggests failure of persuasion. There is also a discontinuity between expression of *anger* with passion and the embodiment of *compassion* in material goods. A change in prosperity is provided with an increase in material goods associated with a glorious house in which the LORD can dwell. In such a fine dwelling in a time of renewed prosperity the LORD will no longer leave in an angry rage. He will be present; it will be possible to speak to him. He will be speaking in a world in which messengers assure immediate communication. Yet the portrayal of the history of the LORD's anger does not lead the reader to welcome interaction with the LORD. The LORD's anger seems to be a device to explain the discontinuity between expectations as defined by the messenger and reality, but it undermines the desire for communication that would give the messenger his role.

The oracles, as I have argued above, undermine the view of the world presented by Zechariah—including what he claims about the extent of the LORD's power. Perhaps that, too, explains the LORD's anger; he is not in control and neither are the messengers. Anger is also evident in Zechariah when he becomes impatient with the shepherds (see 11.8). The voice of the LORD and the voice of the messenger have melded in the expression of anger. By the end of Zechariah, the LORD's anger is again out of control. He will bring the nations to Jerusalem, so that houses will be looted, women raped, and half the city taken into exile.

In my reading of Zechariah, then, I do not see the LORD's return and the messenger's announcement of that return as disinterested compassion. The emphasis on wealth and prosperity that are to eventuate from returning to the LORD's dwelling in the temple in Jerusalem appeals to self-interest and suggests self-interest on the part of the messengers, who see this as a time of prosperity not only for the LORD but for themselves.

The last oracle in the Twelve, Malachi—in the hands of 'my messenger'—is addressed to Israel, those who appear to challenge the temple ideology seen through Zechariah's eyes. This oracle also only tells one side of the story. The community's questions are raised with no right of rebuttal. The community is not only accused of improper worship, but also, as the oracle comes to an end, is accused of robbing the LORD. Malachi continues the message of an angry god denied the wealth anticipated as a result of temple construction.

In order to correct this situation the LORD will separate the righteous from the wicked (also denied a voice) in his book of remembrance. The righteous will tread down the voiceless ones as ashes under their feet, and they will keep the statutes and ordinances of Moses (Mal. 4.3-4). Before this great and terrible day comes the LORD will send his messenger to Israel: 'See, I am sending my messenger to prepare the way before me' (Mal. 3.1). He will send a messenger to Israel as he had sent a messenger to Jerusalem. This messenger is Elijah: 'Lo, I will send you the prophet Elijah before the great and terrible day of the LORD comes'

(Mal. 4.5). He is a prophet/messenger who, in the past, blurred the distinction between heaven and earth, when he ascended into heaven accompanied by horses and chariots of fire (2 Kgs 2.9-12).

Bibliography

Ackroyd, P.R., *Exile and Restoration* (London: SCM Press, 1968).

Andiñach, P.R., 'The Locusts in the Message of Joel', *VT* 42 (1992), pp. 433-41.

Andersen, F.I., and D.N. Freedman, *Hosea: A New Translation and Commentary* (AB, 24; Garden City, NY: Doubleday, 1980).

Baldwin, J.G., *Haggai, Zechariah, Malachi* (TOTC; London: Tyndale Press, 1972).

Barton, J., 'Reading the Bible as Literature: Two Questions for Biblical Critics', *Literature and Theology* 1 (1987), pp. 135-53.

Berry, D.K., 'Malachi's Dual Design: The Close of the Canon and What Comes Afterward', in K.W. Watts and P.R. House (eds.), *Forming Prophetic Literature: Essays on Isaiah and the Twelve in Honor of John D.W. Watts* (JSOTSup, 235; Sheffield: Sheffield Academic Press, 1996).

Blenkinsopp, J., *A History of Prophecy in Israel* (London: SPCK, 1984).

Bosshard, E., 'Beobachtungen zum Zwölfprophetenbuch', *BN* 52 (1990), pp. 27-46.

Butterworth, M., *Structure and the Book of Zechariah* (JSOTSup, 130; Sheffield: JSOT Press, 1992).

Carr, D., 'Reaching for Unity in Isaiah', *JSOT* 57 (1993), pp. 61-80.

Carroll, R.P., 'Prophecy and Society', in R.E. Clements (ed.), *The World of Ancient Israel* (Cambridge: Cambridge University Press, 1989), pp. 203-25.

—'The Myth of the Empty Land', *Semeia* 59 (1992), pp. 79-92.

—'So What Do We *Know* about the Temple? The Temple in the Prophets', in T.C. Eskenazi and K.H. Richard (eds.), *Second Temple Studies, 2: Temple Community in the Persian Period* (JSOTSup, 175; Sheffield: JSOT Press, 1994).

Carstensen, R., 'The Book of Zechariah', in C.M. Laymon (ed.), *The Interpreter's One-Volume Commentary on the Bible* (London: Collins, 1972).

Clines, D.J.A., 'Haggai's Temple, Constructed, Deconstructed and Reconstructed', *SJOT* 7 (1993), pp. 51-77.

Coggins, R.J., *Haggai, Zechariah, Malachi* (OTG; Sheffield: JSOT Press, 1987).

Cohen, N.G., 'From *Nabi* to *Mal'ak* to "Ancient Figure"', *JJS* 36 (1985), pp. 12-24.

Collins, T., *The Mantle of Elijah: The Redaction Criticism of the Prophetical Books* (The Biblical Seminar, 20; Sheffield: JSOT Press, 1993).

Conrad, E.W., 'The End of Prophecy and the Emergence of Angels/Messengers in the Book of the Twelve', *JSOT* 73 (1997), pp. 65-79.

—*Fear Not Warrior: A Study of 'al tirā' Pericopes in the Hebrew Scriptures* (BJS, 75; Chico, CA: Scholars Press, 1985).

—'Heard But Not Seen: The Representation of "Books" in the Hebrew Bible', *JSOT* 54 (1992), pp. 45-59.

—*Reading Isaiah* (Overtures to Biblical Theology; Minneapolis: Fortress Press, 1991).

—'Reading Isaiah and the Twelve as Prophetic Books', in C.C. Broyles and C.A. Evans (eds.), *Writing and Reading the Vision of Isaiah: Studies of an Interpretive Tradition* (Formation and Interpretation of Old Testament Literature, 1; VTSup, 70; Leiden: E.J. Brill, 1997).

Craig, K.M., 'Interrogatives in Haggai–Zechariah: A Literary Thread?', in K.W. Watts and P.R. House (eds.), *Forming Prophetic Literature: Essays on Isaiah and the Twelve in Honor of John D.W. Watts* (JSOTSup, 235; Sheffield: Sheffield Academic Press, 1996).

Davies, G.I., *Hosea* (NCBC; Grand Rapids: Eerdmans, 1992).

Davies, P.R., *In Search of 'Ancient Israel'* (JSOTSup, 148; Sheffield: JSOT Press, 1992).

Day, P.L., *An Adversary in Heaven: satan in the Hebrew Bible* (HSM, 43; Atlanta: Scholars Press, 1988).

Eybers, I.H., 'The Rebuilding of the Temple According to Haggai and Zechariah', *Die Oud-Testamentiese Werkgemeenskap in Suid-Afrika* 18 (1975), pp. 15-26.

Fewell, D.N. (ed.), *Reading between Texts: Intertextuality and the Hebrew Bible* (Louisville, KY: Westminster/John Knox Press, 1992).

Floyd, M.H., 'Prophecy and Writing in Habakkuk 2,1-5', *ZAW* 105 (1993), pp. 462-81.

Frow, J., 'Intertextuality and Ontology', in Still and Worton (eds.), *Intertextuality: Theories and Practices*, pp. 45-55.

Garbini, G., 'Hebrew Literature in the Persian Period', in T.C. Eskenazi and K.H. Richards (eds.), *Second Temple Studies, 2: Temple Community in the Persian Period* (JSOTSup, 175; Sheffield: JSOT Press, 1994).

Glazier-McDonald, B., 'Zechariah', in C.A. Newmand and S.H. Ringe (eds.), *The Women's Bible Commentary* (London: SPCK, 1992), pp. 230-31.

Good, R.M., 'Zechariah's Second Night Vision', *Bib* 63 (1982), pp. 56-59.

Gunkel, H., 'The Prophets as Writers and Poets', in D.L. Petersen (ed.), *Prophecy in Israel* (Issues in Religion and Theology, 10; London: SPCK, 1987).

Halpern, B., 'The Ritual Background of Zechariah's Temple Song', *CBQ* 40 (1978), pp. 167-90.

Hanson, P.D., 'Zechariah 9 and the Recapitulation of an Ancient Ritual Pattern', *JBL* 92 (1973), pp. 37-59.

—*The Dawn of Apocalyptic* (Philadelphia: Fortress Press, 1975).

—'From Prophecy to Apocalyptic: Unresolved Issues', *JSOT* 15 (1980), pp. 3-6.

Holladay, W.L., *A Concise Hebrew and Aramaic Lexicon of the Old Testament* (Leiden: E.J. Brill, 1971).

House, P.R., *The Unity of the Twelve* (JSOTSup, 97; Bible & Literature Series, 27; Sheffield: Almond Press, 1990).

Jobling, D., 'Texts and the World—An Unbridgeable Gap?' in P.R. Davies (ed.), *Second Temple Studies. I. Persian Period* (JSOTSup, 117; Sheffield: JSOT Press, 1991), pp. 175-82.

Jones, D.R., *Haggai, Zechariah and Malachi* (Torch Bible Commentaries; London: SCM Press, 1962).

Kodell, J., *Lamentations, Haggai, Zechariah, Malachi, Obadiah, Joel, Second Zechariah, Baruch* (Old Testament Message, 14; Wilmington, DE: Michael Glazier, 1982).

Laato, A., 'Zechariah 4,6b-10a and the Akkadian Royal Building Inscriptions', *ZAW* 106 (1994), pp. 533-69.

Landy, F., *Hosea* (Readings: A New Biblical Commentary; Sheffield: Sheffield Academic Press, 1995).

Lemche, N.P., *The Canaanites and their Land* (JSOTSup, 110; Sheffield: JSOT Press, 1991).

Long, B., 'Reports of Visions among the Prophets', *JBL* 95 (1976), pp. 353-65.

Love, M.C., 'The Evasive Text: Zechariah 1-8' (PhD Dissertation, University of Sheffield, 1995).

Marinkovic, P., 'What Does Zechariah 1-8 Tell Us about the Second Temple?', in T.C. Eskenazi and K.H. Richards (eds.), *Second Temple Studies, 2: Temple, Community in the Persian Period* (JSOTSup, 175; Sheffield: JSOT Press, 1994), pp. 88-103.

Marks, H., 'The Twelve Prophets', in R. Alter and F. Kermode (eds.), *The Literary Guide to the Bible* (London: Fontana Press, 1987), pp. 207-33.

Mason, R.A., *The Books of Haggai, Zechariah and Malachi* (The Cambridge Bible Commentary; Cambridge: Cambridge University Press, 1977).

—'The Prophets and Restoration', in R. Coggins, A. Phillips and M. Knibb (eds.), *Israel's Prophetic Tradition* (Cambridge: Cambridge University Press, 1982), pp. 137-54.

—'The Purpose of the "Editorial Framework" of the Book of Haggai', *VT* 27 (1977), pp. 413-21.

—'The Relation of Zechariah 9-14 to Proto-Zechariah', *ZAW* 88 (1976), pp. 226-39.

—'Some Echoes of the Preaching of the Second Temple? Tradition Elements in Zechariah 1-8', *ZAW* 96 (1984), pp. 221-35.

Meyers, C.L., and E.M. Meyers, *Haggai, Zechariah 1-8* (AB, 25b; Garden City, NY: Doubleday, 1987).

—*Zechariah 9-14* (AB, 25c; Garden City, NY: Doubleday, 1993).

Miscall, P.D., 'Biblical Narrative and Categories of the Fantastic', *Semeia* 60 (1992), pp. 39-51.

—*Isaiah* (Readings: A New Biblical Commentary; Sheffield: Sheffield Academic Press, 1993).

—'Isaiah: The Labyrinth of Images', *Semeia* 54 (1991), pp. 103-21.

Mitchell, H.G., *A Critical and Exegetical Commentary on Haggai, Zechariah, Malachi and Jonah* (ICC; Edinburgh: T.& T. Clark, 1980).

Niditch, S., *The Symbolic Vision in Biblical Tradition* (HSM, 30; Chico, CA: Scholars Press, 1983).

Nogalski, J., *Literary Precursors to the Book of the Twelve* (BZAW, 217; Berlin: W. de Gruyter, 1993).

—*Redactional Processes in the Book of the Twelve* (BZAW, 218; Berlin: W. de Gruyter, 1993).

North, R., 'Zechariah's Seven-Spout Lampstand', *Bib* 51 (1970), pp. 183-206.

—'Prophecy to Apocalyptic via Zechariah', in G.W. Anderson *et al.* (eds.), *Congress Volume: Uppsala 1971* (VTSup, 22; Leiden: E.J. Brill, 1971), pp. 47-71.

Odell, M.S., 'The Prophets and the End of Hosea', in J.W. Watts and P.R. House (eds.), *Forming Prophetic Literature: Essays on Isaiah and the Twelve in Honor of John D.W. Watts* (JSOTSup, 235; Sheffield: Sheffield Academic Press, 1996), pp. 158-70.

Parker, K.I., 'Speech, Writing and Power: Deconstructing the Biblical Canon', *JSOT* 69 (1996), pp. 91-103.

Person, R.F., *Second Zechariah and the Deuteronomic School* (JSOTSup, 167; Sheffield: JSOT Press, 1993).

Petersen, D.L., *Haggai and Zechariah 1-8* (OTL; Philadelphia: Westminster Press, 1984).

—'Introduction: Ways of Thinking about Israel's Prophets', in D.L. Petersen (ed.), *Prophecy in Israel* (Issues in Religion and Theology, 10; London: SPCK, 1987), pp. 1-21.

—*The Roles of Israel's Prophets* (JSOTSup, 17; Sheffield: JSOT Press, 1981).

—*Zechariah 9-14 and Malachi* (OTL; London: SCM Press, 1995).

—'Zechariah's Visions: A Theological Perspective', *VT* 34 (1984), pp. 195-206.

—'Zerubbabel and Jerusalem Temple Reconstructed', *CBQ* 36 (1974), pp. 366-72.

Pierce, R., 'Literary Connectors and a Haggai-Zechariah-Malachi Corpus', *JETS* 27 (1984), pp. 277-89.

—'A Thematic Development of the Haggai-Zechariah-Malachi Corpus', *JETS* 27 (1984), pp. 401-11.

Redditt, P.L., 'The Book of Malachi in its Social Setting', *CBQ* 56 (1994), pp. 240-55.

—*Haggai, Zechariah, Malachi* (New Century Bible Commentary; Grand Rapids: Eerdmans, 1995).

—'Israel's Shepherds: Hope and Pessimism in Zechariah 9-14', *CBQ* 51 (1989), pp. 631-42.

—'Nehemiah's First Mission and the Date of Zechariah 9-14', *CBQ* 56 (1994), pp. 664-78.

—'The Two Shepherds in Zechariah 11:4-17', *CBQ* 55 (1993), pp. 676-86.

—'Zechariah 9-14, Malachi, and the Redaction of the Book of the Twelve', in J.W. Watts and P.R. Houses (eds.), *Forming Prophetic Literature: Essays on Isaiah and the Twelve in Honor of John D.W. Watts* (JSOTSup, 235; Sheffield: Sheffield Academic Press, 1996), pp. 245-68.

—'Zerubbabel, Joshua, and the Night Visions of Zechariah', *CBQ* 54 (1992), pp. 249-59.

Ross, J., 'The Prophet as Yahweh's Messenger', in Petersen (ed.), *Prophecy in Israel*, pp. 112-21.

Savran, G., 'Beastly Speech: Intertextuality, Balaam's Ass and the Garden of Eden', *JSOT* 64 (1994), pp. 33-55.

Shaefer, K.R., 'The Ending of the Book of Zechariah: A Commentary', *RB* 100 (1993), pp. 165-238.

—'Zechariah 14 and the Composition of the Book of Zechariah', *RB* 100 (1993), pp. 368-98.

Smith, R.L., *Micah–Malachi* (WBC; Waco, TX: Word Books, 1984).

Still, J., and M. Worton (eds.), *Intertextuality: Theories and Practices* (Manchester: Manchester University Press, 1990).

Stuhlmueller, C., *Rebuilding with Hope: A Commentary on the Books of Haggai and Zechariah* (International Theological Commentary; Grand Rapids: Eerdmans, 1988).

Tollington, J.E., *Tradition and Innovation in Haggai and Zechariah 1-8* (JSOTSup, 150; Sheffield: JSOT Press, 1993).

Tigchelaar, E.J.C., *Prophets of Old and the Day of the End: Zechariah, the Book of Watchers and Apocalyptic* (Oudtestamentische Studien, 35; Leiden: E.J. Brill, 1996).

VanderKam, J.C., 'Joshua the High Priest and the Interpretation of Zechariah 3', *CBQ* 53 (1991), pp. 553-70.

Waltke, B.K., and M. O'Connor, *An Introduction to Biblical Hebrew Syntax* (Winona Lake, IN: Eisenbrauns, 1990).

Wellhausen, J., *Prolegomena to the History of Ancient Israel (with a Reprint of the Article, 'Israel' from the Encyclopedia Britannica)* (Meridian Books Reprint; New York: World Publishing Company, 1957).

Wolff, H.W., *Hosea: A Commentary on the Book of the Prophet Hosea* (trans. G. Stansell; Hermeneia; Philadelphia: Fortress Press, 1974).

Wolfe, R.E., 'The Editing of the Book of the Twelve', *ZAW* 53 (1935), pp. 90-129.

Zvi, E. ben, 'Twelve Prophetic Books or "The Twelve": A Few Preliminary Considerations', in J.W. Watts and P.R. House (eds.), *Forming Prophetic Literature: Essays on Isaiah and the Twelve in Honor of John D.W. Watts* (JSOTSup, 235; Sheffield: Sheffield Academic Press, 1996), pp. 125-56.

Index of References

Index of Authors